Nunshigum

On the Road to Mandalay

Nunshigum

On the Road to Mandalay

Arthur F. Freer

The Pentland Press
Edinburgh – Cambridge – Durham – USA

First published in 1995
by The Pentland Press Ltd
1 Hutton Close
South Church
Bishop Auckland
Durham

British Library
Cataloguing in Publication Data.
A catalogue record for this book
is available from the British Library.

ISBN 1-85821-264-2

Typeset by Carnegie Publishing Ltd, 18 Maynard St, Preston
Printed and bound by Antony Rowe Ltd, Chippenham

To

Joan Isabel

without whose love

and nurturing over 44 years

this would never have been written

Contents

List of Maps and Sketches

Foreword

by Brigadier J. R. Fishbourne CBE, DL
Colonel, 3rd Carabiniers, 1957–1966

I am deeply privileged to be asked to write this foreword to Arthur Freer's *Nunshigum*, a very vivid and personal account, in diary form, of the lives of a tank crew of my Regiment and their activities supporting infantry units in Burma. At the end of the campaign I was myself able to talk to many who took part in that very unpleasant series of actions – fought not only against the Japanese but also the terrain, the weather and disease. I heard of their experiences at first hand and I also knew some of the main characters such as Edward Sanford, Tom Dimsdale, Desmond Murphy and the redoubtable Sergeant Major Craddock.

The author's account of his wartime experiences as an N.C.O., over a period of two years, is both fascinating and utterly authentic; and he has hit on an ingenious and original method of combining his diary with an entirely fictional but up-to-date introduction and tailpiece about a serial killer, which must undoubtedly interest a wider readership.

This intimate account of wartime soldiering in Burma is not in any way just a slice of military history. It does, however, paint a very down-to-earth picture of life in an armoured regiment supporting British, Gurkha and Indian infantry units in action. It may not be for the squeamish, as the author omits no detail of his crew's domestic life in the enclosed space of a Lee Medium tank – nor of the torrential

rains, sometimes very inadequate rations, disease and even an earthquake.

The story of the author's personal part in the extraordinary battle
of Nunshigum comes early in the text. This was indeed a unique
action fought by only a single tank squadron and an Indian battalion
of Dogras. It involved the climbing of steep, jungle-covered and
sniper-infested slopes to the summit with the tanks in single file.
Only by getting to the top could the strong Japanese bunkers be
engaged at point blank range. Tank commanders could not see
without putting their heads out – with fatal consequences. At crisis
point and with all officers dead there came the inevitable halt. It was
then that the Squadron Sergeant Major and the surviving Indian
V.C.O. took joint action, neither really understanding each other's
language. The Sergeant Major was an army boxer whose instinctive
reaction was just to "box on" – this he did, with the cooperation of
the Dogras, and after reorganisation the enemy bunkers were destroyed. The successful outcome of this action was crucial to the
campaign at that stage, for had the Japanese managed to consolidate
their position on Nunshigum, the whole of IV Corps concentration
area at Imphal would have been threatened, with potentially disastrous results.

Throughout the book the reader will be aware of the high standard
of training in the Regiment. All tank crew members were completely
interchangeable. It is here that I must pay tribute to the meticulously
detailed training directed by the C.O., Colonel Ralph Younger, and
his second in command, James Whetstone. The former must have
been one of the most experienced armoured corps officers at that
stage in the war, having served with the 7th Hussars in France, in
the Desert and in the retreat into India from Burma. He had a very
penetrating eye for detail and an uncompromising attitude to both
training and turnout (even in battle). Transgressors soon became
aware that he had a very short fuse! The Regiment profited enor-
mously from his leadership.

I make one further point. The Carabiniers had only recently lost
their horses and been mechanised. They had then been literally sliced

in two so as to enable the formation of the 25th Dragoons. The Regiment was then made up to strength by imports of transfers from other arms, from volunteers and finally by conscripts. Yet, all through this completely absorbing book, one is conscious of the close and happy teamwork at all levels and a splendid Regimental spirit which did indeed serve them well in Burma.

I hope that other readers will enjoy this book as much as I have.

October 1994   J.R.F.

"HUNTLEY"
Major Michael Huntley-Wright MC, Officer Commanding B Squadron 3rd Carabiniers
(Prince of Wales's Dragoon Guards) from 14th April to 23rd December 1944.

Preface

The Battle of Nunshigum

Extract from the Order of Ceremonial at the Twenty-Fifth
Nunshigum Anniversary Parade of the 3rd Carabiniers
(Prince of Wales's Dragoon Guards) held at Chester, 1969.

On April 13th, 1944, was fought one of the most crucial actions in
the great battle for IMPHAL, the most fiercely contested battle of
the Burma campaign.

In March of that year, the Japanese 15th Army, moving swiftly
through the jungle and crossing the mountains of the North East
frontier of India, cut the land communications of the British and
Indian troops of 4th Corps. Thereafter, the only link between this
large force, amounting to nearly one hundred thousand men, and the
outside world, was by air. All the supplies, petrol and ammunition
to enable it to fight had to be flown into the airfields on the Imphal
Plain.

NUNSHIGUM, a dominating hill standing almost four thousand
feet above sea level and rising abruptly from the parched fields, lay
six miles from Imphal, around which, besides the airfields, were all
the dumps, the hospitals, the workshops and the 4th Corps Headquarters controlling the battle. The loss of this base could have been
disastrous.

On 6th April, part of the Japanese 51st Regiment attacked NUN-
SHIGUM, the hill was lost and won again and again until finally on
11th April the enemy firmly established themselves upon it. Now,
only scattered defences, largely manned by administrative troops, lay
between the enemy and the hub of the defence. The security of the

whole Corps was threatened and the recapture of NUNSHIGUM was imperative.

The troops allotted for the operation were 1st Battalion The Dogra Regiment supported by the tanks of B Squadron the 3rd Carabiniers, with the artillery of 5th Indian Division and three squadrons of the Royal Air Force in support.

———

The plan involved an advance on two separate company axes up neighbouring spurs of the hill. Each company was supported by a troop of tanks, with two troops in squadron reserve, and half squadron headquarters with the left hand company. The attack began at 1030 hrs. on 13th April, without prior reconnaissance by those taking part, due to shortage of time. Known enemy positions were shelled by the artillery and attacked by aircraft as the attackers climbed the hill.

The enemy occupied strongly defended bunkers on the twin peaks of NUNSHIGUM, one behind the other. Most of the advance was screened from their view by a series of false crests and involved a climb of a thousand feet above the plain.

After an hour the first peak was reached and action joined. The only feasible tank route was astride the crest of a razor-backed ridge along which the tanks had to move, perforce, in single file. So steep were the slopes that one tank, overbalancing, fell a hundred feet but ended its fall on its tracks and the crew survived. The hill was covered with scrub and bushes affording good cover for dug-in infantry and the attackers came under fire at ranges of a few yards. Tank commanders could not close down if they were to guide their drivers and retain control in these circumstances. The first officer casualty was Lieutenant Neale, shot through the head. Shortly after, the Squadron Leader, Major Sanford, whose father commanded the Regiment twenty years before, was similarly killed.

About this time the commander of the left hand company, Major Jones, was wounded. The commanderless tanks were withdrawn with difficulty and Lieutenant Fitzherbert, now in command, continued the attack with the remaining tanks. Within fifteen minutes both he and the commander of his leading tank, S.Q.M.S. Branstone, were killed, as was Sergeant Doe. Other crew members attempting to take over in these tanks became casualties also.

At this moment B Company Commander, Major Alden, was wounded while directing the fire of a tank. All the British officers in the two companies of the Dogra Regiment were now casualties. It became clear that a relieving commander would have to be sent up the hill to take command of the operation, now apparently leaderless.

Meanwhile, deterred by neither casualties nor confusion, Squadron Sergeant Major Craddock assumed command of B Squadron. He and Subedar Ranbir Singh, the senior surviving Viceroy's Commissioned Officer, together replanned the attack. They closed once more with the bunker positions, were forced back, repositioned the tanks, notably Sergeant Hannam's, directly above an enemy bunker, finally destroyed the bunkers and their occupants and gained the day. By 1400 hrs. the peaks were in friendly hands. The enemy fled leaving over 270 dead. An hour later the relieving British Officer arrived to find, in his own words, 'The position entirely satisfactory and consolidation nearly complete.'

Thus as a result of this supremely gallant action, the very serious threat to 4th Corps was removed.

Never again did NUNSHIGUM fall into enemy hands.

This citation continues to be read to the assembled Nunshigum Parade on 13th April each year by the Chaplain of the Royal Scots Dragoon Guards. The Fiftieth Anniversary Parade was held at Stanley Barracks, Bovington Camp on 13th April 1994. More than 100 Old Comrades, members of the Regimental Association, were proud to attend and to join in the March Past.

Acknowledgements

My thanks go to those who have helped me to recall the happenings of fifty years ago.

Major J. Terry Morton and his staff at the Royal Scots Dragoon Guards Museum, The Castle, Edinburgh, who gave me access to the War Diaries of B Squadron, 3rd Carabiniers, for the period April 1944 to June 1945. Some of these were typed and some were handwritten. It was an emotional experience simply to read original reports written by young officers who were killed in action only a few days later.

Major Roger Pickard and his staff at the Royal Signals Museum, Blandford, who helped to correct my recall of the phonetic alphabet used in the Army. This was dramatically changed from Ack, Beer, Charlie, etc., to Able, Baker, Charlie, etc. in 1941.

Charles Warren, who gave me a copy of his poem, "Two Troops B Squadron will move . . ." typed on a blank Army Form C2136 (Large).

Major G. L. 'Dickie' Scott-Dickens, who was wounded near Imphal and who later commanded C Squadron in action in the Arakan Yomas in 1945. He alerted me to some of my lapses of memory of events when he read the first draft.

Army Badges and Insignia of World War 2 by Guido Bosignoli and *The Campaign in Burma* (H.M.S.O., 1946) for the designs of many of the badges used by the 14th Army (Appendix G).

Fellow members of the 3rd Carabiniers Old Comrades Association, who meet at least once a year and remember the past.

Mrs Anne Langley, of Polebrook, Northamptonshire, who typed, and retyped, my manuscripts with amazing patience and encouragement.

A.F.F.

Chapter 1

April 1982.
A Serial Killer in Yorkshire

13th April 1982

"It's funny," she said, peering through her thick lenses into the lane. There was no reaction from Fred, reading his *Mirror*. "It's very funny," she repeated. "He was up here yesterday, as well." Helen Fagin looked down at her husband from her position standing on a chair in the front room of their terraced cottage. He again ignored her except, possibly, for a slight sigh of annoyance at being interrupted. "You're more interested in your bloody paper than what I'm telling you."

Fred reacted to this. He put the *Mirror* down on to his knees. "I keep telling you, woman, you'll fall off that chair one day. What's the matter with you?"

In his first year of retirement from being a colliery clerk at the local pit, he thought he would never get used to having time on his hands. His paper needed only a quarter of an hour's attention each day, being thereafter of no further interest. His garden and pigeons filled more of this time, until he went to the Institute each evening for a few jars and a frame or two of snooker.

Helen's reply was quick and strong.

"If only you'd cut that privet in front, I'd be able to see out without having to climb on to this chair! I was saying, that man has been up the lane twice in two days. He'd know the first time he couldn't get any further, so why does he have to come back again today?"

"What man?" said Fred.

"That jogger," she replied, twisting her body round to look after

1

the running figure going out of the lane towards the Barnsley road. "He looked too old to be doing that sort of thing anyway."

"That's his business," grunted Fred, returning to his paper.

The jogger had left the Grange feeling satisfied with a job well done.

As usual, the careful planning had paid off and no changes had been needed because of any surprises. The only problem now was that he had a sudden feeling that his bladder was too full. "Pathetic," he thought, "I must be getting too old for this. A good job I've decided to make this my last one. I should be able to make it back to the car park and there's a loo just near the car."

He continued running down Field Lane, gaining his usual rhythm with each breathing cycle matching four paces. This had always suited his slow pulse rate of around 50 at rest and rarely exceeding 80 on a run of twenty or thirty miles in a day. He had never been really sure whether he was a good long distance runner because his pulse rate was slower than average, or whether the rate was slow because he had run regularly since his school days. Which was cause and which was effect? That fanatical P.T.I. [a] at Catterick had always claimed the latter.

It started to rain gently. This cooled his face at the same time that it blurred his vision as it settled on his glasses. "No real problem. It'll reduce the number of people who see me and, at the same time, keep their heads down under their brollies . I've made it," he grinned to himself as he ran into the public toilet, "just in time!"

The relieved jogger looked across the half-filled car park, saw only one black Morris Minor being driven away and then trotted across to his red Cortina. He slipped the light rucksack off his shoulders, put it on the passenger seat and drove off in the now heavy downpour, heading towards Sheffield.

---

a Appendix A1

At Barnsley Central Police Station they were no strangers to sudden death. They had their share of reports of heart attacks, pit disasters, domestic strife and occasional muggings leading to premature death, but murder was unusual. Especially when the president of the Colliery Workers Union appeared to be the victim. The report of the 999 call had alerted Chief Inspector James Ackroyd that the body of Vince Hallett, controversial president of the C.W.U. for the past two years, had been found in his office at the Grange in the Barnsley suburb of Greenfields.

The Grange had been built by the colliery owner between the two world wars and had been acquired by the C.W.U. for their headquarters soon after the nationalisation of coal. It was a substantial house, with twenty rooms, standing in its own grounds of ten acres. Access by road was up Field Lane, a cul-de-sac edged with twenty terraced cottages on the south side. The north side was bordered by the six-foot-high stone wall of the Grange gardens.

A patrol car was ordered to the Grange immediately and steps were taken to ensure that no one entered the murder room until the arrival of the investigating team. This would include the police surgeon, Chief Inspector Ackroyd, and his number two, Inspector Harry Bennet.

The two senior police officers arrived before the doctor and found that patrolmen Sergeant Catchpole and Constable Davis had acted promptly and prevented anyone from entering the office of the C.W.U. president where the body lay.

"We've to keep an open mind on this one," said C.I. Ackroyd. "It could be domestic or political. Who found the body?"

Sergeant Catchpole volunteered, "It was Molly White, a clerk here for the past five years. She's waiting in the next room."

"Right, I'll see her in a few minutes."

Dr. Hutchins, police surgeon, bustled into the room and exchanged greetings.

"Sorry for the delay, I was at the other side of town."

"Don't worry about that," said Ackroyd, "I know you need time on this, but can you give me a rough estimate of the time of death and, possibly, the cause and means?"

The doctor grunted "I'll see," and immediately went down on his knees beside the body.

Vince Hallett was lying on his back on the floor next to his black leather-upholstered swivel chair. This was behind a large, leather-topped mahogany desk. The bloodstain on his white shirt front had spread from a wound just below his rib-cage. Inspector Bennet looked around the sumptuous office and murmured, "He did himself well."

It had an air of affluence, with the latest in office equipment for the business executive. Expensive drapes were held back to give a view of the well designed gardens, full of spring flowering shrubs and many hundreds of daffodils and narcissi.

Vince Hallett had certainly been a controversial figure since becoming president of the C.W.U. The four-months-old strike of his union was seen as a threat to the Government. On the other hand, they were confident of the outcome as they had a large majority in the House of Commons.

Following threats of such a strike from the day Hallett was elected president, the N.C.B. had wisely built up stocks of coal on the surface, sufficient for meeting demand for more than twelve months without mining a single ton.

Hallett had stated his intention of bringing down the Government. His 'flying pickets' had clashed with the police wherever he had tried to stop work at power stations, coking plants and at other institutions which were customers of the N.C.B. Press commentators had expressed amazement at his apparent inability to grasp the economic facts of life.

The N.C.B. were steadily selling off their stocks of coal whilst having their costs dramatically reduced because of not paying the striking miners. This could go on for another year, long before which time the C.W.U. would be bankrupt and it's power as a union broken.

Two years earlier there had been many questions asked about the electoral procedures used for both Hallett's selection and the actual voting by the union members. Despite that, he had become firmly entrenched in the top position for the duration of his lifetime. He had joined the local colliery workforce soon after leaving school and had spent only two years down the pit before starting to climb the union ladder, prior to becoming a full-time union employee at the age of thirty.

The media had followed his activities very closely. They had reported fully his visits to Moscow and his virulent speeches, in which he continually criticised the Tory Party policies. During the past ten years he had also often attacked the Labour Party, especially if it had not helped him to press for better conditions for his members. Demands for more and more pay, for shorter working hours and increased holiday entitlement were a basic essential of all his speeches. He had persisted with this theme despite regular warnings from the N.C.B. and industrial and financial experts that spiralling wage bills would soon lead to the ruination of the market for British coal.

Vince Hallett had always ignored economic advice which included any hint of restrictions on wages or perks for his members. It had been reported that he did not, or would not, understand the modern meaning of the word 'marketing'. "Something to do with selling eggs and butter in the Friday market," he was quoted as saying, "nothing to do with men's wages or working conditions in the coal industry. It's just a ploy by the bosses to stop progress."

Now he was dead.

Dr. Hutchins stood up and looked at the Chief Inspector. "I'd say, without any lab. tests, he died about two hours ago, perhaps around ten o'clock, and that the cause was a piece of wood, possibly bamboo, entering his heart and causing massive damage. The post mortem will be more specific and you can then examine the weapon, or at least the piece that was broken off and is still lodged in the chest."

"Bamboo?" asked Ackroyd. "Very strange," he mused. "Let me know as soon as you have finished the P.M. One of us will be at the station. Thanks for your help so far."

The two officers went into the adjoining room to see Molly White, who was seated behind her typewriter. After a few words of sympathy to the upset woman, C.I. Ackroyd asked her to describe what she had found in the next room.

"Well, sir, I was taking a fax through to Mr. Hallett at about a quarter to ten, when I knew he was in the room – I'd just taken his coffee in only ten minutes earlier – and I found him lying there behind his desk."

She put her hands to her face and shuddered.

"Don't upset yourself, Mrs White," said Inspector Bennet. "Just take your time and tell us what you saw, and if you heard anything after taking the coffee in."

"Nothing else seemed to be different from usual. Oh, I thought I heard his voice raised once or twice, but that is fairly normal. You see, he used to shout at folk – on the 'phone, or when they were in the room with him. The walls are very thick, so I could never tell what was said." She paused.

"Did he ever shout at you?" asked Bennet.

"Oh, yes. It was part of the job. He was always quite pleasant afterwards, so I never let it upset me for long. The others all feel the same, but they all work further away from Mr. Hallett's office, in the next two rooms."

"If you will let me have your list of employees, we'll need to see them in turn and take their statements." Bennet looked at Molly White. "Can we use this office for that purpose?"

The results of interviewing the other ten clerical workers were of little use. No one had seen or heard anything unusual until Molly White had screamed and run from the scene of the crime and into the general office. The front door of the Grange was kept open during normal business hours for any visitor to walk in and announce their presence at Mrs White's room. This was indicated with a board marked 'Reception'. Yes, anyone could have walked in and gone straight into Mr. Hallett's office – and gone out the same way – without being seen.

"That seems to be the most likely," said Inspector Bennet, looking towards his superior, "I'll send a team to knock at all the doors near here, especially those cottages we passed. Someone, somewhere, must have seen something."

========

14th April 1982

Inspector Bennet was sitting in Chief Inspector Ackroyd's office summarising a few facts which had arisen since the murder.

1. The cause of death was a sharpened piece of bamboo which had been plunged upwards into the victim's heart. Death would have occurred within a matter of seconds after the blow, at near ten o'clock in the morning of 13th April. The bamboo had been broken off nearly level with the skin just below the ribcage.

2. No one at the Grange had seen or heard anything strange at that time.

3. From all the neighbourhood interviews so far reported, only Mrs Helen Fagin, living with her husband Fred at 19, The Cottages, Field Lane, had seen anything unusual. An older man, perhaps 60 years old, dressed in a black, two-piece jogging suit, had run up and down Field Lane on the morning of 12th April and was seen again on 13th April running down the lane, from the Grange, at about 10 a.m.

No one had found the remainder of the murder weapon, i.e. the bamboo handle.

C.I. Ackroyd looked across at his Number Two.

"You've some useful lines to explore there. What are your plans?"

"This jogger is our best bet. He may have been doing a recce on the 12th and done the deed on the 13th. I'll continue with the 'house to house' all the way into town, especially in the most likely parking spots. I reckon he'd have some wheels at the ready not too far away. A poster campaign might stir a few memories, but I'm intrigued with the bamboo connection. I've never come across it before, not as a weapon."

Ackroyd smiled. "They came across it a lot during the war – before your time – but it is used every day in South East Asia. They use it for making houses, furniture, cooking and eating utensils, and for weapons of offence or defence.

"Do you know that when you split green bamboo downwards, the inside contracts faster than the outside skin leaving two edges that are sharper than a razor? If, at the same time, you whittle one end into a point, that will harden into a very sharp knife point, like a rapier.

"My brother told me that they did this a lot in the Chindits[a] in Burma. They called them 'punjis'.[b] They used to stick them into the ground to make a defensive barrier across the tracks leading to wherever they were camping for the night. If anyone walked on to one it went right through his boot and foot, even British army boots. The Japs wore rubber-soled canvas boots which were no protection from punjis at all.

"Just a point of interest: did you know that their canvas boots were made like our mittens – they had a separate 'thumb' to take their big toe, with the other four toes in their own department? It was supposed to help when walking on rough ground or climbing trees. That's of no value now, but there is a whiff of Burma about this case." He looked rather pensive. "I wish my brother was still with us. He told me many tales about living in the Burmese jungle." He paused again. "Another point which could be of use – I have a recollection of at least one other unexplained death linked with bamboo. It was years ago and it might have been a dagger or a bow-and-arrow job. Somewhere abroad, or it could have been in the U.K.

"Now, I have a suggestion, Harry. When you are ready, and only you will know when you are, why not apply all that knowledge you gained on the Crusoe course and feed all your facts into the system? You could be surprised, and it might even help you in this case."

The Crusoe Course had lasted only three days for senior officers in Regional Crime Squads in order to initiate them into the use of a newly centralised record system available throughout Europe. All

---

a Appendix A2
b Appendix A3

serious crime which was unresolved after twelve months was fed into the Computer Record of Unresolved Serious Crime of Europe – hence the near acronym. It could rapidly produce a brief history of crimes which had a similarity to the parameters specified. A fully detailed report could then be produced for any selected crime.

Harry Bennet, known unfairly as 'Flash Harry' to his subordinates because of his very modern approach to crime detection, nodded.

"Yes, sir, that is one of my possible methods. There are sufficient facts here to produce a reasonable list, and, if this is not the first murder by this jogger, it should prove helpful. Incidentally, on that Crusoe course last autumn, one of the members fed in too little data and the computer churned out the complete list of its records. Very expensive in printing time and paper and a black mark for the man concerned. He couldn't even lift the printout, it was so heavy. I shall see to it tomorrow as I will need to go to Sheffield. The computer they use is in the University." He then continued to study the flow of reports being received.

15th April 1982

The 'outside' telephone extension rang on the Chief Inspector's desk as he was about to walk out of the door. "Yes?" he answered.

"Harry here, sir, I'm still at the University. We've struck oil with Crusoe. There are four crimes listed in the U.K. which include a bamboo weapon. Each one indicates a single operator, and in each case death was caused by a pointed piece of bamboo!"

"Excellent!" congratulated Ackroyd, "what is the spread of dates?"

Bennet was more subdued when he replied. "The first was in 1948 and the others in 1955, 1964 and 1973. It is not likely to be the same man for all five crimes, spread over thirty-four years, but – hold it, the dates!" he exclaimed excitedly. "Each one is on 13th April! They are connected. It must be the same man!"

"Before you blow a valve, Harry, I've just one more suggestion. Have you thought of the possibility that our Mr X doesn't always use bamboo, only occasionally? How about going back to your

Crusoe friends and asking for a printout of all crimes which are dated around 13th April each year since the Second War and which involve a possible lone operator? Bring the lists back here and we'll chew them over together."

"Will do, sir." The phone cleared.

Ackroyd rubbed his hands together with smile.

"I'll have a fresh coffee now please, Mary," he said into the intercom.

That afternoon the two of them studied the computer printout with an awareness of imminent success – up to a point. Each year since 1946 there was the record of an unresolved murder on the 12th, 13th or 14th April. Thirty of them were actually on 13th April. In every case there was no indication of a second person being involved.

In every case the victim was some well known person mentioned frequently in the press for his controversial views or activities. They were mostly reported as being politically to the left but at least six of them were entrepreneurial types who were under suspicion of committing fraud at the time of their deaths.

13th April 1946. East London. Miles Swannick, 46 years, Shot with a .38 pistol, weapon never found, no witnesses. Reputed to be a black marketeer who had avoided service in H.M. Forces due to 'bad health'.

13th April 1947. Glasgow. John (Jock) McFee, 51 years, Fell (suspected that he was pushed) under a train at Strathclyde when returning from a union meeting, no witnesses. He was leading a three-month-old strike despite objections from many of his members and from the owners' organisations.

14th April 1948. Birmingham. Brigadier Charles MacAlister Fitzburn (ret'd), 46 years, Found in the grounds of his country house near Chepstow with a chest wound, possibly from a crossbow. The projectile had been withdrawn but a small sliver of bamboo was found embedded in the heart. Discovered at 7 a.m. Bed not slept in. No witnesses. He had resigned his commission and avoided a possible court martial. Estimated time of death, 11 p.m. 13th April 1948.

13th April 1949. North London. Eric Blackett, 42 years. Found shot
in his own study. Smith and Wesson .38 pistol at his side with only
one blurred fingerprint (his own). Owner of weapon not traced.
Murder suspected.

The list continued with a record of an unexplained killing of similar
people in the news on or near this same date each year.

Ackroyd grunted. "The pattern is developing and I don't like it."

"What don't you like?" thought Bennet. "I'll not ask as he's sure
to tell me."

"If one man has committed a murder on the same date each year
for 36 years, we not only have a nutter, but the entire U.K. police
force can't have been studying these criminal records during that
time. How do you explain that, Harry? And anyway, he will be an
old man by now."

Harry Bennet looked across at him and replied carefully.

"I'm only looking at the facts at this point. There's a murder on
my patch. An unusual weapon, a bamboo dagger, appears to be the
cause of death, but we don't have the complete weapon. There is a
reliable witness prepared to swear to seeing just such an older man
jogging near the scene, not only within half an hour of the crime,
but also the day before.

We've had only one report so far resulting from the poster campaign. A local man saw a jogger in 'a dark blue (?) outfit' running
from the public loo near the library to a red Ford in the parking area
and driving off – mid-morning on 13th April. He only thinks it was
a red Ford but he is sure the man was grey haired and wearing
glasses. It must be this jogger we want. What are your views, sir?"

"You're probably right there, Harry."

Ackroyd looked wistful.

"Of course, you must pursue all possible lines to find him, but he
could be anywhere in the country by now. If there is a '13th April
serial killer' he could be based anywhere at all, or he could be an
itinerant. Let's find this red Ford – not exactly an unusual car or colour."

He paused, tapped his desk with his spread fingers. "Would you
like me to follow up on another possible line? I keep thinking of the

bamboo connection and the many tales I've heard my brother tell about the Burmese jungle. There must be some significance in the date of 13th April. It's been unlucky for so many of these forceful characters who have become victims. There's a link there some-where. I'll make a few 'phone calls and then let you know if I can find anything." He raised his eyebrows.

"Of course, sir, thanks a lot. I'll get on with all the routine enquiries and see you in the morning." Harry Bennet returned to his own office, taking the computer lists with him.

C.I. Ackroyd called his secretary into his office and gave her a list of various telephone calls he wanted to make. This included the Ministry of Defence, Whitehall, the Imperial War Museum, the Burma Star Association, Sheffield City Library.

Within two hours he had noted more facts ready for Harry Bennet.

1. The significant wartime connection between Burma and 13th April could only be for either 1944 or 1945. He could eliminate 1942 and 1943. In 1942, our army in Burma, a mixture of British and Indian troops with some Burmese levies and thousands of refugees, was retreating from the central plains, over the mountain barrier into India.

Few detailed diary records were kept and the histories were mostly written from memory at a later date. 13th April had no special significance in that year.

During 1943 there was sporadic contact with the enemy along the eastern borders of India and Burma. Patrol activity, from both the British and Japanese armies, kept both sides aware of each other in the Akyab Peninsula and to the north along the Chindwin river. Similar patrols from General Stilwell's Chinese army in the extreme north of Burma had the same affect. Again, 13th April 1943 had no apparent importance.

1944 was much more interesting. 13th April 1944 was highlighted by the battle of Nunshigum. This angular mountain, rising sharply from the dried paddy [a] fields of the Imphal plain, had been secured

---

a Appendix A4

by a strong Japanese force a few days earlier. They were eliminated by eight tanks from B Squadron, 3rd Carabiniers, leading and supporting 1st Battalion the Dogra Regiment, Indian infantry led by British and Indian officers.

Earlier in the month, on 5th April, General Sato's 31st Japanese Division had attacked Kohima, some 50 miles north of Nunshigum, and had been unable to remove the much smaller force of the 4th Battalion the Royal West Kents. They were still in action around Kohima on 13th April.

These were just two vital actions taking place to secure the base of the British 4th Corps in Imphal.

Japanese forces were also attacking the defenders in the Kabaw Valley to the east, at Bishenpur and other villages to the south and west of Imphal. It was all part of the Japanese plan U Go, invading India in the start of the 'Glorious March on Delhi'. General Bill Slim and his 14th Army were surrounded for almost three months. They stood fast, depending upon all supplies coming in by air, and fought the Japanese to a standstill.

The Chindit 77 Brigade, commanded by Brigadier Michael Calvert, reported in their war diaries that their West Africans had a very successful action on 13th April 1944, capturing part of Mawlu, a Japanese-held village on the railway line in northern Burma. These black troops were commanded by white officers and N.C.O.s.[a]

Yes, 13th April 1944 was a very significant date.

13th April 1945. The reinforced and refreshed 14th Army was still fighting the Japanese, who were retreating to the south and east along their original lines of communication towards Rangoon. Our confident, experienced troops were widespread over northern and central Burma, rushing south. Mandalay and Meiktila had been recaptured using a brilliant strategy which misled the still active Japanese forces. The race was against time. It was essential for the 14th Army to reach Rangoon and its port before the monsoons [b] made it impossible

---

a Appendix A5
b Appendix A6

to air-supply the growing number of men and units involved. At the same time, they must not miss the opportunity to eliminate the remains of a once proud Japanese army.

No. 13th April 1945 had no outstanding significance.

1944 was the year – 13th April 1944 was the vital date of the turning point in the battle of Imphal. Nunshigum or possibly Kohima?

The Chindits could be held in reserve as a third possible source of enquiry if necessary.

He looked up as Harry Bennet knocked and walked into his office, raising his eyebrows in query. Harry smiled, "Good news, sir. Sheffield Police found a red Cortina this morning during a routine check on car numbers left overnight in their multistories. It had been reported missing from a house in the suburbs days ago. Looks like our man used it for the job and then switched back to another vehicle before disappearing. Yes, it's already been checked for prints – wiped clean inside, nothing useful left behind."

He pulled a sour face. "Looks like we're up against a wall now." He saw the sparkle in the boss's eyes.

"You've found something?"

Chief Inspector Ackroyd hesitated.

"I've not been wasting my time. You know I was going to check out on the date, 13th April, and any possible link with the South East Asian war? If our man is a nutter, which seems likely, then his 13th April madness could be linked with the battle of Nunshigum on 13th April 1944!"

"Nunshigum? Never heard of it."

"No, most people never have. At one time the 14th Army was known as the Forgotten Army and Nunshigum was a very important battle near Imphal in Eastern India. The Japanese had actually invaded India early in 1944 and they claimed to have started their March on Delhi. At that time the Brits controlled the whole of India, which included what we now know as the three countries of Pakistan, India and Bangladesh. End of history lesson.

"Tonight, the two of us are eating with an old friend of my brother, a veteran from the 14th Army called Alan Fenner. He was in the ranks at Nunshigum and continued fighting the Japanese for fifteen months, until he became a casualty and was flown out of Burma." He paused, looking reflective. "He was a tank man in the 3rd Carabiniers, an old cavalry regiment, and, when you think that they were in action two months before the Second Front opened in Europe and they were still in action weeks after it had finished on V.E. Day, he'll have a tale to tell – and he might help us to find a lead to this murderer."

The two policemen met Alan Fenner as arranged at the Hen and Chickens Hotel, near the centre of Sheffield. They were familiar with the welcome and comfort of the public house, which had been popular with the Sheffield police for many years, based as they were at the station next door.

The old soldier shook hands with Ackroyd, whom he had met a few times before, and looked keenly at the younger Bennet when introduced.

"I'm glad to meet you and hope that I can help you with this Burma business. It goes back a long way but I can, in fact, remember more details about that time than I can about the things my wife asked me to buy at the shops yesterday," he laughed. "What can I get you to drink?" It was a pleasant start to a fascinating evening.

Alan Fenner (they were soon all on first names) had salt and pepper hair, which would have been brown a few years earlier. He was 5' 9" tall, weighed perhaps 10 stones 7 lbs and looked quite lively and in good health.

During the excellent dinner, served smoothly by the hostess, he gave a clear resumé of his wartime service prior to arriving in India.

After volunteering for the Royal Armoured Corps on his nineteenth birthday, (I had enough footslogging in the Hymers College O.T.C.[a] in Hull and only fancied riding into action), he spent nearly a year at the R.A.C. Depot, Catterick.

---

a Appendix A7

In 82A Squad at the 56th Training Regiment he had the usual square-bashing, followed by gunnery, driving and wireless training. A wireless instructor's course at Bovington was a success. Then he returned to Catterick to train new recruits. The others in his squad had already been spread to other units, some to OCTUs [a] but mostly to tank regiments in the U.K. and overseas. Many were to meet up again in various parts of the world.

Teaching beginners the rudiments of radio telephony (R.T.) [b] and wireless telegraphy (W.T.) [c] together with the intricacies of the No. 19 set,[d] all in a rigid two weeks' programme, to be repeated with a new squad each fortnight, began to drag for Alan.

The war news was rarely encouraging. The U-boats were sinking too many Allied ships, the R.A.F. were inflicting heavy losses on the German raiders on our homeland, and in North Africa the German and Allied armies yoyoed backwards and forwards across the deserts. Libya and Tunisia were a testing ground for armoured fighting vehicles and our old Valentines and Matildas, with their 2-pounders, were being outgunned by the enemy.

Alan Fenner volunteered for a transfer to his local Territorial Regiment, the East Riding Yeomanry, stationed at Bingley near Bradford.

Two weeks after joining them he realised how foolish it was to volunteer. He was sent home on embarkation leave before being drafted to North Africa.

That journey took ten weeks in the Esperence Bay, sister ship of the Jarvis Bay which had been sunk when she attacked a German battleship with her single 4-pounder manned by Marines. She sailed, in convoy, from Liverpool to the east coast of the U.S.A. and South America, then across to Freetown for refuelling. They did not see Capetown when they rounded the Cape and eventually docked at Durban for two weeks' leave ashore.

---

a Appendix A8
b Appendix B
c Appendix B
d Appendix B

"We were all told the night before docking that we must remember our wives and loved ones and not be tempted by the fleshpots, nor must we fall for the invitations we were sure to receive to go into the Boer country to stay and work on a farm, i.e. to desert. It was not to be.

"The next morning we were marched, with our kit, along the dock, straight aboard the Nieuw Amsterdam and sailed that night. This new Dutch transatlantic liner had an American and Dutch crew who treated their 'passengers' extremely well. The ship was very much larger than the Esperance Bay and the food was a marked improvement on our wartime rations.

"The 1st South African Armoured Division, without their vehicles, travelled with us and we had our first experience of apartheid when we saw their treatment of the Kikuyu servicemen who walked near. White fists and boots were freely used to move them out of the way. Trouble with the British troops started when a large blond South African beat up a coloured East Riding Yeoman who foolishly asked him 'Have you got a light, mate?' The contingent of Military Police quickly moved between the two sides and kept us apart for the rest of the voyage.

"Excluding that problem, we all enjoyed the luxury and were sorry to disembark at Port Tewfiq at the northern end of the Red Sea. It was a bitterly cold night and we were soon bussed to Giza on the outskirts of Cairo to join the 47th Royal Tank Regiment. They had been severely battered by the Germans a few weeks earlier at El Alamein. Our draft consisted of reinforcements prior to their going back into the desert to rejoin Monty and the 8th Army, the Desert Rats.

"Our tents were in lines on the sand in front of the Sphinx, near the Pyramids, and this was where I blotted my copybook.

"The S.S.M.[a] had given us a long lecture on how to survive in the cold of the night with six blankets issued per man, how the locals would help themselves to anything not chained down and had warned us that they would even creep into the tents at night and steal the blankets off our beds!

---

a Appendix A9

"On the first night, after imbibing two pints of a strong Canadian Black Horse beer, the first ale for nearly three months, I had to get up for a pee. This I did well away from the tent at the feet of the Sphinx, as I hadn't found any urinals, and then I crept back into my tent.

"Problem. My bed was occupied.

'Wake up, chaps,' I shouted, 'there's a wog in my bed.'

Half the men in the tent, perhaps a dozen or so, leapt out of their blankets, grabbed a boot or something heavy and belaboured the shape in my bed. Horror – the shape pulled back the blankets over its head and we all saw the irate face of the S.S.M. emerging. I managed to creep quietly out of the tent, which I now realised was the wrong one, and entered the next tent where I found my own bed exactly as I had left it. The S.S.M. was rather bad tempered for the next few days, until a large group of us were drafted for immediate transfer to the Poona depot in India. This is the first time that I've confessed to the mistake. I think that even the Sphinx might have smiled at the time."

The meal was now finished and the three men ordered coffees and brandies which they took to the corner near the fire.

"I wonder, Alan, if you could lead us up to 13th April, 1944 and Nunshigum?" murmured James Ackroyd.

"Of course," replied Alan Fenner, "the next eight months led me through a spell of more wireless instructing at the Poona Depot. I did a guard duty on Gandhi, who was imprisoned there, but that is another story. Then I joined the 26th Hussars at Secunderabad. I'd volunteered again – I never learn – and within three months that regiment was broken up. Some of the men with an infantry background went to join the Chindits – you've heard of them – Wingate's lot? But a good number of qualified tradesmen, mostly tank crews, went to join the 3rd Carabiniers (Prince of Wales's Dragoon Guards) at Trivellore near Madras. They were known throughout the Royal Armoured Corps as the 'Carbs' and were second to none for their 'bull' or spit and polish. However, you want to hear about them?"

"Yes," agreed Ackroyd, "we think that the man we're seeking

went through some traumatic experience in Burma in the war, probably on 13th April, and we would appreciate hearing something of your own knowledge of the Carabiniers' action at Nunshigum and beyond. If he is a Carabinier, it will be a great help to know what he went through that might have triggered off his unusual activity. Of course, we hope to find him from the information already in our hands. Could you start from the time the Carabiniers went from India to the Burmese border, please?"

Chapter 2

October 1943.
The 3rd Carabiniers Move
from Madras to Manipur

October 1943

Trivellore, Madras.

There was a "holiday air" amongst the tank crews of B Squadron, 3rd Carabiniers. Their sixteen Mark III General Lee[a] tanks were to travel by train, via Calcutta, to the state of Manipur, Assam, on the North East Border of India and Burma. They could be going into action for the first time since the start of the war.

The fifty N.C.O.s and men selected to travel, three per tank, were paraded in the lines [b] for briefing by the second in command (2 i/c) Captain Murphy, a peace-time schoolmaster.

"Now, pay attention, men. You have been selected to take the squadron A.F.V.s [c] many hundreds of miles in complete secrecy. You will deliver them safely to a map reference to be advised, taking possibly two weeks on trains, both standard and narrow gauge, using ferries over rivers and on tank transporters for the road journeys. Once again, you will observe the strictest security. You will not wear any Carabinier insignia and will travel as 123 Workshops, Royal Army Ordnance Corps. Side hats with R.O.A.C. cap badges will be issued and worn at all times.

"Each tank will be covered completely with a 40 by 40 tarpaulin,

---

a Appendix E
b Appendix A10
c Appendix A11

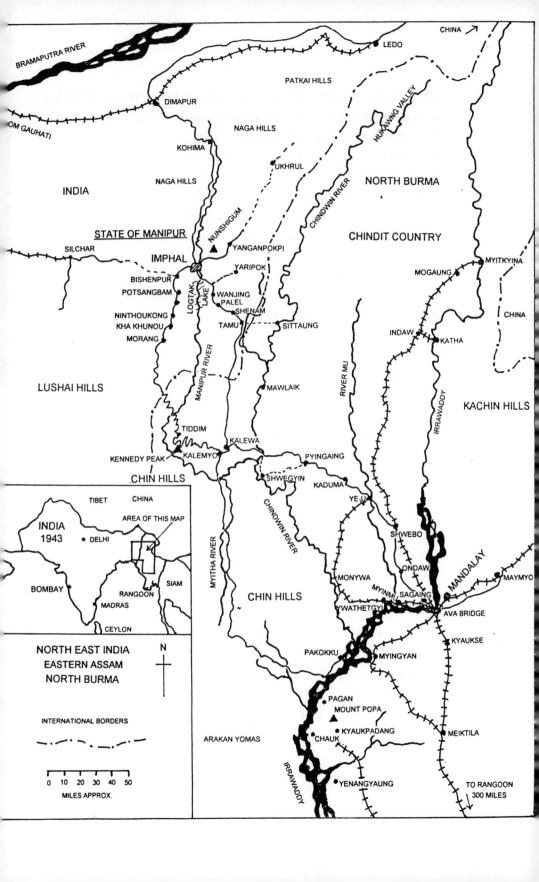

tied down so that no one will realise that it covers an A.F.V. If any stranger approaches you with questions you will not disclose anything about your unit, the equipment or your destination. Is that understood? Sergeant Major Craddock will now give you further details of timing, rations and procedures."

The S.S.M. stepped forward in the bright sunlight and looked steadily into the eyes of each man standing at ease. He knew that he was not liked. He did not wish to be liked. He was there to ensure discipline by whatever means he thought necessary. His being an army boxer of light-heavyweight grade certainly discouraged most men from showing any desire to disagree with him. Any man showing what he called 'dumb insolence' was likely to be challenged to a 'sporting contest' with the gloves on, but reports of previous such punishment deterred all but the most stupid from accepting a challenge.

There were no takers that day.

Sgt. Major Craddock read out a list of the names of those detailed to accompany each tank. Two motorcycles were to travel with the first two tanks. Two weeks' rations were to be drawn immediately, water containers filled, small arms and ammunition to be inspected at 1600 hrs. B. Squadron A.F.V.'s were to be loaded on to transporters at 0700 hrs. tomorrow.

He looked at the men again, looked straight at me and said, "Trooper Fenner, you set a high standard on picquet[a] duty last night. That's what I expect from all of you, two hours on guard, four hours off, 24 hours a day, for the next two weeks. Any one of you might have to make a decision for action without having a senior N.C.O. near to give you an order. Make sure that you each make the right decision. The 3rd Carabiniers expect it and rely on you. Dismiss."

As we fell out, Paddy Ryan, a London bus driver, caught my elbow, drew me to one side and asked, "Hey, what's all that about 'last night'?" Some of the others heard him and gathered round.

"Well," I said, "you remember the warning we were given by one

---

a Appendix A12

of the old Carbs, when our 26th Hussars draft joined B Squadron, that the S.S.M. was a bully? I was warned that he made a habit of leaving the Sergeants' Mess after 2300 hrs. and then prowling around the lines looking for the guard, hoping to catch him napping.

Last night I was on mobile picquet from 2200 hrs. to 2359 hrs.[a] and I was looking for him. I heard him leaving the Mess as usual, then he went very quiet and I saw him tip-toeing between the bashas.[b] I followed him behind the Orderly Room, along the perimeter of B Squadron lines, to the back of the Guardroom and then I challenged him: 'Halt, who goes there?'

He spun round and started walking towards me.

'Halt, or I fire.' He hesitated then started towards me again.

'Halt' I shouted again, loud enough for the Guardroom to hear, and then I cocked my pistol, loud enough for him to hear. He halted and answered, 'Friend'.

I had him then. Keeping the cocked, loaded pistol pointed at his chest, I said 'Advance friend, to be recognised'. He said he had been looking for me, so I told him exactly where he had walked, where he had hidden in the shadows, and that I had followed this 'shady character' as he was obviously up to no good. Of course, I recognised him now, but I had only obeyed orders and done my duty. Yes, I said, I was quite prepared to shoot him if he had not complied with my order to halt."

The others clapped me on my back and one, an old Carb, said, "You may have beaten him this time but he'll get you for it!"

"I wouldn't be so sure," I replied, "I think we both now have a certain respect for each other." He looked at me. "You know what the Carbs call his tank? Zero tank! The first time the Squadron goes into action the other fifteen will zero their 75s[c] on him and blow him to hell!" There was real hate in his voice. I looked at him. "What about the rest of his crew – the other six? They are all old Carbs,

---

a Appendix A13
b Appendix A14
c Appendix E

muckers [a] of yours?" He looked a bit shifty over that. "They will be warned to get out first."

We all laughed and went off to draw two weeks rations for our tanks and to fill up with water.

———

The next morning we were off on what was to be an epic journey. It was good to get away from Trivellore, with the recent history of burst dams, tanks lost in floods, cholera in the next villages, the departure of many of the old Carabiniers on Python [b] after six years or more of service in India – service without any action against the enemy. Those of us from the 26th Hussars were nearly all trade-tested [c] tank crews, well trained and ready for some effective action.

We had been told that the Japanese had reached the border of Burma and India, having moved by land and sea from Singapore and Siam. I had met two of the 7th Hussars at the R.A.C. Depot, Poona, where I spent some months as a wireless instructor, giving refresher courses to officers and men passing through to reinforce regiments such as 3rd Carabiniers, 26th Hussars (now disbanded) 25th Dragoons (formed from the 3rd Carabiniers). Corporals Joad and Hemstock D.C.M. [d] of the 7th Hussars had described the appalling conditions experienced during their retreat in 1942, under General Slim, from central Burma, having to leave their Stuart tanks at the Chindwin river and continue the journey on foot through Imphal to a safe base in India.

The 25th Dragoons had recently joined an attack on Jap positions in the Akyab peninsula but had not made much progress. Both sides had been hampered by natural land barriers, rivers, chaungs, [e] and jungle-covered hills. They had learned that fighting in such country

———

a Appendix A15
b Appendix A16
c Appendix A17
d Appendix A18
e Appendix A19

depended as much upon good engineering support as on the determination to survive and succeed.

During the first days of the journey the train moved steadily northwards with the mountains of the Eastern Ghats on our left and occasional views of the Bay of Bengal on our right. We saw lush jungle and tidy, well-worked fields, dotted with the bent backs of labourers. We adjusted to the dramatic change in living conditions, cooking and eating on the open 'flats', washing, shaving and relieving ourselves as and when it was possible, depending on the speed of the train.

Clickety-click, clickety-click, – the rhythm of a slow-moving goods train could send anyone to sleep, particularly after the first few days of guard duty on the move. Each of the sixteen flat open wagons, carrying one covered tank, was 'home' for the three B.O.R.s [a] who were guarding their own tank. We stuck rigidly to being alert and on duty for two hours and then having four hours for sleep and relaxation. Sometimes the train speed was less than five m.p.h. and we would jump down on to the track side and trot along level with our own tank or chat with the crews of the other flat wagons. At other times the train would be stationary, held up by signals, for a few hours – on one occasion all day. Any such halt gave us the opportunity for a brew-up, whatever time of day or night. One of us would walk up to the engine with our tea and draw boiling water with the approval of the driver – usually a cheerful Anglo-Indian.

Sometimes the two men off duty on one flat would join their opposite numbers on another flat for a game of cards – brag or pontoon were the favourites. This worked out very well – until the train moved off, rapidly picking up speed, with the card players spread all along the train. They could continue to play cards where they were but each man was required to be on his own flat when it was his time for guard duty. No excuses were accepted for not being there on time to relieve his colleague.

We all became quite adept at crawling over the top of each covered

a Appendix A20

tank and leaping across the gap between two wagons in order to rejoin our own flat when due for guard duty. The only one to fall off the train in motion did so whilst asleep one night. He rolled off still wrapped in his blankets and awoke when he hit the earth at some five or six miles an hour. He managed to clamber aboard another flat and rejoined his own crew later that night – none the worse for his experience.

4th Night. "Fire! Fire!". The shouts of our own guard and the sound of machine gun ammunition exploding brought us out of our dreams instantly. I had been sleeping just under the canopy formed by the tarpaulin pulled forward over the 75 mm gun on the tank.

The sight of the first three tanks, apparently on fire, was a shock. Flames leaping into the night sky, with sparks blown back in the wind, looked likely to spread along the whole train which was moving at some 10 m.p.h. Shouting men could be seen beating at the flames with their blankets. The train slowed down and halted.

Everyone was now awake. Sergeant Willis yelled, "Get off with your buckets and make a chain down to that pahni[a]", pointing to the small pond at the side of the track. "You lot, unfasten the ropes and pull off the burning tarpaulins. You others, get forward with all your water and put those flames out – watch that ammo!"

It worked.

Thanks to the pond water, the men who had been asleep only minutes earlier were now formed into an efficient chain carrying full buckets up to the fires and passing empty buckets back to be refilled. The burning tarpaulins were lying on the trackside, exposing three General Lee tanks and two burnt out motorcycles for all to see. But, there were no strangers near.

Recovery was quickly achieved. A bright Q.M.S.[b] had ordered five spare tarpaulins to be loaded on to the last flat of the train before leaving Trivellore. Perhaps he just wanted to be rid of them, but they saved the security that night.

Sergeant Willis belatedly ordered each crew to get a fire extinguisher

---

a Appendix A21
b Appendix A22

out of their tank and keep it in the 'living area' at the front. Paddy Ryan made some comment about cavalrymen closing stable doors, but luckily no one heard him. One man who had been on guard reported seeing a mass of sparks coming from the engine funnel just before the fire started and that was accepted as the most likely cause of the trouble. After that excitement the journey continued more or less as before – periods of travelling slowly, with a few hours stationary, until we changed to the narrow gauge railway well north of Calcutta.

This was done between 0200 hrs. and 0500 hrs., with the tanks being uncovered, driven off the original standard gauge flats and on to the meter gauge flats, then re-covered with the tarpaulins. No security problems were reported.

On day fourteen the train arrived at Gauhati, travelling east. Our food and tea rations were almost expired. We faced a ferry trip across the Brahmaputra river, which flowed from the mountains of Tibet south into the Bay of Bengal. This was again done at night.

A further week's rations were drawn from a truck sent back to meet us from our advance party, who were already at Dimapur. The new train then took us into the hills at Dimapur at the start of the Manipur Road.

It was at Gauhati, where we had halted after reloading and covering the tanks in the marshalling yard, that a Sikh officer came up to me and demanded, "Tell me, please, are those tanks carrying 57 mm or 75 mm guns?"

Remembering the security talk so many days ago, I took off my side hat, plucked the hair on the top of my head and said in my best Stan Laurel voice, "I've no idea. I understand it is just a load of equipment to be delivered somewhere." – and moved on. His fellow officer, another Sikh, said to him, "I still bet you that they are 75s." I reported all this to Sergeant Willis, but there was little we could do.

We were glad to reach Dimapur at the end of our train journey, after all the restrictions of living on a flat wagon, with never more than four hours sleep at a time and every transfer carried out in the small hours of the morning.

Dimapur was a hive of industry twenty-four hours a day. All the needs of the growing army based in the Imphal plain were shipped through this small town. Transferring reinforcements and thousands of tons of supplies from the narrow gauge railway on to trucks was a continual and noisy process. There were sixteen huge transporters awaiting our arrival and each one weighed 40 tons with a Lee tank on board.

The Manipur Road to Imphal, winding through the Naga Hills, mountains of up to 7000 feet, had a newly improved metalled surface for 130 miles. The hairpin bends were not designed to take such large vehicles and negotiating each bend required some reversing and shunting before we could drive the short distance to the next one. Most bends showed signs of some earlier vehicles having missed the corner and gone over the khud [a] side. The wrecks of three-tonners and 15 cwt trucks could be seen hundreds of feet down into the jungle. I asked the Scottish transporter driver how it happened.

"We take a villager out of his paddy field and we give him a 3-tonner to go to Imphal. He usually manages to leap out before it goes over!"

"Do you mean it's sabotage?" I asked.

He shrugged his shoulders. "Maybe. There are Gandhi-wallahs [b] all over India. Just be careful if you have to be driven by one!"

After that, our tank crew dismounted before every bend in the road. We told the driver that we enjoyed walking after such a long train journey.

The drive, firstly to Kohima and then to our destination, was complicated by the narrow road being one-way, with the direction changing every twelve hours. This created delays, with more shunting, reversing and waiting at prepared parking areas.

At Kohima we reached a bridge over the river which was simply not able to take a 40 ton load. We had to uncover the tanks, unload the transporters, cross the bridge separately and then reverse the process before continuing the journey. All this at midday. Bang went

---

a Appendix A23
b Appendix A24

security. Hundreds of locals observed the exposure. Any Japanese sympathiser would now know that some heavy tanks were being moved to the border area.

Twenty days after leaving Trivellore the B Squadron tanks arrived at 108 milestone, almost twenty miles north of Imphal, and were reunited with the remainder of the Squadron who had travelled by train and road. B Echelon [a] had driven their vehicles all the way from Madras over the very varied roads. They had spent the past week preparing the camp site on the west side of the road. The gently sloping open land was ideal and, although the monsoons had ended, any sudden storm water would quickly drain away. The jungle-covered higher ground rose to craggy peaks as far as the eye could see in every direction.

It was good to be welcomed back into the 'family' with a hot meal of bully [b] and vegetables supplied by the squadron cooks. The cry of 'come and get it' [c] was never more welcome. The new arrivals were excluded from guard duty that night and we slept right through until 0600 hrs. reveille.

The irreverent words to the cavalry trumpet calls confirmed that feeling of belonging. 'The Carbs have got no hiloes,[d] no hiloes, no hiloes, the Carbs have got no hiloes, they flogged them for beer'.

---

a Appendix A25
b Appendix A26
c Appendix A27
d Appendix A28

Chapter 3

In the Naga Hills

0830 hrs. Squadron Parade.

The grass-covered open land was no help to smartness of drill, neither were the previously given orders not to polish brasses, nor the fact that some of us still wore the R.A.O.C. caps and badges. I expected the S.S.M. to give us hell – but he did not. He formed us into three ranks, called us to attention and handed over to the Squadron Leader, Major Edward Sanford.

His father had been Colonel of the Regiment between the Wars. The Major, known as 'Dizzy' to the old Carbs, was a short man, perhaps 27 years old, with a 'cheese cutter' cavalry officer's hat on the top of a large head. Most of the old 26th Hussars had seen him only once or twice before and we were looking forward to assessing him for ourselves.

The old Carbs had judged him as an 'officer',[a] which put him into a class apart, never to be helped, welcomed or admired – only to be obeyed. (And jump to it, man!) His batman,[b] Trooper Richardson, had certainly turned him out well. The new jungle green battledress was immaculate with gleaming green-painted webbing and highly polished brasses.

"B Squadron, Stand at – Ease! Stand Easy."

We relaxed and looked at him.

"I want to welcome you all back together after three weeks of being spread over most of Eastern India on your various journeys to reach this place. Firstly, I want to thank and congratulate the tank crews who safely brought our sixteen tanks all the way from Madras

---

a   Appendix A20
b   Appendix A29

30

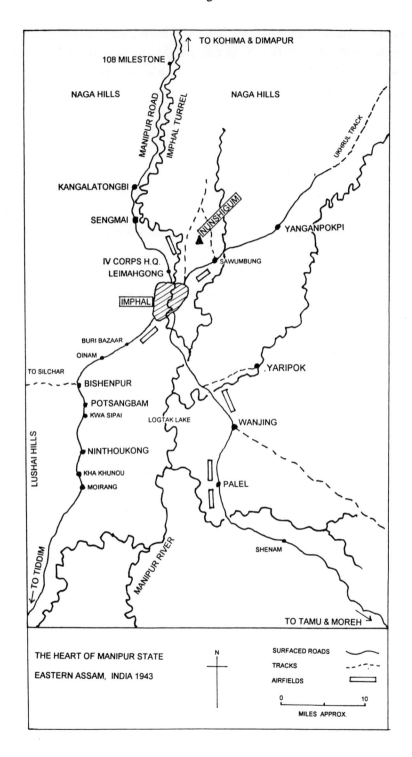

THE HEART OF MANIPUR STATE

EASTERN ASSAM, INDIA 1943

under difficult circumstances. Your continual guard duties were very testing and your reaction to an unfortunate fire in transit was superb. We were all relieved to learn that you had no casualties. The two damaged motorcycles have already been replaced.

During the months ahead, when we meet the enemy, that sort of attitude and action will help you win through to a successful end of the war.

Now, about the enemy. They are known to be at the other side of the Chindwin River, about 50 miles east of us. The Japanese 15th Army in Burma has six divisions to support their attempts to invade the eastern borders of India into Assam and Bengal. As you know, our daughter regiment, the 25th Dragoons, has been in action in Akyab, 300 miles south of here, but the country was not suitable for the deployment of tanks. We learned many lessons from their experiences which will help us.

To meet this threat from the east, we have 4 Corps and 15 Corps – a total of eight divisions. 4 Corps, based at Imphal, has the extra support of 254 Indian Tank Brigade comprising the 3rd Carabiniers in General Lee/Grant tanks and 7th Indian Cavalry in Stuarts.[a] They are already here near Imphal. 15 Corps continues to defend Bengal.

We already have a number of organisations active behind the Japanese lines – General Wingate's Long Range Penetration Group known as the Chindits, also the intelligence-gathering units of Chin Levies and the Lushai Brigade. They are all helping to weaken the Jap efforts, which are hampered by very long lines of communication. They will really have problems when we meet them."

He looked around the listening men. "This may be in only a very few months, but, in that time you must all be ready and trained to a point of excellence. Captain Murphy and your troop leaders will see to it that every member of a tank crew can do every job in the tank – firing the guns accurately, driving, changing the tracks, using

---

a Appendix A30

the wireless, commanding the tank in action. Every day counts. We may have only a few weeks before being tested.

Fall out the officers. Carry on, Sergeant Major."

"Parade – parade, 'shun." He saluted the Major, who walked away with the five other officers on parade. Then he turned back to face the men.

"Tank inspection 1400 hrs. Parade, dismiss."

"Bloody hell," said Smudger Smith, as we walked back to the tank lines. "He doesn't give us any time to sort things out." But he need not have worried. All the crews went back to their tanks and started stripping the guns, checking the tools and recounting the ammunition, ready for the inspection.

Sergeant McDonald, the dour Scot from Edinburgh in charge of the L.A.D.,[a] went from tank to tank with his clipboard and list of kit already issued. He checked the heavy tools strapped on to the top engine cover – crowbar, 28lb persuader, long-levered box spanner, spade, pick and spare track.

"We're going to have some mods[b] done in the next few days. Extra ammo racks and containers, an armoured box above the engine doors for an R.T. extension," he told us.

"That's my field, Sarge," I said, "What's the purpose?"

"You 'sparks' will soon find that out," he admitted rather grudgingly, "something to do with talking to the infantry."

It sounded a good idea to me as we had no experience of tank/infantry communications in jungle where trees were likely to blank out any wireless signals.

We pressed on with cleaning and reassembling the 75 mm, 37 mm guns and the two .300[c] Browning machine guns. We then had an ammunition check against the lists and indented for the extra needed to complete the minimum stock to be carried into action. It made us all realise that we would soon be using it for real.

I was told by the armourer to hand in my Smith & Wesson .38

---

a Appendix A31
b Appendix A32
c Appendix A33

pistol and holster and draw my new side arm – a .45 Thomson submachine gun.

Talk about excitement, I could hardly believe my luck. I had seen plenty of gangster films with James Cagney and Edward G. Robinson and the Chicago gangs wiping each other out with their 'Tommy guns'. The thought of having one of my own with the big round drums of 50 (or was it 100?) rounds to be sprayed into the enemy was soon changed to more sober reflections.

My 'Tommy gun' was the real thing but there was a penalty. The magazines were simple and straight, holding 20 rounds each, but there were ten magazines, to be carried in webbing pouches, five aside, fixed to my belt. The full kit was very heavy and was to prove a problem when getting in and out of the tank. It would become too heavy to carry when I lost my strength over the next six months. I did not realise this immediately.

"When can I test fire?" I asked the armourer.

"Tonight, if the Japs come," he joked, "but in the next few days, when you are told."

I thought that the Japs had arrived that night when I was on perimeter guard at about 0300 hrs.

It was a clear night, the monsoons well past, with the huge tropical moon lighting up the entire camp. I saw something moving on the track leading down from the khud. Three or four figures were coming quietly towards me. They looked about 4 feet 6 inches tall but did not appear to carry any weapons. I stepped back into the shadow of a tree and cocked my new Tommy gun. They continued to move in my direction. One of them coughed and they halted, looking straight at me. The sudden gripe in my gut was a shock and I clenched my sphincter in a panic, gripping my gun ready to spray them. Then they were gone.

As they ran past me I recognised the doglike jaws of four baboons who were farting and crapping in their own frightened exit.

At 0900 hrs. next morning all driver/operators (the tank wireless operators, whose secondary trade was driving) were called for a squadron net [a] by big Bill Pride, the corporal in charge of Squadron wireless communications. He was also the Squadron Leader's personal driver/operator when in his tank.

The daily net was to become a routine procedure at which all the wireless sets in the squadron would be locked on to two different wavelengths. This enabled them to be used on the first wavelength all day if required, or the whole net could be switched to the other if desired for reasons such as security or interference from another 'net' nearby. Such a change could be ordered by control using a prearranged code word.

Corporal Pride's cheerful baritone voice saying "All stations Able report my signals" was usually answered smoothly – "Able one strength five over". "Able two strength five over". "Able three strength five over". etc., through to "Able seven strength five over".

This gave a check of the accuracy of net to the four tanks of H.Q.A. troop and to the troop leader's tank of each of the four troops. In order to check the sets of all the other fifteen tanks, the net would start with the call, "All group stations Able report my signals".

This system gave each operator the opportunity to tune his variometer for maximum strength of transmission and, at the same time, gave Bill Pride, as control, an accurate check of each set's locking on to the wavelength. Occasionally a small number of operators would be told to unlock and relock on to another brief transmission from control. Then, "All group stations Able, roger, out." This told them all to close down and return to crew duties.

Most of us had become very much aware of a subtle change in attitudes on the part of the officers and N.C.O.s since we had arrived in Manipur. It was difficult to define, but they seemed to have realised that we were all in it together, all necessary to each other. The spit and polish included in the expression 'bull' had gone. During the tank and kit inspections there were none of the usual 'needling'

a Appendix A34

criticisms. Any deficiencies, which would have been an offence two months ago, were simply and quietly replaced with new kit.

The officers made sure that they knew a man's name before speaking to him – and then they looked him in the eye when doing so.

Army Education Officers and Sergeants visited occasionally to address groups of men, perhaps only one troop of twenty men, giving them the background of the current situation. Question and answer sessions became a weekly item on Squadron Orders.

One A.E. Sergeant explained the build-up of the Indian Congress and the part played by Mahatma Gandhi. I had seen Gandhi when he was imprisoned in the palace of the Nizam of Hyderabad at Kirkee near Poona and told the sergeant that he had looked an insignificant little man, just a bag of bones.

"You wouldn't say that if you had seen one of your friends soaked in petrol and then set alight," he snapped. "Never turn your back on a civilian anywhere in India. Even those in Indian Army uniform may be wanting to see you off. One of Gandhi's Congress wallahs is trying to form an Indian army to help the Japs. He's called Subhas Chandra Bhose and has already recruited from the Indians taken prisoner when we retreated from Burma a year ago. We understand that they are called the Japanese Indian Force – Jifs, for short – so you may well find yourselves up against them."

This raised another question. We had just been told that we would soon have an Indian Company of Bombay Grenadiers allocated to support us in action – mainly to prevent any Japs from climbing on to the tanks or getting near enough to fix sticky bombs (magnetic mines) to the armour plates. Sergeant Connor, an old Carb, butted in. "There should be no problem. We will be working with the 'Grinders' for a few weeks before going into action and it's up to us to make sure that we know and trust each other. Any Jifs we meet will be facing us and probably shooting at us. 'Nuff said."

That night, Squadron Orders listed men for guard duties as usual but also had a list of groups of five or six men, including a junior N.C.O., for patrols into the surrounding hills. I was included in the

next day's patrol under Corporal 'Dinty' Moore and I looked forward
to testing my tommy gun at last.

After reveille at 0530 hrs. we had our first 'stand-to'. This was
to become a regular first job of the day, based on a belief that the
Japs always attacked a defended strongpoint just on or before dawn.
The last of the night guards would creep up to each sleeping tank
crew and awaken one of them who, in turn, would nudge all the
others, usually with some highly amusing question. "Do you want
to buy a battleship?" or "Get up, your wife has just arrived with the
kids." The answers were mostly unprintable but we all slipped into
our stand-to positions – commanders, gunners and loaders into the
tank, driver ops and spare files would jump into the slit trench with
a tripod-mounted Browning machine gun.

And there we waited. Very quietly.

The tropical dawn always arrived suddenly. Soon after that, the
Sergeant Major, or an officer, would walk around giving us the
'Stand down'. A quick wash, shave and breakfast put us all into a
good frame of mind for the day's efforts.

This morning, the five of us, with Dinty Moore, were taken to the
armourer's truck first so that the others could each draw an Enfield[a]
.303 rifle – "You can't attack a Jap road block with a pistol," said
the Corporal with a laugh. "Is that what we're going to do?" asked
'Sherley' Holmes. "We'll see what we can find 'cos Alan here wants
to test his gangster gun."

Dinty led us up the track leading into the rising cloud and we all
followed in single file, chattering happily at the thought of a day
without much discipline. We were mostly old 26th Hussars and talked
of our different experiences since joining the Carabiniers.

"It's funny how we were all put into tank crews," said Busty Bain,
a big strapping fellow who would make a good weight lifter, "I see
that Dizzy Sanford has kept some old Carbs in his own crew."

"That'll change soon," said Dinty Moore, "his operator, Bill Pride,
is overdue for repat under Python, and I hear he was told he could

---

a Appendix A35

go as soon as he has trained his replacement. Most of his crew are about due for repat."

That rang my alarm bells because I knew that I was well over-qualified as a tank operator and also for the job of Squadron wireless N.C.O. I had qualified as a P1 [a] wireless instructor from Bovington, Dorset, and, more recently, with the 26th Hussars as a Q1 from Ahmednagar, Deccan. Both courses were very similar and had been essential for training wireless operators of all ranks during my year at the R.A.C. Depot, Catterick, and, later, at the Poona Depot. I kept quiet about this because I did not want to be transferred from 4 Troop, full of established friends, to go into the Major's crew.

Just then, as we followed a narrow track round a rocky col, we all heard it – a sharp cough that sounded like a bark from a big dog. Everyone froze. Then we moved forward slowly, with our loaded weapons at the ready, but we had been seen first. At least six baboons were running away along the track. We saw them for only a few seconds and then they were gone.

"That's what I saw the other night," I cried, "they're not so bad in the daylight." "Especially when they are running away!" said Dinty.

We continued climbing up through the jungle, enjoying the exercise and freedom. There was always something of interest. Twenty feet above our heads at one point we spotted a bunch of small bananas. This was where I tested my tommy gun. Aiming at the thick stalk, I fired two magazines before I severed it so that the bunch dropped to the ground. Busty Bain rushed to pick up the fruit. "What a bloody waste of effort," he said and threw it down on the track. The plantains were yellow, nearly ripe, but as hard as wood when we cut them with a knife.

"And it's done my tommy gun no good either," said I, "It's jammed solid and I can't move the cocking lever."

Dinty Moore told me not to try to use it again. A later examination,

---

a Appendix A36

back at camp, proved that a faulty round had jammed in the barrel which had bulged when the next round had rammed into it.

After a halt for tiffin,[a] using our haversack rations and part of our water supply, we carried on walking up the khud side. The jungle noises continued without a break – like our conversations – until we suddenly realised that we were surrounded.

Completely unprepared for this, we stopped in our tracks facing eight naked black men. Each one was pointing a brand new Lee Enfield rifle at us. They obviously not only knew how to use them but were ready to do so, when one of them gave the well known Indian greeting in Urdu, "Tikh hai,[b] Sahib?" and, smiling, lowered his rifle. They all followed suit and stood grinning. Most of them were wearing old leather bandoliers full of clips of .303 ammunition for their rifles, but not much else.

This was our introduction to the Naga hill men. Their leader pointed his rifle at me and asked, "Japani wallah hai?[c]" indicating my steel army issue glasses. This raised a laugh from everyone. They were very fit, lean and happy folk. Their Indian interpreter emerged from the jungle and, in a mixture of Urdu and English, asked us where were we going and where were we based. They were on a regular patrol and had no news of any Japs to the west of the Manipur Road, but they had heard recent reports of Jap patrols on the east of the road – only a few miles from our base at 108 milestone.

As it was now only two hours before we were expected to be back at camp, we set off in that direction following paths heading downhill.

The only other incident on the way 'home' was finding the decaying carcass of a tiger near the path. The stench was overpowering and the large body had obviously been there for a few weeks. We poked at the rotting skin with interest and found that the huge claws had separated from the pads. There were no volunteers to take the claws for souvenirs.

As we were crossing a stream of rushing clear water, we all

---

a Appendix A37
b Appendix A38
c Appendix A39

decided to take a bath in turn, with at least two of us staying on guard. That's when I spotted some dark brown pods, the size of marrows, hanging from a creeper over the water. They were dried loofahs which I proudly demonstrated when taking my turn to bathe in the stream.

The many black seeds fell out on being shaken but some natural residue in the loofah made a good lather when soaked and rubbed on our bodies. With 'all mod cons' supplied, we emerged feeling very refreshed and packed our haversacks with all the spare loofah pods we could find.

We all had a tale to tell when we were back in camp having a bully stew for the evening meal with our own tank crews. Dinty Moore had pointed out to us the weaknesses of the patrol. "Just imagine that the baboons and the Nagas had been Japs. We would have been wiped out on each occasion. There was too much noise and chatter and we were grouped far too closely together most of the time. We may not get another chance to learn without cost, so just be warned. We are not on holiday!"

We had all accepted the criticism as well justified.

I also had to explain to the armourer why I needed a new gun. He admitted that it was not the first 'bulged barrel' and had probably been caused by old ammunition which had been affected by damp.

Chapter 4

Training for Close Action

December 1943

The four squadrons of the recently reassembled 3rd Carabiniers were ordered to continue training in new locations. HQ and A Squadrons moved nearer 4 Corps H.Q., just north of Imphal. C Squadron headed south, through Imphal, towards Tiddim and the Fort White area. All the tanks were carried on transporters. B Squadron moved to Yaripok, which was a most attractive village of clean, wholesome bamboo bashas with smooth hard mud floors. The few hundred residents had moved elsewhere but their fields of sugar cane and pineapples were flourishing and almost ready for harvesting. The locals visited regularly, checking their crops and property whilst bringing a small supply of chickens, eggs and sugar cakes for barter. We quickly established a pleasant arrangement to supplement our army rations.

Some of us ordered bamboo charpoys [a] to be made by the Manipuri craftsmen – each bed required only one hour's work with materials growing at the corner of most fields. They were good value for two rupees (about 3 shillings) and gave us a feeling of real luxury and space under the mosquito nets each night.

The days were full of sheer hard work and the rapid assimilation of skills to make all members of each tank crew interchangeable. The awesome 75 mm [b] gun, fitted in the right sponson, was very accurate up to 3000 yards.

We all, drivers, wireless operators, gunners, loaders and commanders,

a   Appendix A40
b   Appendix E

practised until we could hit a tree trunk over a mile away with our third round. Using A.P. (armour piercing with tracer) allowed the gunner and observers to follow the flight of the shell, make any slight adjustment for side winds, and bracket the target with the second round. The third round usually hit the target. On the odd occasion when the first round did so, the gunner was subjected to some good natured legpull. The only disadvantage with the 75 mm was that it could be traversed no more than 15 degrees to either side of centre. Any bigger movement to either side required the tank to be slewed to the left or right. Similar training, but for a shorter period, was carried out with the 37 mm gun (turret mounted with a 360 degree traverse and also co-axially mounted with a .300 Browning machine gun). We all became very adept at stripping breech blocks, clearing jammed rounds or, more warily, misfires. Brownings were rapidly withdrawn from their mountings, fixed on to a tripod on the ground, and then fired as if by infantry, ready for night defence positions.

The driver/operator had responsibility for another Browning .300 in a mounting on the left of the driver's position in the tank. Unfortunately this gun could only be elevated or depressed while being fired forward – traversing required the driver to slew the tank to one side or the other. Because of this snag the 'hull' Browning was the one usually mounted on the tripod at night. (I was to fire it only once in the hull [a] mounting and that was up Nunshigum, some four months later).

All this training, with such good results, gave us a surge of confidence that we would sort out the enemy whenever we met him. His few smaller tanks would be hit and destroyed before they were able to get within range of us. Our four inches of armour plating, admittedly only on the front of our Lees, would deflect any of his A.P. rounds that might reach us.

A Company of 1st Seaforth Highlanders moved into Yaripok to start their training with us. They were mostly regular soldiers who

---

a Appendix E

had spent the past two years in Hong Kong. The plan was that we would all train together and then we would support them in their future attacks on established Japanese positions. They were training with us for only two weeks before they were moved east, towards the Kabaw valley, where increasing Jap patrols were being reported.

They were soon replaced by another Company of infantry, but our new neighbours and colleagues were a 'first' for most of us.

We had heard of the legendary Gurkhas but we had not worked with them before. The 2nd/5th Gurkha Rifles, like all their other battalions, had been recruited in the independent state of Nepal, in the Himalayas in North East India.

These happy, smiling little men – some appeared to be boys of only fifteen or sixteen years of age – were commanded by British officers and Gurkha V.C.O.'s (Viceroy Commissioned Officers). The officers all appeared to be handpicked and showed outstanding qualities of leadership. The men also were handpicked from large numbers of volunteers, as the Nepalese villagers considered it a great honour to serve under the British Crown. Most of their pay went straight home to Nepal. It was a basic essential element of the economy of the villages scattered over the mountains and valleys, where walking and climbing were the only means of public movement.

The British Gurkha Captain, who introduced his men to us with a fascinating talk about their background, had only one hand. He wore a hook strapped to his wrist and declined to discuss the matter.

We learned later that he had lost his hand in action two years earlier and had pressed to rejoin his battalion despite the handicap. He used a smooth rounded hook normally each day, but on exercise or in action he wore another hand-substitute in the form of a miniature kukri, some four inches long. In his 'good' hand on these occasions he carried the full size issue kukri.[a]

He was an awesome sight running forward, leading his men, with a deadly blade at the end of each arm yelling 'Ayo Gurkhali'.[b] We

---

a Appendix A41
b Appendix A42

saw this a few times during our 'bunker busting' exercises, designed to clear the enemy from their reinforced foxholes or bunkers.

It was at the end of this first day of training with the Gurkhas, long, tiring but still very interesting, that I heard the news that I dreaded from the Orderly Room Corporal.

"Trooper Fenner, report to the Major immediately."

I saw Major Sanford dismounting from his tank as we all returned to the village for the usual maintenance before cooking our meal. (Cavalry training – always feed and bed your horse before looking after your own needs – was a good system.) The tanks would then be refuelled and all guns cleaned and rearmed, ready for any night action.

I saluted. "Trooper Fenner reporting as requested, sir."

"At ease, Fenner." The Major drew me to one side. "You may be aware that Corporal Pride has been my driver/operator for some time and is now due for repatriation – in fact, he is overdue for it. He leaves later this week and recommends you as his replacement."

He looked quizzically at me. "Do you feel capable of running Squadron communications?"

"The decision is yours, sir. I have spent almost two of the past three years as a qualified instructor, training men and officers to use wireless in tanks. You will have my records. I even trained as a signaller, including the use of heliograph[a] in my school O.T.C., but —."

"But what, Fenner?"

"But, I have been very happy these past few weeks in 4 Troop. I have been training with friends who came with me from the 26th Hussars and I am looking forward to going into action with them."

"None of us are here to be happy, Fenner. We are here to obey orders and help win this war."

He put out his hand which I accepted with a shake.

"Congratulations, Corporal. Arrange to put up your first stripe tonight and now come and meet your new colleagues."

---

a Appendix A43

Corporal Pride was beckoned across.

"I have promoted Fenner to Lance-Corporal in order to succeed you, Corporal. Take him to meet the other members of my crew."

"Sir," saluted Bill Pride.

"Congratulations, Alan. Come along," he beamed.

My transfer into his tank crew meant that he could pack his kit and start the long journey back to Blighty and Blandford in Dorset. He was about to leave his Regiment and miss all that the future held for the Carabiniers. He did not appear to be at all sad. In fact, he was even more exuberant than usual as he introduced me to the others.

"You'll know most of the crew.[a] Paddy Ryan, driver, Ginger Whiteley, 75 gunner, 'Joe' Nussey, his loader. You complete the downstairs crew, then, 'Sherley' Holmes, 37 gunner and young Norman Dimmock, his loader. 'Dizzy' Sanford completes the crew. You don't call him 'Dizzy'. No one does. But I think he knows his nickname and probably rather likes it."

"You'd better return to 4 Troop for tonight," Bill Pride went on, "and report to me with all your kit at 0830 hrs. tomorrow. You can then take the Squadron net and move in."

It proved to be an easy move and transition. I already knew all the other squadron driver/operators; some of them had attended training courses which I had supervised at the R.A.C. Depot at Poona. The main difference that I noticed was that there were only six of us to handle the routine maintenance jobs in the Squadron Leader's tank. The Major disappeared each time that we returned from exercises. He would check at the Squadron Office and often drive off in a jeep to visit R.H.Q.[b] a few miles away.

His crew received a certain amount of respect from the other crews. It was certainly not envy, as we tended to be out on training longer than the other tanks each day – or so it seemed.

When the time came for any of B Squadron tanks to go on a

a Appendix E
b Appendix A44

shoot, mostly only one or two troops, the Major would also be there in his tank and, usually, join in the shoot. In the meantime, the other tank crews would be doing routine maintenance or resting.

Throughout all this time, we were supported by the technicians in B Echelon. Sergeant Jock MacDonald, with his L.A.D. team, ensured that the tanks were mobile and reliable. Signalman Shand, attached from the Royal Signals, was constantly answering calls for help with the maintenance of our No. 19 wireless sets.

That morning, during Squadron parade, the Major stood us all 'at ease' to give his occasional sitrep. "We are receiving regular intelligence from beyond the Chindwin where we have more and more forces in contact with the enemy. The Long Range Penetration Group, commanded by Brigadier Wingate, is attacking Japanese lines of communication with much success. They will not stop the Jap advance into the borders of India but it will be a weakened enemy force when we meet them during the next few months.

"Now, on the subject of training. I have been well pleased with some of the gunnery seen on the ranges. We will need to conserve ammunition from now on. Firing will be on a reduced scale and mainly applied to a new concept of attacking the enemy. Wireless procedure used, particularly by gunners and loaders, needs to be improved. Corporal Fenner will see to that.

"Back to gunnery. Most of the shoots we have practised have been designed for squadron or half squadron strength at ranges of one to two thousand yards – a job that you do well and will, no doubt, do effectively when required. It is also a job that can be done by the artillery and at much greater ranges than we can achieve with our 75 mms. But now we have a new challenge." He looked along the lines of attentive faces. "We must now learn to use our fire power at a closer range – a much closer range of down to ten yards!"

There was a gasp from the ranks, quickly stifled.

"The enemy have proved their ability to master one or two techniques which will require some thought, skill and determination to beat. They are very quick to build a reinforced defensive position from which it is not easy to move them by our usual infantry attack, especially if they are given a few days in which to extend and strengthen the bunker system. Using felled trees, rocks and earth to protect their slit trenches, they can, in a short time, build a large chain of such strong points, each covering the others with machine gun fire, making it a very expensive task to clear them out. From this we have learned two important facts.

"One. We must attack him before he can become established in a system of bunkers, such as I have described and, two, we must be trained and ready to lead and support an infantry attack on a strongly held bunker position.

"Today, H.Q.A. Troop will practise this method of attack on a dummy bunker which has been built for us by the sappers.[a] Tomorrow, we will demonstrate it to the remainder of the Squadron and to the 2nd/5th Gurkhas. After that, this attack method will be practised until we have perfected it, with the actual infantry unit with whom we will be going into battle. Stand by, H.Q.A. Troop. Remainder, Dismiss."

There was a rumble of chatter as the others fell out and walked away.

H.Q.A. Troop, totalling 28, including the Major and Captain Murphy, remained. Some of us were looking apprehensively at each other. Major Sanford walked nearer and continued, "It's quite simple, really. We all know that when the H.E.[b] shell leaves the muzzle of the 75 mm gun at high speed and explodes, even if only 15 to 20 yards away, all the shrapnel continues to move forward at approximately the same speed. It can do no damage to any person behind the point of explosion. Therefore, anyone crawling forward from a position at the side of the tank, under the shell's trajectory, can safely move ten yards towards the point of shell burst whilst a total of three H.E. rounds are fired – provided he keeps his head down," he added casually.

"Now, if the fourth and last round fired is armour-piercing, it will

a Appendix A45
b Appendix A46

encourage any surviving Japs in the bunker to keep well down in the bottom of the trench whilst the infantryman puts up a hand to stop the 75 from firing again. He can then jump up, rush the bunker and finish off any Japs with grenades or with his kukri."

"Rather him than me," muttered Paddy Ryan.

"What do you think of that?" asked the Major.

"Very efficient, sir," said the S.S.M., scowling at the rest of us in order to deter any criticism. He knew we had experienced an airburst a few days ago when an H.E. shell had exploded a few yards from the muzzle after hitting a twig.

Trooper Dimmock raised a hand rather diffidently, "May I ask a question, sir?"

"Of course," nodded the Major.

"What happens if the gunner doesn't see the hand signal to stop firing and the Gurkha jumps up for the last dash?"

"That is a question of training, which we are about to start. You will realise that the tank commander is in a better position to watch for that signal. He is in charge. Another safeguard is the fact that the number of rounds fired will be fixed at a total of four – no more, no less."

"But, it's the poor bugger on the ground who has his head shot off, if there's a mistake," whispered Ginger Whiteley. He would be the 75 mm gunner involved in the first trial.

The S.S.M. went red in the face.

The Major then laid it down that the procedure would be started by the infantry speaking on the tank intercom system from the newly-fitted rear box, advising the tank commander when his men were ready at the sheltered side of the tank. The 75 mm gunner would be ordered to fire three individual rounds of H.E. followed by one round of A.P. – and then cease firing. Fire cover could then continue from the much higher mounted 37 mm and co-ax [a] Browning.

The four tanks of H.Q.A. Troop drove the mile into the maidan [b]

---

a Appendix A47
b Appendix A48

where the Sappers (Royal Engineers) had built a bunker for these initial tests. It was made of two straight tree trunks, one on top of the other. Across the top were some smaller logs, holding up another thick trunk, making a dark gap for a firing slit. Over the lot had been piled earth, grass sods and leaf-covered branches. Access to the slit trench was from one side.

If it had been built amongst other trees or in the jungle, and occupied by the enemy, it would have presented a formidable stronghold, particularly with the approach covered by one or more machine guns sited at either side.

"Well, men, who is going to be first?" cheerfully from the Major. The silence was very loud.

We looked at each other. We looked at the bunker, then at the 75.

The S.S.M. butted in, "You are all going to do it in turn, so you can show our Gurkha friends that there is nothing to worry about."

There was a shorter silence this time.

"I don't mind being first," I whispered. And the Major heard me.

"Good show, Fenner. Let's get started."

Lying prone, in front of the right hand track of the silent tank, I realised that the muzzle of the 75 was only some three feet above my head. When given the order to fire, Ginger Whiteley would squeeze the pistol-grip trigger and a 14lb high explosive shell would be expelled at high speed from the muzzle and immediately explode on hitting the target bunker, only 15 feet in front of me. I was aware that a premature detonation could occur if the shell hit a bird or some other solid matter, but that was unlikely. I hoped.

"You all right, Fenner?" called the Major from his turret.

"Right, sir." I tried to sound confident.

It was strange, hearing the orders to the gunner being given over the intercom whilst I was in a totally alien position for action, lying in the open, with a breeze on my face.

"75, How Easy." [a]

---

a Appendix D

The 75 loader slammed home an H.E. shell, which automatically closed the breech as he tapped the gunner on the shoulder.

"75, How Easy," confirmed the gunner to the commander.

"75, bunker target immediately ahead. Fire."

The noise of the gun firing and the shell instantly exploding was simply just one big bang. The dust cloud, from around me and the damaged bunker, had not settled when I heard the shouted order from the Major, "Commence crawling forward," and the second shell went over my head and exploded. I had crawled eight or nine yards when the third H.E. shell exploded, quickly followed by an A.P. shell. This sounded similar to the other three but did less damage to the now ruined bunker.

I held up my right hand and rapidly jumped up to the left of my path and away from the track of any possible fifth round.

In something of a daze, with my head ringing with the noise from the past few minutes, I went through the motions of running to the left side of the bunker and throwing a rock into it, representing a grenade.

"Excellent," cried the Major, jumping down from the tank, "Congratulations, Fenner! A very good show!"

We all looked at the smashed bunker. It was doubtful whether any Jap could have survived the shelling alone, apart from the immediate infantry attack. "No need to go through that any more," the Major said, turning to the Sapper officer, Lieutenant Ken Ryman, "can you get the bunker rebuilt ready for the Gurkhas tomorrow, 1000 hrs?"

Lt. Ryman nodded, "We'll have to make it more substantial, or build a few more for spares, if the Gurkhas are going to have a few goes at it. Will do."

He was a small, wiry and very fit man who carried, as his side arm, a captured Japanese rifle with the barrel reduced in length by ten inches. Declining to give any detail of how he had obtained it, he showed us the clips of ammunition, pointing out that each round was almost the same size and length as our rifle ammunition but that the projectile was only a little more than .22 inches in diameter.

One of the R.E. other ranks told us later that Lt. Ryman had met a solitary Jap on the road to the Kabaw Valley when he was driving in his Jeep to see A Squadron, and he had won the fight. He had later fitted a new foresight and helped to supply the Officers' Mess with the occasional wild fowl. We were to see a lot more of this sapper officer and rely on his help and expertise during the coming year.

<hr>

The next morning only the Squadron Leader's tank was required for the demonstration and training of the 2nd/5th Gurkha Rifles. It went very smoothly.

I was still very deaf, suffering from a loud whistle in each ear, and pretended not to hear Major Sanford when he asked me to repeat the performance. I explained the cause of my hesitance but he assured me that the hearing problems would soon go away, so I again volunteered.

This time I started from the left front of the tank and I felt more confident that a shell would not hit me. Again, I counted three H.E. and one A.P. shells as they hit the rebuilt bunker, and then casually stood up and ran to the side of the bunker. Lobbing the rock (grenade) into the opening was greeted with shouts of approval from the watching Gurkhas, including their officers. "Shabash,[a] shabash!" I felt twice my size and enjoyed the next two hours watching the Gurkhas, all volunteers, go through the procedure. They greatly improved the show by charging the bunker with their drawn kukris, screaming hate for the enemy.

I said to the Gurkha Officer, "I'm very impressed with the eagerness of your men, sir. They volunteered much more readily than I did."

"Of course, Corporal, they can sometimes embarrass us by volunteering 100% for almost any dangerous job. There was a time, last year, when I asked for volunteers to be flown into southern Burma

___

a Appendix A49

and dropped from 2000 feet to attack a Japanese divisional H.Q. and I was surprised when only half of them volunteered. This figure improved quickly when I explained that they would be supplied with parachutes. Immediately, 100% volunteered."

We all enjoyed the story, which only confirmed our admiration for the Gurkhas.

We looked forward to going into action with these happy little men. It was not to be with this battalion. Two weeks later they were moved forward and we soon learned that they had suffered heavy casualties. The one-armed officer had been killed leading an attack on to a Jap bunker without tank support.

The inter-trade training continued for a few weeks into December, when the Squadron moved back to 108 milestone for a brief rest. We were all more competent when taking each other's job in the tank. Driving the 30 ton giant over the bunds [a] at the edge of a paddy field required balancing on the top and then gently rocking forward to reach a lower, or higher, level without loosening the teeth of the rest of the crew. Ammunition rationing had stopped all firing practice on the guns. Most of us were able to strip them all quickly and reassemble them, knowing that a stoppage could be cleared in the minimum time.

Loaded sidearms were carried day and night. The stand-to was a strict routine from half an hour before dawn and dusk until the O.C. was satisfied that no attack was going to take place – usually each stand-to lasted just over three quarters of an hour.

Christmas 1943 came and went almost unnoticed during the move back to 108 milestone. H.Q.A. Troop were split between the two camps. Two crews were in the rearguard remaining at Yaripok in order to complete the tidying up of the site. They received their rations, including a bottle of beer for each man, and enjoyed a quiet singsong, mostly of carols.

---

a Appendix A50

Norman Dimmock gave his 'always requested' version of 'The Barrow Boy'.

"They say I ain't no good because I'm a barrer boy,
A barrer boy I've always wanted to be.
As I wheels me barrer,
I walks along with pride.
I'm a coster, a coster,
From over the other side —."

On this occasion we had a duty visit from Major Sanford, who appeared a little more relaxed than usual, and he asked us to sing his current favourite.

"You are my sunshine, my only sunshine,
You make me happy, when skies are grey.
You'll never know, dear, how much I love you.
Please don't take my sunshine away."

He seemed to enjoy it and left after a few minutes.

"I didn't know he could be so sentimental," was Paddy's later comment.

The next day we were all reunited with the Squadron at 108 milestone, feeling ready for action. This was not to be so soon.

The days were filled with 'internal economy' – cleaning and checking kit, digging more latrine trenches, vehicle inspections and the occasional hill patrol in the mornings. Afternoons were for athletics and football matches.

We were all issued with new shoulder badges, which we sewed on to our green battledress blouses. The 14th Army shield, designed by General Slim, was worn just below the 254 Tank Brigade badge. This was simply four tapering black lines running downwards on a red background, leaving five red parallel lines, then crossed with two more black lines to give the numbers 2, 5 and 4. The comment from our local cynic was "blood on the tracks", which soon came true.[a]

a Appendix G

During our relaxed evening meals we talked about every subject you could imagine. Some tank crew members would say that their job was similar to that of the aircrew in an R.A.F. bomber. "We do the same sort of job," stressed Bob Greendale, another old East Riding Yeoman from Hull. "We have a go at the enemy taking bombs, shells and machine guns, hit them as hard as possible, and then return to base to refuel, rearm, and set off for another go. The main difference is that we do our own refuelling whereas the R.A.F. have it done for them by the ground crew."

"And they are based near a town or village in Blighty, not in the middle of the jungle," added another, "I could just fancy a pint in the local."

"Only those flying in Europe," said a third.

"But at least if a tank is hit the crew don't have so far to fall."

"And all the aircrews are officers or sergeants," from another.

"I'd be satisfied if they paid me the same."

There was no lack of comment, some of it critical of the "Brilcreme Boys", but we were mostly all satisfied with the life we were leading in the relative security of our own tank crews, and, also, some of us had lost brothers in the R.A.F.

"I've an idea," butted in Sherley Holmes, "why don't we give each tank a name and paint it on the side? There are some paints in B Echelon, and you do a bit of painting, Alan." "Wilco,[a] " I said, "we'll have to get the O.K. from Dizzy, but I'll ask him in the morning. What names shall we have in H.Q.A.?"

When I approached Major Sanford he was quite amenable.

"You see, sir, there is a growing pride in each tank crew for their own tank. It is their home as well as their workshop, and, I think, there could even be a little jealousy of the R.A.F. idea of each aircraft having a cartoon character as its mascot."

"That's fine, Corporal. My only comment is that it should be small

---

a Appendix B

and well painted. Remember, they will be seen by many senior officers, including General Slim and Lord Louis Mountbatten. What are you suggesting for our tank?"

This was the crunch.

"Well, sir, with the greatest respect, there is a rather likeable Walt Disney character called 'Dizzy' and your crew have asked me to see if you will agree."

He smiled and, to my surprise, said, "I see, yes, go ahead, bearing in mind all that I've said."

The next day I did the job.

With a few colours I painted a character based on Goofy, the Walt Disney dog, skiing madly downhill, and put the name Dizzy just beneath it.

The only comment from the Major was, "Oh, I always thought it was spelt 'DISSY'"

"Perhaps you were thinking of Disraeli, sir?"

He accepted that and walked away.

I remember painting a potato on the side of the second in command's tank. Captain Murphy knew quite well that all 'Murphy's' were known in the army as 'Spud'. Most of the other tank crews copied the idea.

———

A few days later – surprise, surprise – we had an E.N.S.A. concert. We were first alerted when told to erect a wooden stage in the lines where the ground sloped up the hill to form an auditorium. It was to be for only two performances – one each day at 1700 hrs – planned to finish before evening stand-to. The cast included a standup comedian who raised a few laughs and two singers who plucked at the heartstrings with songs of loved ones far away. The highlight of the show was billed as Commander Stephen Kinghall, an ageing comedian who earned the cheers of the men with his criticisms of officers and N.C.O.s.

"I'm told you have a famous Sergeant Major in B Squadron?"

The crowd roared their approval.

"He's a bit of a boxer, so they say?"

More cheers.

"Well, I was boxing for the Royal Navy when your Sergeant Major was still in nappies. I also hear that he is rather quick at putting a man on a fizzer!"

Louder cheers.

In a cultured 'officer' voice. "Take that man's name, Sergeant Major." In a deeper voice. "Clang, he's in, sir. His feet didn't touch!"

The laughing audience all turned to look at the S.S.M. to assess his reaction and were mostly surprised to see that he was laughing also.

Before the cheers for Stephen Kinghall had finished there was a burst of machine gun fire from perhaps two miles away, from the east of the Manipur Road. The tracer rounds appeared to be floating upwards and over the stage. Everyone went very quiet.

The comedian addressed the audience. "What was that?"

"Don't worry," someone called out, "probably some Indian sentry who has tripped over his gun."

But we were wrong.

We learned later that a Jap patrol had bumped into an Indian unit who were alert, standing to, as we should also have been with the quick fall of dusk, almost instantly going into night.

The incident was enough for the E.N.S.A. party, who immediately closed the show and did not stay to give the second performance the next day. There were no more incidents.

We were offered some more professional entertainment a few days later. Half the Squadron strength were taken in trucks into Imphal for the first time to see a performance by the Rajah of Manipur's private dance group. The leading dancer, Mambi, was reported to have been a great friend of the Rajah some twenty or thirty years earlier, and she controlled all the much younger dancers with a very firm authority.

Most of us had been in India long enough to have formed an opinion on Asian music but we were not experts on either that or eastern dancing.

The show was colourful, with the lovely young girls in their bright saris, but the British soldiery were not trained to appreciate the subtle nuances of these traditional dances. They expressed some noisy interest when one of the wooden swords used in a particular dance broke at the hilt and the blade flew into the audience. The Indian soldier whom it struck carried it to the stage and placed it there for all to see.

Mambi quickly picked it up and used it to strike the unfortunate dancer across her behind.

The show continued for another hour, as long as there were rupee notes and coins thrown on to the stage – mostly by the Indian soldiers present in the audience.

Our next highlight was a visit from the General Officer Commanding 14th Army. We were all paraded under our C.O.,[a] Lt. Col. Ralph Younger, who presented us to General William Slim. This was the man who had led the British retreat from Burma two years earlier. He had recently replaced General 'Pop' Giffard – a man reputed to believe that there was no alternative to the strategy and tactics of massive frontal attacks on enemy strongholds.

General Slim addressed the entire B Squadron, who were all eager to see the man responsible for ordering them into any future action. We were all most impressed.

He put us at ease, stand easy, and jumped on to the bonnet of a conveniently placed jeep, with the men standing around him. He was dressed in lightly starched and pressed khaki drill,[b] wearing his Gurkha hat and two rows of decoration ribbons. He was weathered, mature and experienced. Looking around at us, eyeball to eyeball, he started:

"I've heard a lot about the Carabiniers and I'm impressed with what I've heard. I'm aware of your abilities and high standard of training to use the tremendous fire power of your General Lee tanks to destroy any enemy who are in your way. Your Commanding

---

a Appendix A51
b Appendix A52

Officer, Colonel Younger, has much experience in action and he will soon be ordering you to attack and destroy the Japanese who are now invading India. You will succeed for a number of reasons.

"You have been thoroughly trained to use the superb modern equipment in your possession to destroy any enemy foolish enough to attack you. I led the British forces who retreated from Burma in 1942 and I can assure you that the retreat would not have been necessary if the 3rd Carabiniers had been there with me. That is no exaggeration. You have this enormous firepower and your officers will lead you to beat the enemy into the ground.

"Now, a word about the Jap. I have fought him before and he is, firstly, predictable and, secondly, persistent. He does not learn from his mistakes. He rarely makes a frontal attack, preferring to go past a strong point and then attack in force from the rear. He is brave – have no doubts about that – and he never gives up until he is dead. He prefers to die rather than be taken prisoner. Think of him as a soldier ant. Fixed in his intentions and only stopping the attack when he is crushed. That is what we will do. We will crush him here, around Imphal, when he attacks us in our strong points. He will be at the end of very long lines of communication, stretching from Rangoon, through the jungles and crossing two major rivers, whereas we will be here with our stockpiles of food and ammunition at the end of short L. of C.[a] from Dimapur, and with one very important trump card up our sleeve.

"Don't worry if we are surrounded. We may well be. We will be supplied by air. Don't worry if you are surrounded and separated from the other units. You will be supplied with your needs. We are already stronger in numbers of men and guns and aircraft – and we will grow stronger.

"Just one point. I have heard that there are some of you who say the 14th Army is the Forgotten Army. Well, you can forget that! How can you be a forgotten army when no one has ever even heard of you? But, they will do.

---

a Appendix A53

"I have no doubt about the outcome of the approaching battle. I know you will all be proud to have been part of the 14th Army. Looking around me today, I can see that you have your share of that stalwart of the British Army – the lance corporal.[a] "

Cheers and laughter.

"You may laugh, but, let me tell you that I have the greatest respect for men of that rank and I appreciate all the hard work done by the lance corporal. I know! I was one myself – a few times!"

This raised more laughter. There were many amongst us who had experienced being promoted for a short time and then demoted for a minor misdemeanour or even when transferred to another unit.

"Now, a word about your officers. I know your Colonel Younger – a very capable, experienced officer – he has seen action a few times already and proved himself. Your other officers I will get to know in the coming months. I have one word of warning for them."

His jaw jutted out even more.

"If I ever find an officer lying down on his bed, after an action, when his men are still busy replenishing the tank with fuel and ammunition, he will be back in the ranks as a trooper before he can blink!"

Cheers from the ranks.

"We are all in this together, and, success comes to those who pull together. Good luck with all your efforts. I will be visiting you again."

Col. Younger called us all to attention, saluted the General, who had jumped down from the jeep, and walked away with him and the other officers.

R.S.M.[b] Wingrove quickly took over the parade and dismissed us. The cheers and laughter would have carried to the officers and assured General Slim that he was fully accepted by the other ranks. He was warmly referred to as "Uncle Bill" by the men who would now follow him anywhere – to hell if necessary.

---

a Appendix A54
b Appendix A55

The next day, after morning net, I started to give a spring clean to my area in my new tank and found the vehicle log book wedged under the wireless set. It made interesting reading. The inside cover, on which were details of the place of manufacture and original engine number, was clearly stamped: 'Training purposes only. Fort Worth, Texas, 1922.'

This was a shock. Here I was in 1943, thinking I was in a modern tank,[a] only to find that it had been condemned for 'training only' in the year I was born.

We had one more important visitor before going into action. He was the new Supreme Commander of South East Asia Command, based in Ceylon.

Lord Louis Mountbatten, in his spotless white tropical admiral's uniform, was a very impressive sight. One of our more gentle troopers standing in the rear breathed, "Oh, how simply gorgeous!" when he appeared.

Our C.O., Lt. Col. Ralph Younger, was always considered to be an impressive soldier in both style and appearance but, standing beside Lord Louis, he faded into mediocrity. The near-royal personality was overwhelming.

We had all seen the Noel Coward film 'In Which We Serve' with the story of the sinking of the Mountbatten ship Kelly and we now had the real personality of that epic story here as our Supremo. His speech was brief and presented with just the right amount of confidence without being at all 'gungho'.[b] It had basically the same content as that given by Bill Slim a few days earlier but the charisma stayed with us long after he had moved on to the next unit.

The C.O. then reassured us that everything was going 'according to plan'.[c] The Japs were stretched to their limit. We were not surrounded – although that "may well happen".

He then told us of a Japanese trait, with the obvious intention of building morale.

---

a Appendix E
b Appendic 56
c Appendix A57

"We all know that the average Jap is very short in stature – perhaps around five feet – and, also that he has poor eyesight – many of them have to wear thick glasses in order to find their way about – well, it is now reported that they cannot close one eye without closing the other one! This, of course, makes it impossible to aim a rifle accurately. Add this to the fact that their rifles use ammunition that is only slightly larger than the .22 inches you all know from your days of playing with airguns at home, and you will appreciate all we need to do now is to concentrate on crushing him out of existence wherever we find him."

He looked around to gauge our reaction. There were many raised eyebrows. Many of us had seen and handled the Japanese rifle ammunition and we knew that it packed a punch similar to our own .303 rifle, even if the bullet was slightly smaller. A quiet Scottish voice was heard clearly from the rear. "Balls!"

We all tensed, expecting an immediate strong reply from the Colonel, but he was either deaf or he chose not to take issue at that point.

He continued, "In order to conserve stocks and ensure a successful outcome, there will be some immediate reduction in rations issued:- Meat to 50%, fats to 50%, tea to 75%. Extra supplies of grain and vegetables are now available from local suppliers, so you will feel no shortage. The reduction in rations is simply a temporary measure."

This raised a few groans, but most of us knew that we had our own reserve stocks of many items, including a few luxuries, tucked away in the odd corners inside our tanks.

14th March 1944

The B Squadron orderly room clerk, Trooper Charles Warren, wandered through the tank lines looking even more lugubrious than usual. He had what was considered a 'cushy job' in the right place to get all the 'pukkha gen',[a] but he was trusted by the officers not

---

a Appendix A58

to spread it around the squadron. Although he had received the basic training as a member of a tank crew, he did not expect to fight the enemy at any stage.

He had been given the job because he had been educated, he could spell correctly and, it was rumoured, he could even do joined-up writing and use a typewriter. He was not the only one who could do this. There were many other ranks who had held responsible jobs in civvy street but Charlie was respected by all for his honesty and basic decency.

"What gives, Charlie?" called Dimmock, as he looked up at him.

"Bad news, I'm afraid; we've just heard that Trooper Thomas, despatch rider, has disappeared somewhere between R.H.Q. and A Squadron in the Kabaw Valley. There seems to be no doubt that he is our first casualty. Sarnt Major wants you all to know and not wander off anywhere in small numbers."

This hurt. It brought it home that there were risks for us all. Thomas had probably been knocked off his motorbike with a stretched rope, or gunfire, and was already a prisoner or dead. He would be reported 'missing', with all the subsequent anxieties for his family.

Chapter 5

The Battle of Nunshigum

15th March 1944

"At 0900 hrs. B Squadron will move to a new location, fully prepared for action at any time."

Squadron Orders were terse and simple. The move on transporters was smoothly and efficiently carried out and a rear party tidied the familiar site on the Manipur Road, filled in the latrines and pulled down the few semi-permanent tents and bamboo shelters. The dried and worn ground would soon return to nature.

The new camp site was at Wanjing – a village only a few miles south of Imphal.

We were ordered to be 'dug in' before dusk with slit trenches at prescribed points for defensive fire cover. All sleeping areas, next to the tanks, had to be dug down a minimum of two feet. Despite the usual grumbling, all this was achieved before stand-to.

We did not immediately feel any different living on the reduced rations. Each tank crew grew closer within itself, sharing carefully allocated tins of food including such items as Maconochie's Meat and Vegetable (M. & V.), corned beef, and beans with pork. This was a tin of baked beans in tomato sauce in which, on very rare occasions, there was a small piece of pork fat.

Two strange introductions to our rations were mutton and onions, both dehydrated. We were supposed to soak them in fresh water overnight before stewing them with vegetables. In practice the dried granules were sprinkled into the pot, whatever that happened to contain. The awful taste is still with me and I remember complaints of stomach gripes and wind for twenty-four hours after eating either mutton or onions.

We also had packs of dehydrated mixed vegetables, which were more acceptable. The real complaints about these new additions to our diet arose when we had very little water to drink and none for washing or for rehydrating dried foods.

We were kept informed of any news by three methods.

Squadron sitreps [a] from Major Sanford or Captain Murphy made us realise that tension was building up throughout the 4th Corps based in and around Imphal. Japanese infantry, with some artillery, were established on many of the mountains surrounding us, particularly in the Naga Hills to the north, up the Ukhrul Road, on the Manipur Road, near our old campsite at 108 milestone, and to the south at Shenam, near Palel.

Secondly, we had regular deliveries of SEAC,[b] a newspaper for the 14th Army edited by Frank Owen, which gave us censored news reports from various parts of India and the Burma front. World news was meagre and old. A cartoonist often raised a few laughs and we realised that there were many others griping about the usual irritants in armies the world over – officers, bull, N.C.O.s, rations and leave, especially the shortage of both the last two items.

Thirdly, those with access to wireless sets could listen to broadcasts of news from Radio Seac in Ceylon. The smooth presentation from the young David Jacobs made his voice a welcome reminder of the far distant civilisation which many of us would never again experience. We all realised that these news reports, indeed all transmissions, were sent in the full awareness that the enemy were listening, and that many items of news were omitted.

All our wireless operators were warned against using their sets when the tank engines were not running. The steady drain on the tank batteries could cause difficulties when trying to start the engines later in the day or night, and a flat battery during a night attack could endanger not only the crew but all the others depending on support in that part of the box. The Lee tanks were fitted with a small two-stroke petrol-driven Homalite dynamo for recharging the

---

a Appendix A59
b Appendix A60

batteries without running the tank's seven-cylinder aero engine, which used high octane fuel. The Homalite was the responsibility of the wireless operator, who started the motor by pulling a cord whilst crouching on the floor of the turret – not easily done if the turret crew were in position. Another problem was that the noise of it running could be heard, on a quiet night, from more than a mile away – a signal to any Jap patrols.

25th March 1944

The morning sitrep was dramatic. The Major was more serious than usual when he gave us the news. "You all know of the large force of Chindits recently flown into northern Burma and their success in establishing themselves in a number of places on the Japanese lines of communication? They are already effectively reducing the pressure on General Stilwell and his Chinese army; at the same time they have started to destroy the Japanese supplies being moved north to support the enemy. This morning we learned that General Wingate, commanding the Chindit operation, was on an aircraft which was reported missing last night. That aircraft has not yet been found.

"The Chindit operation will continue under a new commander and we can rely on them to harass the enemy in every way possible. Nearer here there are targets presenting themselves and we will be in action very soon. Your Commanding Officer and I have already selected some targets where we can help the infantry by shelling Japanese positions.

"Tomorrow, 4 Troop will move to the south of Palel and engage the enemy dug in on the Shenam Saddle. I know they will have a good shoot. From now on each troop will have plenty of opportunities to do the same on selected targets."

And we did.

26th March 1944

The three tanks of 4 Troop under Lieutenant FitzHerbert and Major Sanford's tank drove south a few miles until they met an infantry officer on the roadside near Shenam. The two tank officers dismounted and studied the hilltop, which was emerging from a cloud cover, and were soon back in their tanks.

"Able 4, proceed to the chosen position, over."

"Able 4, wilco, all stations Able 4 follow me, out."

It was very simple. The four tanks moved a hundred yards, slewed to the right with their 75s pointing up the khud side. Inside the Major's tank, I had a very limited view of the outside world, improved only by Paddy Ryan having his driver's [a] visor wide open.

"Able 4, fire when ready, out."

The Major might have been on the training range, his orders were given so calmly.

The crash of Lt. FitzHerbert's 75 mm gun made me jump, as I had not heard his I.C. [b] order to his crew. We could follow the trace of his shell as it appeared to float up the hill until it created a puff of smoke on impact, just below the target. A second shell followed and hit higher up the hill, near the ridge.

"Able 4, in your own time, five rounds Howe Easy, fire, out."

The lieutenant appeared to be a competent tank commander. His three tanks were quickly spreading high explosive shells, each approximately 14 lbs., in the crevasses and bunker positions along the ridge of the Shenam Saddle.

The Squadron Leader was not going to be left out. He gave Ginger Whiteley and Joe Nussey their chance to fire their 75 mm and spread ten rounds of H.E. on to the target area.

We all felt good. Our first shots 'fired in anger', except for Paddy!

"What a waste of ammo," he commented after we had returned to Wanjing.

"What do you mean?" I asked

"There we were, sat on our bottoms, at least a mile away, and we fired forty odd rounds into a khud. How do we know if we killed any Japs? If I had been a Jap up there, when the tanks arrived, I would have walked over the top of the ridge and waited until the

---

a Appendix E
b Appendix A61

tanks had gone home. Then, I would have walked back into my bunker, none the worse for it all."

His words made us all think as we helped clean the 75 and replenish the ammunition.

In fact, Paddy had spotted the secret of the Japanese resilience when they were defending a hill top. They used the ridge top as a defensive barrier. This technique was to become a problem whenever we attacked them on high ground.

27th March 1944.

We learned that the Japanese had crossed the Manipur Road at Kanglatongbi and also at 108 milestone on our old home ground, blocking the road to Dimapur. We were now cut off by road from our supply base there.

———————

The next few days were spent accompanying one or two troops of tanks going to various points on the road to Dimapur, Ukhrul and Palel in order to have long range shoots on to hill positions. We were being used as artillery from reasonably safe positions, although one tank returned from a shoot near Kanglatongbi with a deep gouge cut into the front armourplating by a Jap anti-tank shell. The crew showed it off with pride as their first scar.

The Major took our tank on almost every such attack, letting Captain Murphy take control on perhaps one day out of every six. This resulted in the Squadron Leader's crew being in action on four or five days each week.

Whilst the shooting might take only half an hour, the crew were 'mounted' [a] and driving or waiting for six hours or more. The crews of the other tanks were spending four or five days each week actually in the box [b] and being more relaxed. My crew began to feel that they were paying the price for the privilege of being in the Major's tank.

---

a Appendix A62
b Appendix A63

5th April 1944

B Squadron moved to Yaingangpokpi on the Ukhrul Road and applied their efforts to shooting the Jap defences on the high ground, especially on the Saddle, another wooded ridge.

We were told that the Japs had attacked and surrounded Kohima, where the Royal West Kents were defending strongly. This sounded like bad news for Dimapur, which would be the next target, only a few miles further north. We began to wonder if the R.A.F. would be able to keep us supplied with all our needs.

Our shoots continued.

Lieutenant Archie Weir, 6 Troop Leader, walked up to me one day. I had spoken to him many times recently, mostly trying to help him improve his use of R.T. procedures, and I had always found him co-operative.

"Ah, Corporal, I notice that you often smoke a pipe."

I hesitated.

"Yes sir, I prefer it to smoking the Victory Vs.[a] "

"Well, perhaps we can help each other."

I wondered what was coming.

"When I was on embarkation leave, I was smoking a pipe for the first time and this must have impressed an ancient aunt of mine because she has sent me a two-ounce tin of Players 'No Name' every week since then. It put me in rather a fix as I only smoked the pipe for a week and then reverted to cigarettes. Not wanting to embarrass the old dear or myself, I have not told her that I am not using her presents so that now each delivery of mail brings me a pile of tobacco. Could you enjoy some of it?"

"Delighted, sir! Thank you very much!"

He nodded and gave me two tins.

"I'll drop them in as they arrive, if you like the tobacco."

It was beautiful and cost about twice the price of the brand I was smoking then. He kept me supplied with 'No Name' until I was flown out of Burma more than a year later.

---

a Appendix A64

The daily shoots continued with at least two troops firing each day. Routine maintenance proved its value in preventing or minimising faults on all the equipment. One tank engine, with a serious breakdown, was replaced very smoothly by L.A.D. on the roadside whilst the 75 was being fired on to a target half a mile away. All part of the service. No tank missed a shoot for mechanical reasons.

We noticed that our drivers and operators tended to close their visors and portholes more during these attacks because the Japs sometimes gave us a spray of machine gun fire when we were hitting their positions.

Also, the dusk and dawn stand-to was taken very seriously. We had received reports of Jap infantry attacks at these times with machine guns and grenades and were warned about 'jitter parties'. Apparently, English-speaking Japs would crawl near to our positions at night and call out, trying to locate our officers and N.C.O.s

"Are you there, Sergeant?"

"Where is the company commander?"

"Come and help me, Sergeant."

These were all very eerie when heard at 4 or 5 a.m. and any answer from our side would result in a shower of grenades on to our positions. It was even more weird when some of the Japanese voices had American accents. These warnings were given to us at least three weeks before we first heard the voices in Bishenpur.

8th April 1944.

Half of B Squadron moved back towards Imphal to join R.H.Q. at Sawambang on the Ukhrul Road, near one of the airstrips. The supply Dakotas were landing and taking off in a steady stream – bringing in stores and flying out the wounded and the few remaining 'non-essential' personnel. We felt very essential.

We found our positions in the Box on the left of the track running due north and were immediately ordered to drive up the track for a shoot on to Nunshigum on our left. The mass of this solitary mountain rose from the dry, hard paddy fields which surrounded its four-mile length. The Japs were established along the ridge connecting its three peaks, the highest of which, at 3800 feet above sea level, rose steeply to 1000 feet above the paddy. The enemy would have a dominating view of Imphal with its roads and airfields and it was essential for both sides to occupy it in order to control Imphal and its plain. 4th Corps H.Q. lay only five miles to the west. This Japanese stronghold was the most immediate threat to the security and the very existence of 4th Corps.

An Indian regiment, the 9th Jats, had been fighting on the mountain all that morning only to be pushed back along the southern spur with its small peak named Pyramid. Their call for help was answered by our half of B Squadron who gave a long shoot of H.E. on to the two highest peaks of Twin Bumps, which were joined by a sharp ridge.

Japanese bunkers could be clearly seen through binoculars, with individuals walking along the ridge. Our shelling drove them out of sight but not off the peaks. Using hindsight, we might have been more effective with the other half squadron firing at the same time from the west side of the mountain. Our infantry were not able to make any more progress and we withdrew our tanks to the new box. Our guards on duty at 0200 hrs. the next morning heard the noise of the Jap counter-attack which drove the 9th Jats off the Pyramid.

9th April 1944.

A squadron of R.A.F. fighter-bombers flew over us as soon as the clouds lifted and strafed the peaks of Nunshigum. We could see the 'planes flying just above the paddy fields and then turning upwards to place their bombs only a few feet below the ridge and the peaks. It was all over in ten minutes.

As it was a Sunday, there was a church service but without the usual parade. It was held in the open area of the village and was attended by a dozen officers and men, with communion offered by our C. of E. padre. It seemed very odd to hear the familiar words of the service with the rattle of machine guns only a mile or two away. We had not seen the padre since leaving 108 milestone a few weeks earlier and we had all been in action many times since then.

Perhaps this was one of the benefits of being next to the R.H.Q. Box, but being here also meant that we were more likely to see Colonel Younger unexpectedly. We could always rely on the C.O. spotting any minor error in appearance or occupation and pointing it out very forcefully. He set and demanded a very high standard in all our activities.

10th April 1944.

The entire squadron went out to attack two separate targets. One half shelled a feature identified as Turtle on the Ukhrul Road and the other half again attacked a spur on Nunshigum. Some of our tanks fired 50 rounds of H.E. on to the mountain so the Japs must have felt the effect of all this attention.

They reacted quickly. A rain of mortar shells fell around us on the road and, when we moved a hundred yards away, the mortars following us but with no hits or damage.

At 1800 hrs., back in the box, a few shells fell inside the perimeter. These were probably fired from guns based miles away. They were much heavier than the mortars, possibly 105 mm, and very unpleasant. We squatted in our slit trenches feeling more secure than the crew members who were in the tanks. Again, there was no serious damage. Perhaps the Japs were running short of ammo?

11th April 1944.

Once again the 9th Jats were going to try to recapture Nunshigum, and this time they asked for our support from below before they attacked. There we sat in our tanks in the paddy fields firing a stream of 75 mm shells on to the same peaks of Pyramid and up to the Two Bumps. Firing was interrupted to allow another airstrike, which was right on the target.

As we watched the infantry walking up the slopes, we moved the shell-bursts along the ridge, about thirty yards ahead of the leading files. We ceased firing as soon as they were near the top but as they went over the peak they were in immediate trouble. The Japs were waiting for them and wiped them out as they topped the ridge.

The few who moved sideways, trying to move behind the enemy, were caught by machine guns before they could make any progress. We felt helpless down below, especially when the attack was called off, leaving a strong Japanese force even more firmly in control of the mountain.

That night, we heard later, there was a meeting of top brass at 4th Corps H.Q. Included were Brigadier 'Cully' Scoones, of 254 Tank Brigade, Lt. Col. Ralph Younger, our C.O., plus various senior officers of infantry, artillery and the R.A.F. Col. Younger made the point, which was confirmed by Brig. Scoones, that our Lee tanks were capable of being driven up the slopes of Nunshigum in order to attack the Japs on the summit. The crews had been trained for just such close work – 10 yards from the target bunkers – and could knock out all resistance. The sceptics who doubted our ability to drive up slopes of nearly one in one were assured that our R.E. support would be there to overcome any problem of terrain.

General Slim agreed to go ahead and issued the order. It was vital to regain control of Nunshigum before the Japs could take their artillery up to this vantage point and so endanger Imphal.

12th April 1944.

We heard about these decisions late this afternoon. Each of the four troop leaders was advised by the Major so that the officers could inform the men in their own troop.

Major Sanford called the crews of H.Q.A. Troop together – 27 men from his four tanks. He knew that we were not going to have an easy shoot from the road but that we were going in ahead of the infantry and, literally, putting into action all we had practised with the Gurkhas at Yaripok.

"Gather round, men, I can tell you now what we will be doing tomorrow. You have all been involved in firing on to Jap positions on Nunshigum. Tomorrow, half of you will go up the hill, leading the 1st Dogras into action, and we will take the positions at the summit and keep them. The Japanese up there must be eliminated and any counter-attack repulsed."

He paused to see our reaction. It was non-committal.

"4 and 5 Troops will make the attack and 6 and 7 Troops will give supporting fire from below, as and when we need it. Sergeant Major Craddock and I will climb the southern spur, towards Pyramid, together with Lieut. Neale and 5 Troop, and B Company of the 1st Dogras.

"Lieut. FitzHerbert's 4 Troop will climb the southwestern spur, together with A Company of the Dogras, aiming to join up with us on Pyramid before we attack the highest peak of Twin Bumps. The other two tanks of H.Q.A. Troop will be in reserve here.

"Before we climb, starting at 0900 hrs., there will be a heavy concentration of fire from the Indian Artillery and bombing by three squadrons of the R.A.F. The aircraft will continue strafing the peaks until we are almost there and then they will continue making 'dummy runs' over the target area. They will be flying very near to the leading tanks at that time, but don't worry, they will not bomb near us. They will make the Japanese keep their heads down. A squadron of the 7th Cavalry, in their Stuarts, will create a diversion during the action in the valley of the Iril River. They will deter any attempts by the enemy to reinforce their positions on Nunshigum. Any questions?"

"Yes, sir," said Paddy Ryan, "are we only shelling one side of the peaks? We've seen the Japs run back and shelter behind a ridge so many times."

"You can be sure that we will cover all sides of the peaks with shelling and airstrikes. Any more questions?"

There were none and we resumed our preparations. Final checks on guns, ammunition, including 37 mm canister,[a] which we had not yet used. Hand grenade split pins were nipped with pliers and eased ready for pulling, side arms were once again cleaned and reloaded.

I said to our crew during supper, "I think Dizzy looked rather apprehensive tonight. He spoke as though he really depended on us and that he is just one of the team."

"Too true," said Joe Nussey,[b] usually a very quiet, self-contained Yorkshireman, "tomorrow will probably test us all."

---

a Appendix E

Not wanting to be left out, Paddy put in his penn'orth. "You lot are all hoping to kill a few Japs when you get close tomorrow, but I don't have a gun. I still intend to get me a Jap or two with our Brigade badge."

We all looked puzzled – as he expected.

"Yes, I'm going to crush a few under the tracks, as long as Dizzy doesn't stop me. Perhaps he will be too busy."

We each had two hours on guard duty that night and heard the noise of constant rifle and machine gun fire in the surrounding hills.

13th April 1944.

Stand-to at dawn, as usual, followed by a cooked breakfast, led to our crew being mounted, ready to go at 0800 hrs.

The sun was well up in a cloudless sky and the pre-monsoon humidity [a] was beginning to make long hours inside the tank less comfortable.

Major Sanford climbed into the turret on time and picked up his handset, putting on a cloth helmet holding his earphones under a new type of steel helmet. It was rather like a paratrooper's helmet, fitting closely to his head. We wondered why he wanted to wear it inside the tank.

The call sign for the day was B for Baker.

"Are they all on net, Corporal?"

"Yes, sir, checked only ten minutes ago, including R.H.Q." (For the C.O.'s tank.)

"All stations Baker, delay three zero minutes, out."

The brief message, without any check on its being received, left no one in any doubt of the tension we all felt. The Major told us on the intercom that the airstrike had been delayed an hour and therefore the whole exercise was affected. We were to remain mounted and the engine was switched on so that fresh air could be drawn in from outside. [b]

---

f Appendix A65
a Appendix A66
b Appendix A67

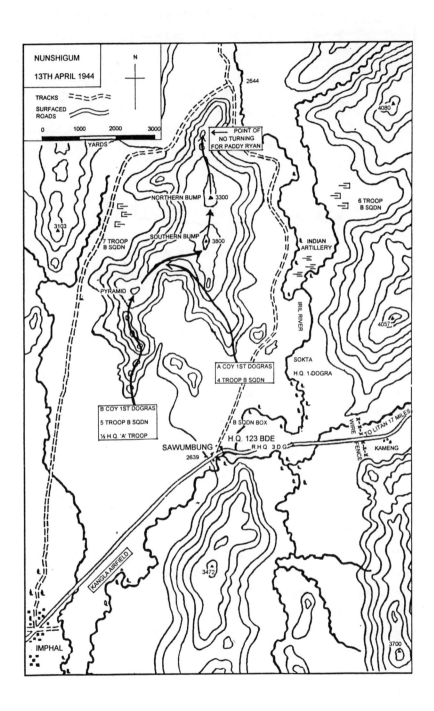

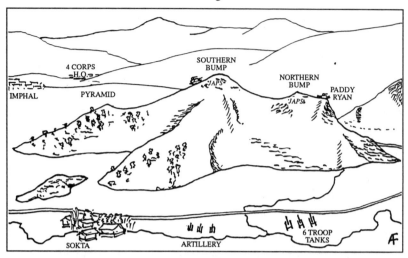

NUNSHIGUM 13th APRIL 1944. VIEW FROM THE EAST.

At 0930 hrs. we moved off. "All stations Baker, advance as planned."

The tank engines started up and we immediately drove on to the paddy field, aiming for the point where the southern spur of Nunshigum climbed sharply upwards, less than a mile away. B Company of the 1st Dogras marched casually in sections, parallel with the tanks, outside the dust clouds that we created. Looking through my porthole on the left front, I could see their weapons – rifles, Bren guns, 2″ mortars and grenades. It looked just like another exercise until we met Lieut. Ryman waiting for us at the start of the climb. There seemed to be no hurry. We were ready well before the planned time.

1030 hrs. The Major gave the brief order, "Baker 5, commence climbing, out."

This started Lieut. Neale and his other two tanks climbing the slope of about one in two in first gear. The Dogras went with them, on either side and behind each tank. The Squadron Leader followed closely with the Sergeant Major's tank behind us. Our speed was about one mile an hour as we picked the easiest gradient through rough jungle. There were no trees big enough to divert the tanks from their chosen route.

1100 hrs. We all jumped as the Vultee Vengeances and Hurri-bombers tore past us at about 200 m.p.h. after flying across the paddy behind us. Roaring up the hillside, as on previous raids, they flew up to the summit and threw their bombs at the peaks. They repeated the process and it was all over in five minutes.

And our climb continued.

Lieut. Ryman walked ahead of the leading tank, giving the signals 'right hand down' or 'left hand down' when necessary to keep the tank from tilting to either side. I was amazed to see him being exposed to the danger from Jap snipers. We were getting near to the first summit of Pyramid.

1115 hrs. Another bombing run from the R.A.F. hit the target area well ahead of us. They must have been flying from an airstrip nearby in order to reload with bombs and return so quickly.

"Baker 6 and 7, are you in position? Over."

"Baker 6 ready, over."

"Baker 7 ready, over."

"6 and 7 roger, out."

The replies from Lieut. Weir and Lieut. Steward of 6 and 7 Troops told the Major that these two troops, who were not intended to climb today, were located respectively on the east and west of Nunshigum, ready to give supporting fire from the paddy when ordered.

Lieut. Steward was an unusual officer in the Carabiniers because he wore the cap badge of the IXth Lancers – as well as a large black moustache. He was often referred to as 'the jam man' because of the IXL being a well-known brand of jam at home. He quickly became a respected Carabinier officer, despite being on temporary transfer from that other regiment.

Lieut. Weir's father was another old Carabinier who had become Colonel of the Regiment in his later years. The son, Archie, had joined us at a very early age and was well-known throughout the Regiment.

Soon after the bombing finished we reached the flattened peak of Pyramid and became targets for snipers from the highest peak to the north. This was the nearer of the two known as Twin Bumps. The infantry and Lieut. Ryman took cover. Our five tanks moved forward to protect them and the Major jumped down to confer with the Major commanding B Company of the Dogras.

This coincided with a third airstrike on the Two Bumps. Surely, no one could survive in that hell. The 'planes flew off and the artillery then started their efforts, blasting the peaks and approaches to the Jap positions. Added to this, 6 and 7 Troops fired H.E. from below on to both sides of the peaks and ridge. I was beginning to think that we would find nothing larger than a pebble when we reached the summit ahead of us.

Just in front of us we could see the three tanks of Lieut. FitzHerbert and 4 Troop, which had climbed up from the south east, together with A Company of 1st Dogras, to meet us on Pyramid. Beyond them was a narrow ridge leading up to the main peak, most of which was wide enough to take only one tank at a time. The steep slopes on either side could not be used by the tanks, and the infantry would have problems walking on them without falling down to the rough hillsides fifty feet below.

The Major gave the order to advance, with Sergeant Doe (Baker 5 Able) [a] leading 5 Troop. Lieut. Neale (Baker 5) was next, then Corporal Coram (Baker 5 Baker). The Major in our tank was fourth, followed by the three tanks of 4 Troop. Finally came Sergeant Major Craddock (Baker 2) who carried the F.O.O. [b] as a passenger, seated behind the driver.

This advance, in 'line ahead', resulted in only the one leading tank having a clear view of the target area.

On our left and right the ground fell quickly away, at about 40 degrees, down to the paddy fields below. There was no room to manoeuvre or to change the sequence of the tanks. It was a one-way system without knowing of any outlet at the other end.

The voice of Lieut. Weir came from his position below. "Baker 4, reporting seeing enemy running away from southern Bump, over."

"Baker 4, roger, keep the air clear, out."

The Major left no doubt that he was in charge. He was standing in his turret with his head and shoulders out. Now I knew why he was wearing a steel helmet.

---

a Appendix C
b Appendix A68

Looking forward through the open driver's visor, Paddy and I could see the three tanks ahead of us, each with their commander's head and shoulders out of the turret cupola. I shouted to Paddy, not using the intercom, "Hadn't we better have the oven door closed? It looks as though things will hot up soon. They haven't all run away."

He said nothing but slammed his visor shut and locked it. This left him with a periscope giving a slit view of about 4 inches by 1 inch. He could just see the ground in front, but nothing to either side. My side porthole was also closed and locked, giving me a similarly restricted view of the sky. My front periscope gave me the same 4 by 1 inch view of the sky.

At that point we heard the roar of yet another airstrike, this time without the bombs. I could just see the Hurribombers sweeping up from below us towards the peak ahead. They passed only thirty feet ahead of our tank and I clearly saw the head of the pilot of the last one to fly over. His black beard and moustache, together with his perfectly bound white pugaree,[a] told me that we had the help of a Sikh of the Indian Air Force.

We continued our slow progress northwards with the infantry just behind each tank when all hell was let loose.

The tanks were sprayed with rifle and machine gun fire. Hand grenades rained on to us from the shallow slit trenches on either side of our path.

I could see a bunch of huge Japs running up to the left side of the three tanks in front of us. They were all about six feet tall and heavily built – not the five foot runts described to us so many weeks ago.

Without waiting for an order to fire, I put a burst of Browning into them and, because the gun would not traverse, I was only able to spray up and down about six feet from the sides of the tanks. Three of the Japs fell but the leading one survivor tried to climb up the side of Corporal Coram's tank which was still moving. He put a foot on to the top part of the track which was moving forward at

---

a Appendix A69

twice the speed of the vehicle. He lost his balance and fell heavily to the ground.

Paddy followed closely and he went under our tracks.

"Baker 5, Number 9 shot, over."

The operator's voice from Lieut. Neale's tank was pitched high. We all heard him. Colonel Younger down below us knew what it meant and waited for the Major to reply.

"Baker 5, give him what help you can. Continue the attack, Baker 5 out."

I could see the Japs on the west side of the ridge, standing well out of their slit trenches, firing at us all, then one jumped out holding a long bamboo pointing towards the tanks. There was a dark object on the end of it, probably a magnetic mine or 'sticky bomb', and he ran with it uphill to the side of the tank. Someone behind us shot him and the mine fell to the ground without exploding.

Only the leading tank of Sergeant Doe was able to fire the 75 without endangering the others and this he did at the reinforced bunker positions.

There was a heavy thud in the turret behind me and I looked back to see the Major slumped on the floor.

"What is it, Sherley?" I asked our turret gunner.

"God! He's had it. Right through the head."

Sherley Holmes was bent over the Major trying to hold his head upright. I could see the damage. A bullet had gone upwards under the chin and then out through his helmet. The exit hole in the metal was curled outwards.

"Shut that turret flap and lock it. We don't want any grenades dropped in," I said, thinking of what I had just seen outside. "Can you still operate without standing on him, Sherley?"

I found a packet of morphine tubes in the first aid box and passed two up to Dimmock the loader. "Here, give him these in case he can feel any pain."

Dimmock passed them to Sherley Holmes who exposed the needle of one tube, pushed it into the Major's lower arm and squeezed the tube. He repeated the procedure with the second and then got back into his own seat and looked out through the periscope. By this time Paddy Ryan had continued driving forward and had somehow overtaken the stationary tanks of 5 Troop and reached the top of the first peak of Two Bumps.

Time to report facts to the C.O.

"Baker 9, over."

Colonel Younger's voice came back immediately.

"Baker 9 here, over."

"Baker 9. Regret report Number 9 hit and out of action, over."

"Baker 9, what do you mean by Number 9,[a] over."

"Our own Number 9, Dizzy, hit in the head, over."

"Baker 9, is he dead? Over."

"Baker 9, he's in a bad way but still has a strong pulse, over."

"Baker 9, pull out of the action. Hullo Baker 4, did you hear all that? over."

"Baker 4, roger, over."

"Baker 4, you take command. Out."

The C.O. was calm and decisive after hearing that two of his three officers in the action were probably dead. The survivor, Lieut. FitzHerbert, was at the rear. He could not use much of his available fire power because of the tanks being in line and not being able to manoeuvre.

Sherley Holmes, on the I.C., asked Paddy if he could turn the tank around in order to pull back but Paddy had the bit between his teeth – to use a cavalry expression.

"No way of turning on this ridge. I'll go forward and try to turn on the next peak."

This was at least 200 feet lower and access was down another narrow ridge running north, joining the Two Bumps. I could see the full length and it appeared, in parts, to be even narrower than the width of a tank. The razorback ridge continued beyond the north peak.

Paddy drove along steadily as we were pelted with grenades from

---

a Appendix A70

both sides. We reached the northern peak and continued another thirty yards – then we had to stop.

We had reached a sheer drop in the front and on either side. None of us in the hull could see anything but sky – and we all knew what would happen if we slipped in any direction. We would roll over and drop nearly 1000 feet.

"Baker 4 and 5, pull back towards Pyramid. Out."

Lieut. FitzHerbert's voice clearly told all eight tanks that we were too far forward.

I asked Sherley Holmes if he could see the path back, by traversing his turret 180 degrees, and guide Paddy backwards along the path we had just used. He could, and Paddy went into reverse. There was little adjustment needed for the steering until the tank started to tilt slowly over to my left.

"Left, left," shouted Sherley. The tank tilted even more steeply.

"Halt!" he screamed at Paddy. "Go back!"

The tank rocked and teetered on the ridge, ready to take a dive backwards.

Paddy's acid voice came over the I.C.

"I was going back, you had told me to reverse. What do you want?" He was pulling hard on both 'sticks', holding the 30 tons load on the brakes.

"Pull forward a bit." Sherley realised that he had been giving exactly the opposite instructions to what were required, because he had not allowed for the tank being in reverse.

Paddy then got the tank more evenly balanced across the sharp ridge and we appeared to be stuck – unable to move in any direction without falling off the mountain.

The Japs were still dug in, mostly between where we were and the other tanks. We felt useless. We couldn't depress or fire our guns at them.

Sherley called out, "Alan, can you see a way of getting back to the Two Bumps?"

"I'll have a look," I replied, thinking he wanted me to get out of the tank and guide him back along the ridge, surrounded by these big Japs. I climbed across, behind the driver and the 75 gunner, and tried to lift the hatch cover so that I could get out.

Joe Nussey looked at me. "Are you barmy, Alan?"

I thought I must be and tried again, but the hatch seemed to be jammed, so I went back to my seat. "Sorry, Sherley, I can't get out."

"You must be mad, I don't want you to get out, you'd only be killed. Can you see any way of moving us back?" Paddy butted in.

"I can get back on to the ridge facing the same way as before; you'll have to guide me backwards." He stressed that, "and I think I might be able to spin it round 180 degrees on the top of the peak when we get there."

"O.K.," said Sherley, "do that, but drive very slowly. This thing won't fly."

Paddy pulled on his left stick and slewed us back along the ridge facing north, put it into reverse and gave Sherley the 'go ahead'. Very gingerly we moved backwards as before, and, this time, Sherley gave the correct instructions to adjust the direction of movement. He could see the north peak easily as we climbed back up to it in reverse and he called a halt as soon as we squatted on top of the Jap bunker positions.

We all looked out of our periscopes and portholes and agreed that we were centrally placed and on the level. Paddy then did a perfect seven-point turn on the spot, only moving three feet in any direction each time.

The tank was then facing south, looking along the ridge leading back to the southern Bump. The other tanks were jockeying for position there and some were moving off that peak in order to return to Pyramid.

"Just look at that !" We were alerted to an amazing sight. Only six feet in front of us we saw another six-foot Jap frantically digging in the bottom of his very shallow slit trench. He was bent over using his short, pointed spade and rapidly flicking stones and soil away from him. Paddy didn't wait for him to make the trench deep enough. He quickly moved forward, running the left track over the Jap and the trench, continuing along the ridge to the south.

"Baker 5 Able, over."

The tense voice from Sergeant Doe's tank calling Lieut. FitzHerbert brought his immediate response.

"Baker 5 Able, yes, over."

"Baker 5 Able, our own Number 9 hit in the head, over."

"Baker 5 Able, roger, pull back as ordered, out."

We continued to move back towards Pyramid and hear the same story repeated for Sergeant Doe's No. 2 in his tank. Corporal Hubbard had taken over in the commander's position, put his head out of the turret and had also been killed instantly.

Then reports came over the wireless of other casualties – all tank commanders who continued to keep their heads out of the turrets.

Lieut. FitzHerbert had ordered all the tanks containing casualties to pull out of the action, climb down the mountain and return to base. We were very relieved to hear this and had nearly reached the flat paddy fields when he made another advance up to the Twin Bumps.

Three tanks made the attack. S.Q.M.S. Branstone was leading, then the Lieutenant followed by Sergeant Hannam.

They passed the first Bump and approached the northern Bump.

Once again they were attacked from the three bunkers – one on each side of the peak and one behind it. All three tank commanders advanced into this hellfire looking out of their turrets, throwing grenades and firing their pistols, and all three were killed within a minute. The 37 mm gunner in S.Q.M.S. Branstone's tank, Trooper Hopkins, moved into the commander's position, looked out, and he also was killed instantly.

By this time, our tank was safely down and returning to base. All the crew were feeling shattered and very glad to be out of the fight. We ate some biscuits and drank water on the way and were soon back in the spot which we had left some five hours earlier. It all seemed very unreal and quiet after being up Nunshigum, although we could hear the continuous sound of machine gun fire broken by the roar of 75 mm H.E. fire on the mountain.

Our first job was to lift the Major's body from the turret floor and out of the cupola, six feet above. We then lowered him to the ground, where two members of the medical team carried him away on a stretcher.

Paddy and I took a bucket of water into the turret, in order to clean up the floor, when I looked down in horror. Lying to one side was a Mills hand grenade. There was no handle on it. This lack of handle meant that it could and should explode within a few seconds of releasing the handle, but, we knew that it had been lying there much longer. It must be one that the Major had been about to throw when he was killed two hours earlier. Paddy picked it up, saying, "This is interesting. I must find out why it didn't go off."

"Not here, Paddy, take it out very carefully and go out into the field with it. We don't want anyone else hurt."

He did this and used the special key to unwind the baseplate, exposing the U-shaped detonating device. He pulled it out very slowly and we both looked at the small cap. It had been struck by the firing pin but, though the short fuse was burned black, it had fizzled out just where it entered the fulminate of mercury detonator.

We looked at each other. Paddy gulped and blinked. "If that had gone off in the tank it would have blown us all to pieces – and the tank, too!"

I agreed with him. We were very lucky. A grenade exploding inside a tank would have detonated all the shells and there would have been some problems in finding any trace of our remains.

Paddy then asked me to look with him at the tank's tracks. "I want to see if I had any success today – there should be some sign of those Japs I ran over." He was right; he had been successful. On the left track we found bloodstains with pieces of bone and Jap uniform wedged between the steel and rubber plates which made up the flexible tracks on which the tank moved. "At least we revenged Dizzy," he commented.

The six of us carried out our usual system of replacing all the ammunition used that day, including the tedious chore of refilling the empty belts from the Brownings with .300 rounds.

The 75 mm rounds were individually packed in thick, compressed card tubes with tight-fitting lids. We always carried a couple of these empty tubes inside the tank as they made ideal portable urinals, which were disposable when nearly filled. They became essential when we were trapped inside a tank for many hours with the enemy killing anyone who even looked out – as had happened today on our first of many close encounters.

Whilst this was going on, Major Sanford's batman came to collect any of his kit which was still on the tank and he gave us an update on the battle continuing on the mountain.

The two infantry company commanders had both been wounded so that all British officers, Dogras and Carabiniers, were out of the action. Apparently, S.S.M. Craddock was put in command and he had continued to attack the enemy with the support of the Dogras, led by their senior V.C.O., Subedar Ranbir Singh. The last three tanks, with dead commanders, had been pulled back with the greatest difficulty. No. 4 Troop Leader's tank had run down a slope and stopped on the brink of a precipice, where driver Smudger Smith found that his engine had jammed. He had jumped out and connected a towrope whilst exposed to possible fire from the Japs above him on the ridge.

1400 hrs. Despite all these delays, S.S.M. Craddock was able to pursue the action and blast the Jap bunkers so that the infantry could reach them and complete the job using bayonet and grenade. They were now fixing Dannert [a] wire which had been carried up on the tanks, ready for the expected counter attack.

1500 hrs. A relieving officer, who had climbed the mountain to take over command of this 'officerless' group, found that he was too late to do other than report 'position satisfactory and consolidation nearing completion'.

1700 hrs. Colonel Younger came up to our tank as we were cooking a meal and we started to stand up. "At ease, men, I just want to thank you all for your magnificent efforts today. First class show. I am proud of you. Your guard duties tonight will be taken over by others and you have all tomorrow to relax. Your new Squadron Leader will join you then. Goodnight." And he walked away.

---

a Appendix A71

A few of us raised our eyebrows. "I thought it was a complete balls-up," came from Sherley Holmes. Others agreed. "I can't understand why they all had to ride into action with head and shoulders out of the turret," I said, "especially after the first two were killed."

"That's cavalry training for you," said Paddy, "if they had had longer swords or lances they would have used them. The charge of the Light Brigade all over again."

We all fell quiet at this comment which was almost sacrilege.

Paddy came in again. "And, anyway, if an experienced tank officer had flown over Nunshigum before we were sent up there, he would have seen that three tanks were the most that could have operated on that ridge and the most that were needed to kill a hundred Japs at close range. Any more than three were surplus and just got in the way of the others. They could have operated with the turret closed, as we did after Dizzy was killed, and just as the Sarnt Major did, without having his head shot off. He'll be the hero of Nunshigum now, so what price 'zero tank'? We'll never hear that mentioned again."

He was right on that point. We all had a new respect for the Sergeant Major.

14th April 1944.

A subdued B Squadron were rested for the day. That meant a complete strip of all weapons, ready for instant action, and a complaint to the armourer that our grenades were not reliable, fortunately for us. Captain Murphy took the morning parade, as acting O.C. B Squadron. He told us that our new Squadron Leader was Major Huntley-Wright, from A Squadron, and that he would be with us that evening. Two new troop leaders were also expected within the next 24 hrs. and until their arrival, the troop sergeants of 4 and 5 Troops were in command.

News from the north, where the Jap 31st Division were still attacking Kohima, told of the Royal West Kents holding out against enormous odds. They had been under fire at very close range for more than nine days and nights. This appalled us when we compared that length of time with our two hours yesterday. The good news was that the British 2nd Division was fighting its way down from Dimapur to relieve the Kohima garrison and later to clear the road through to Imphal. Help was at hand but there would be a few weeks of fighting before we could look for relief.

1200 hrs. The Japanese made the expected counter attack on the Dogra position on the peaks of Nunshigum. It was not a strong effort and was easily resisted by the confident infantry.

During the past four days fighting on the mountain there had been 277 Japanese bodies counted on the steep slopes. Out of the 56 Carabiniers who had climbed and fought in the eight Lee tanks, 49 came down alive to continue fighting the Japs for the next fourteen months. Not all of them survived to the end. Never again did any officer mention short-sighted little Japanese who couldn't aim straight. Rumour had it that the giants we had beaten in our first close action were possibly Koreans from an élite company of the Japanese Imperial Guard. I remember them as being fanatical soldiers who continued to fight when they knew that they could not beat us and who gloried in being killed in action for their god-emperor. We were to meet many more like them.

Chapter 6

Bishenpur, Pots and Pans

15th April 1944

We met our three new officers at the morning parade, which was taken by Major Michael Huntley-Wright. Some of the old Carbs had expected a huntin', shootin', fishin', county type – "double-barrelled name, double-barrelled lah-de-dah" came from one of them. But, how wrong can you be? 'Huntley', as he became known by all, generals down to troopers, was a very straight, down-to-earth young man of about 26 years. He required no running-in period before being accepted. Everyone felt that they had always known him from day one. Rumour had it that he came from a theatrical family, with his sister, Betty Huntley-Wright, well known on the stage. His parents are remembered from pre-war vaudeville and you can still see one of their old bills in the Olde Tyme Bar in the Merion Hotel in Leeds. Huntley-Wright senior is shown on it blacked up for a song about 'My Little Chi'chi', a song that would not be permitted today.

In our tank, as in the whole of B Squadron, we were delighted to have him as our leader. It was our gain and A Squadron's loss. The two new lieutenants, Cole and Kerridge, also settled into 4 and 5 troops quickly. They had to, because we were only just beginning a long spell of close action. Lieutenant Cole was on temporary loan from C Squadron.

Norman Dimmock came back to the tank for tiffin. "I say, I've just seen Ben Galli and Pete Phyllis, from Sarnt Major's crew. They gave me the gen about Thursday. There were two tanks left up on Nunshigum. They had to be emptied and abandoned all night!"

"How was that, Norman?"

"Well, Lieutenant Neale's tank ran down a slope, as we heard, and the engine jammed. Then, after the fighting had stopped, Lieut.

Steward climbed his tank from down below and tried to tow it back, but he got stuck as well. L.A.D. and Smudger Smith got them both off the mountain yesterday afternoon."

"Good for them. Any more gen?"

"Yes. It's on Squadron Orders. Immediate awards of the D.C.M. for the Sarnt Major, and M.M.s [a] for Sergeant Hannam and Smudger. Oh, and yes, Ben Galli has been made up to Corporal."

"There'll be more of that," I said, "if only to replace casualties. Who wants promotion?"

That afternoon, both 6 and 7 Troops were out once more, this time with Captain Murphy, having shoots at nearby hilltops, including Sausage and the Saddle.

═══════════════

This procedure went on smoothly for two weeks with only the occasional hazard of broken tracks, jammed 75s, Jap mortars and artillery shells landing near or amongst us.

Broken tracks were repaired by three of the crew jumping out and taking orders from the driver, usually a job of only a few minutes, using a heavy persuader and spanner, some strong language and muscle, unless the tank was tilted or in a nullah. [b] Jammed guns could take more time, especially if there was a live round in the breech.

It was noticed by the armourer sergeant that the rifling on some of our 37 mms was damaged and that the accuracy of this turret gun could become suspect. He believed that the damage was caused by using canister ammunition. The steel pellets had an abrasive action on the bore, as well as on the targets. He advised the use of canister in future only in emergency, if and when the tanks were being rushed by a large number of Jap infantry.

25th April 1944

The morning sitrep informed us that the Japanese 33 Division had moved in strength from the south to be nearer Imphal. They were

---

a Appendix A72
b Appendix A73

established on the Lushai Hills to the west of the Tiddim Road, near the Silchar Track, and, also in the villages south of Bishenpur. Their aim was to cut off our 17 Division,[a] the Black Cats, which was pulling back from the Tiddim area in order to join up with the main force of 4 Corps in Imphal. They had temporarily succeeded. The Japanese tanks and heavy artillery were a very serious threat to an infantry division whose biggest gun was the 25 pounder. To meet this threat, the Lee tanks of A Squadron, 3rd Carabiniers, had been withdrawn from the Kabaw Valley where they were also in danger of being cut off. Now established in the village of Bishenpur with 20 Division, they were having daily shoots at the Japs on the hill tops.

27th April 1944

Jap artillery shelled Bishenpur from their hill positions on the south side of the Silchar Track. Supported by tanks, they attacked this large village and were brought to a halt by the fire from 20 Division, A Squadron and the R.A. 25 pounders. The fighting was continued for more than three days with very little ground being gained or lost. Tanks from both sides were destroyed and captured. Casualties were high but we were told only the briefest of details.

C Squadron were already back in the Imphal area and were supporting the efforts to push the Japs away to the north and to clear the Manipur Road. One report came down the grapevine about a troop of C Squadron supporting 5 Division in an attack on Japanese bunkers on the roadside near Kanglatongbi. They had attempted to leave the road in order to get closer to a bunker when one Lee tank rolled over and landed upside down. All the exit and entry flaps were jammed closed and the crew were unable to leave the inverted tank. The petrol tank emptied inside, with the fumes from the many gallons of high octane spirit making breathing difficult. Some of the crew could be heard singing and shouting in the poisonous atmosphere.

The risk of fire was ignored by the crews of the other tanks. They managed to fix tow ropes and pull the tank on to its side, giving

a Appendix A74

access to the turret and the men inside. They found that the driver
had died from the fumes.

When we heard this horror story, we examined the floor of our
own tank and loosened the four bolts holding down an escape hatch
in the well of the 75 loader's position. No one had envisaged the
possible need to use this exit until that day.

═══════════════

One night I was asleep beside the tank when there was an appalling
explosion which made us all jump up and into the slit trenches. But
it was not the enemy – it was the start of the monsoon storms.
Lightning flashes made the night look like day and we were treated
to a noisy electrical display – without a drop of rain.

Then, an hour later, it started. We must have had an inch of rain
in the first hour. The water was soon forming puddles and running
into our trenches. There was no more sleep that night and we were
glad to dry out in the hot sun the next morning.

28th April 1944

Our medical officer, Lieutenant Griffiths, known by all as 'Doc
Griffiths', attended the morning parade in order to give us one of
his regular pep talks. He was a G.P. from Bangor, North Wales, and
had a very good bedside manner with men who were really ill. "Now
the monsoons have started, I must stress once more that the need to
take precautions to prevent disease is paramount." There were a few
sniggers at that. That was how he usually started his lectures on
prevention of V.D. and we had not seen any women for weeks.
Surely he wasn't going to give us another talk about remembering
our wives at home! Anyway, most of us were single.

"You already know that it is an offence not to take your Mepacrine
tablets every day, to prevent malaria, and also it is essential that you
roll down your sleeves and fasten the cuffs before dusk and until
after dawn each night. Any man not obeying these orders, including
sleeping without a mosquito net, will be reported by any N.C.O. or
officer and punished."

It was a harsh message from a kindly man – no doubt, for our own good. One man commented afterwards, "It's easy to tell that he doesn't stand guard for two hours every night being bitten to buggery by a few thousand mossies. He'll be telling us next that it's a self-inflicted [a] wound to get malaria!"

8th May 1944

I had all the operators together for an hour and a half's training, including a question-and-answer session. Some need had been identified for tightening up on R/T procedure, timekeeping on the morning net, and a refresher on using morse with W/T procedures. I reminded them of a few of their responsibilities.

"It is easy for us to get into sloppy ways, particularly when many of our other disciplines have been relaxed, but I am not going to let any of you relax your operating procedures. There are a number of reasons for this.

"Firstly, you will be letting down your own crew, your troop and your squadron. The lives of you and your mates will depend on wireless communication all the time.

"Secondly, all your R/T signals are heard by senior officers at Brigade and R.H.Q. They are very interested in hearing the nitty gritty of our actions and I don't need to remind you that Colonel Younger is a very strict disciplinarian. If any of you or your fellow crew members inadvertently switch to 'send' when you are talking on the intercom, all these top brass hear what you say. I can tell you that they fully understand all your chatter; they probably use some of the words themselves, but only in private. I will hold each one of you responsible for any such transmissions from your sets, whether it is from yourselves or, more likely, from your tank commanders, especially your troop leaders. All your voices are easily recognised so there is no difficulty in knowing who is at fault. We have all heard our new lieutenants getting excited on a shoot when they see the enemy for the first time. Well, if they continue to transmit when

---

a Appendix A75

they don't intend it, and jam the wavelength, I can tell you that the Major will get rid of them. And you also, if you are responsible.

"Think about it. B Squadron are building up a good reputation and we don't want to spoil it by any such disgrace. Each one of you must sort out this problem with your own crews, and don't be shy of discussing it with your troop leaders.

"Next problem – timekeeping. You each have your Army Issue pocket watches and you are responsible for keeping them dry and in good order. I appreciate that we are now starting the monsoon rains and that we can easily be soaked through in a storm. I will now show you how to keep your watches dry."

There was a buzz of chatter when I pulled out a pack of Army Issue french letters – thick, dependable passion-killers. "Is there anyone who doesn't know what these are for?" There was a burst of laughter.

"No chance of using those here, Corp," said one.

"Haven't seen a woman for months," said another.

"Kutchnai bibi,[a] kutchnai chute," came from an 'old Carb' (aged about 25).

"You've all got one-track minds," I replied, "and you're all wrong. Just look at this."

I pulled out my 'issue' pocket watch. It was a good reliable timepiece, intended for fixing in a holder on the front of the No. 19 set, but it was usually kept in the blouse pocket, secured with a buttoned flap. Taking out and unrolling a french letter I dropped the watch into it and then tied a knot in the rubber. This completely waterproofed the watch but there was an immediate critical comment.

"Do we have to untie the knot to tell the time, Corp?"

I didn't speak and merely pulled the thick rubber tube until it was two feet long when the rubber became thinner and translucent.

"What time is it now?" I put to them. They could all see it. "And, what's more, it will not jump out of your pocket if you lose a button, and you can wind it up whilst it's inside."

---

a Appendix A76

They all liked that one and quickly knotted their own watches inside the novel containers.

This was followed by a half hour of morse practice using a buzzer. W/T was only to be used for night transmissions back to R.H.Q. and Brigade, because speech became hopelessly distorted after dusk in the jungle-covered hills and valleys of Assam and Burma. Thunderstorms added increased static to these problems. All the operators had achieved ten words per minute in morse, running hand [a] and cipher, in order to pass their trade tests, but they rapidly lost even this poor speed if they did not practise regularly. My aim was to train at least one operator in each troop to send and receive at thirty words per minute, so that they could deputise for me on the evening calls to the Royal Signals operators at Brigade.

When the training finished, Trooper Warrilow, one of the faster operators, asked me, "Tell me, Corporal, what did the actress say to the bishop in morse?" I had heard this one from nearly every W/T class I had ever taken.

"Tell me, Warrilow, what did the actress say to the bishop?"

He smiled, thinking he had caught me out. "George William, dah dah di, di dah dah." I dutifully laughed knowing that G.W. was the international morse signal for 'I am being interfered with' or, more correctly, 'I cannot hear you very well because of interference.'

Not many of these men achieved 30 w.p.m. in morse simply because we did not practise often enough. Those who did so complained of dreaming in morse, and I still do this nearly forty years later.

9th May 1944

The Major took the morning parade and told us we were moving to Bishenpur in order to 'help' A Squadron. They had lost a few tanks and suffered casualties whilst resisting the Jap advance. They were the first Carabiniers to be involved in a 'tank versus tank' battle, and they had clearly won. Some of the tanks that they had knocked out were Stuarts, known to us as 'Honeys', which the 7th Hussars

---

a Appendix A77

BISHENPUR MAY 1944.

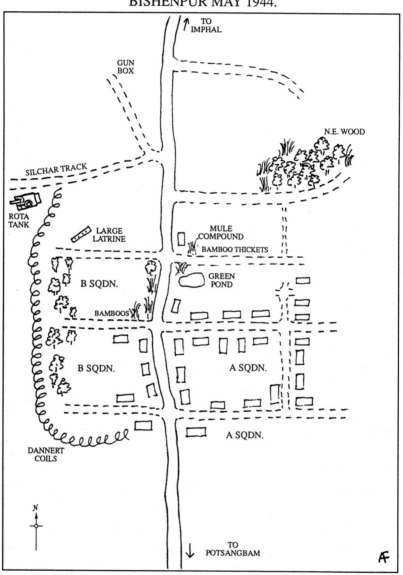

had had to leave at the Burmese side of the Chindwin in the 1942 retreat. Colonel Younger, who had been a major in the 7th Hussars during that retreat, had taken it as a personal affront that the Japs had used his old tanks against us. He was pleased to hear of A Squadron's success.

We moved on transporters into the Bishenpur Box that afternoon, and found our allocated space on the gentle wooded slope facing the road. The Silchar Track was on our north side. A Squadron were also in the village having a few days well earned rest. The surfaced road from Imphal ran through Bishenpur and continued south through the smaller villages of Kwa Sipai, Potsangbam, Ninthoukong, Kha Khunou and on to Moirang, where it became a dirt road to Tiddim, high up in the Chin Hills.

Bishenpur was well designed, with a rectangular layout of wholesome bamboo and timber bungalows. These had been built with the floors raised about three feet above the level of the hard dirt roads. On one side of all these roads was a deeply cut nullah which served as a drainage ditch to take any flood waters during the monsoons. Many of the nullahs were too deep and wide for a Lee tank to cross without the use of a bridge and we were fortunate in being able to call for help, when necessary, from the Royal Engineers. They could supply the services of the Valentine Scissors Bridger.[a] This was a novel invention using the hull of an old Valentine tank, on which was carried a hinged bridge which could be opened and placed across an obstacle such as these nullahs, even under enemy fire. Our tanks would then drive over it and pursue the action. We were to spend the next ten weeks based in this attractive village, where we would become just as stubborn as the Japanese in resisting their efforts to remove us.

10th May 1944

Whilst A Squadron were receiving replacements for their damaged tanks and new crews from Imphal, B Squadron were ordered into action at Potsangbam, a few miles to the south. This village was

---

a Appendix A78

better known as 'Pots and Pans', or 'Pots' for short. The tanks had harboured for the night at a small village only a quarter of a mile north of the Jap stronghold of Pots.

0430 hrs. After a quick breakfast in the dark, the squadron were driving across the paddy fields with two or three Bombay Grenadiers sitting on the back of each tank. It was still before dawn when we met up with the infantry at a new start line. They were, I think, Punjabi Muslims of the Frontier Force Rifles – excellent soldiers and very reliable. They had been pushed back from near the original start line planned the previous day and were now standing-to,[a] about 50 yards inside the northern edge of Pots and Pans.

All these villages looked the same in that light. Bamboo clumps, rising over twenty feet, were at the corners of each basha, giving sufficient material for many of the villagers' needs. Some deciduous trees gave more cover and we knew that the Japs were waiting for us only a few yards away.

The Major got out of his turret and disappeared.

"Where's he gone?" I asked Sherley Holmes.

"Dunno, probably to find the infantry officer."

All was quiet for five minutes.

"Fox 4, over." Lieutenant Cole was wanting Huntley. I answered.

"Fox 4, over."

"Fox 4, have reached the main road. No entry to the village, culvert blown, over."

"Fox 4, will inform Number 9 when he returns, out."

A few minutes later the Major climbed back into the tank and I gave him the report from Fox 4.

"Fine, we can get over this bund in front."

He switched to 'send'.

"Fox 4, report received, move nearer me, access here, over."

"Fox 4, wilco, out."

4 Troop had just started to move in our direction when there were explosions around their position.

---

a Appendix A79

"Fox 4, am being mortared, over."

"Fox 4, can you see any targets, over."

"Fox 4, am engaging, out."

We could hear the familiar noises of 75 mm and Browning gunfire, adding to the noise, as the infantry started to move forward. I could see them through my periscope and didn't envy them. They were moving at the 'high port',[a] ready to use either the bullet or the bayonet.

"Fox 5, advance and keep to the left of Fox 4, Fox 5, over."

"Fox 5, wilco, out."

Machine gun fire was spraying the tanks but the commanders were following orders to keep their heads down. They were inside their turrets with all flaps closed. We could not afford to have a repeat of the Nunshigum casualties.

The rain from the last two days had drained away into the nullahs and the surface of the side roads and land was again baked hard. It was very humid waiting inside the tank. That is what we seemed to do for a large part of the time in these villages. We waited for something to happen or for someone to report a situation.

"Fox 6, am engaging bunker position on the other side of a nullah which is too big to cross, over."

"Fox 6, roger, out."

The heavy roar of 75s firing H.E. at short range was reassuring but there seemed to be no co-ordinated movement of tanks and infantry.

"Hallo, there." A strange voice came on to the intercom. The Major answered. "Hallo, who are you?"

"Captain Jenkins, Frontier Force Rifles, on your rear 'phone. Can you help us to clear a bunker in the other side of the nullah?"

"Yes, Captain, with pleasure, where is it?" The Major sounded as though he had been asked for a light for a cigarette. The perfect gentleman. The Captain described the bunker position, a little to our left front, and the attack was agreed. "Very well, Ryan, you heard all that, advance and turn left at the nullah. 75, How Easy."

---

a Appendix A80

"75, How Easy, ready, sir."

We moved forward, up to the nullah, and saw the cut log at the top of a dark slit in the bank opposite. Our tank was being sprayed by a machine gun at either side of the bunker, but Ginger Whiteley was ready for the order. "Fire three rounds." And they were there.

The simultaneous gunfire and exploding shells roared destruction of the target. It was noisy inside our tank but it must have been much worse on the receiving end of the shells.

"There is another bunker further to the left. Driver, left hand down," and we slewed to the left.

"Can you see it 75?"

"Yes, sir."

"Fire – and two more in your own time."

Ginger was in good form. He put the shells in exactly the right place. I could see it happening through my periscope. Paddy was watching too through his visor periscope.

"Can you see a way across, Ryan?"

"No, sir. Can I move more to the left?"

"Yes, but don't go more than twenty yards."

We couldn't find a way to cross the nullah in that direction.

All four Troops were now quiet. The Japs seemed to have pulled back in amongst the bashas and bamboo thickets. The infantry had waded across the nullah, nearly waist deep in muddy water, cleared the smashed bunkers and had now passed out of our sight. They were on their own. We were stymied. The Major called back to base wireless set in Bishenpur. "Fox 9, Valentine required. How soon available here, over?"

"Fox 9, Wait, out."

The operator at the box would soon let us know. He was back to us in five minutes. "Fox 9, With you in thirty minutes, over."

"Fox 9, thank you, out." The Major acknowledged.

"All stations Fox, you heard that, over."

"Fox 4, roger, over."

"Fox 5, roger, over."

"Fox 6, roger, over."

"Fox 7, roger, over."

"All stations Fox, we must wait, out."

"Right, men," to our crew, "I suggest a quick tiffin and keep our front covered."

We were all feeling weary, especially after an early reveille at 0330 hrs., and were glad to have our rations and a drink of water. Our supporters from the Bombay Grenadiers [a] were behind us, near to the tank and lying down, alert and ready for any surprises. I could see two of them eating their own rations.

1430 hrs. The Valentine Bridger arrived on its own tracks. I remembered training on the Valentine tanks at Catterick in 1941. They were small compared with the Lee and had been designed and built between the wars, carrying a three-man crew, with the main armament of a 2-pounder gun and a Bisa coax machine gun. They were too small and were completely out-gunned by the German tanks and a few had now been modified to carry and lay the scissors bridge over tank obstacles like this nullah.

As it was not on our wireless net, the driver drove up to the first tank he saw. This happened to be Lieutenant Cole's.

"Fox 4, Scissors Number 9 with me. Shall I use him here? Over."

"Fox 4, you will be first over it. You select site, out."

Within fifteen minutes Fox 4 reported crossing the nullah successfully. We soon heard his Brownings and 75s. The three tanks of 5 Troop quickly followed over the water barrier and were giving a lead to the infantry.

"Fox 5, track blown off, over."

"Fox 5, roger, will move nearer and ahead of you with 5 Able, out."

The Major ordered 4 Troop to keep in contact with 5 Troop ready to give any support required. "Fox 4, keep Fox 5 in sight and look out for mines, Fox 4, over."

"Fox 4, wilco, out."

The two H.Q.A. Troop tanks then moved to halt near the bridge

---

a Appendix A81

over the nullah. The Valentine hull had moved back away from it and was looking very vulnerable. Its only weapons were the side arms of the two-man crew and a few grenades, so the Major told the S.S.M. to stay there guarding the bridge and the Valentine. We went over the bridge to join up with the six tanks ahead of us.

On the intercom the Major told us, "I'm worried about Lieutenant Kerridge and his crew. I don't want them to be trying to repair a blown track under fire and we might have to take them out of it inside this one. Can we pack another seven men [a] into the hull, Corporal?"

"O.K. for a short journey, sir, a bit like an Aberdeen taxi, but we'll manage."

We crossed the gardens behind some bashas and spotted Fox 5 with its right track off. He was alone and tilted sideways.

"Fox 5, we are behind you giving cover. Stay inside, over."

"Fox 5, wilco, thank you, out." The crew must have felt reassured.

The other five tanks of 4 and 5 Troops were helping to make slow but steady progress and were now about 100 yards ahead of us.

"Fox 4, have reached another nullah. Am searching for a crossing to my left, over."

"Fox 4, roger. Fox 5 Able, can you see any crossing to your right, over?"

"Fox 5 Able, will search. Out."

Neither troop found any possible crossing place over the deep barrier but they had some good shoots at well built bunkers on the opposite side. The Japanese reaction was frequent heavy machine gun fire and mortaring. This was supplemented by shelling from their artillery placed in the mountains to our west.

6 and 7 Troops were also having a productive time more to our left front. They regularly reported the destruction of bunkers, the slow advance of the infantry and that they had come up against the impassable barrier of the nullah, which seemed to go from the east side of the village right through to the west side.

---

a Appendix A82

Sergeant Major Craddock was feeling very frustrated at being left out of the action, guarding the bridger, and he soon showed this. "Fox 2, may I rejoin you? Local foot support sufficient for this job, Fox 2, over."

"Fox 2, if it is quiet there, O.K. rejoin us up here, out."

He was with us in a few minutes and moved forward, nearer to 4 Troop's position. He was an eager beaver, and again proved the wisdom of the old army advice – 'never volunteer'.

He came up against a Jap anti-tank gun and was hit on the turret. His 37 mm loader, Arthur Wright, was wounded in the arm so he was helped out of the turret by gunner Ben Galli. The two moved back on foot to take Arthur for medical help and they had to run for their lives when the Japs fired at them.

6 Troop were then directed to deal with some strong bunker positions nearer the centre front but they had difficulty negotiating the many wide and deep bomb craters which had been left after earlier R.A.F. raids. Lieutenant Archie Weir and his troop sergeant, Bill Shuker, eventually dismounted and went searching for the Jap on foot. They were looking for trouble and found it when they became targets. Some rapid sprinting and crawling took them back to their tanks where they mounted and caught their breath. Now that they knew their targets, 6 Troop quickly moved into position and blew the Jap bunkers to pieces.

It was late afternoon by this time and the Major was very concerned about the lack of time available for bringing another Valentine Bridger for this new nullah. He also wanted our sappers to look at the obstacle to assess whether any engineering work was required before the bridge could be laid successfully. If he ordered the first one to be moved forward he would be closing the tank exit from the village and it was obvious that we could not clear the Japs ahead of us before nightfall. The last thing he wanted to do was to keep his squadron 'in situ' for the night. He well knew the limitations of vision from inside a tank in daylight. During the night we could be an easy target for a Japanese attack.

He decided to withdraw after giving Lieutenant Kerridge a chance to decide about fixing his track. Fox 5 had been firing its guns with some difficulty after being stuck but the Japs had been driven away during the afternoon. In a lull during the shooting the driver had been out of the tank, examined the damage and decided that he needed the help of the technicians to repair the track and idler assembly and also to pull the 30 ton tank out of the hole. The crew would need to evacuate, bringing their machine guns and kit. They did this on foot, moving to the northern edge of the village.

A section [a] of the F.F.R. were resting in firing positions under the basha near us, watching these antics with some interest and occasionally giving the thumbs up sign. Huntley spotted one with a No. 38 wireless set on his back and he dismounted and ran across to them. None of the section had any English and the Major's Urdu was doubtful.

"Tumara officer kidder hai?" [b] he asked. The word 'officer' was recognised. The answer "Nai malum sahib," [c] was understood by us all but the situation was saved by the bright wireless operator. He pushed his microphone into the Major's hand and said: "Humara officer idher hai,[d] sahib."

Huntley took the mike and called, making his own procedure for speaking to a stranger.

"Hello number 9 footsloggers, I am number 9 tanks, over."

The reply was immediate. "Number 9 tanks. Thank you for your help. What next? Over."

"We are ready to pull back until tomorrow. How does this leave you? Over."

"We will stay put. More help on its way now, over."

"Roger. Good luck. Out."

He ran back and climbed into the turret. "All stations Fox, prepare to return to base, over."

The replies were very mixed and raised some questions. Some of

---

a Appendix A83
b Appendix A84
c Appendix A85
d Appendix A86

the transmissions were very weak and Fox 4 and 5 did not answer at all. "What's the trouble, Corporal?" the Major asked me.

"Some of it sounds as though the aerials are damaged but some could be out of action completely. May I suggest you call 'all group stations' and I'll check the replies." He did. "All group stations Fox, report my signals, over." Eleven of the other thirteen tanks answered. They were all 'on net' although some of them had very weak transmissions and were later found to have had their aerials damaged by gunfire. We knew that Fox 5 had been evacuated and would not answer, but we learned from Fox 4 Able that Fox 4, Lieutenant Cole's[a] tank, had been hit and abandoned. The crew had retired to the northern edge of Pots with their Brownings.

We learned later that the tank was hit on the door, already welded in position, and that the Homelite had ignited. The crew had baled out immediately, unable to inform anyone, and taken cover with the infantry. Despite the risk of the ammunition exploding in the fire, the last one out had sprayed the inside with the contents of a fire extinguisher before joining his mates on the ground. This had done the trick. After twenty minutes the smoke had cleared and they had been able to remount and get back into action. But not for long. Driving between two large craters had not proved to be possible and the tank had slipped down the side of one of them and rolled over, ending up with the turret cupola jammed into the muddy bottom. Once again, the crew of Fox 4 were on foot.

As the other tanks pulled back and came over the scissors bridge, I could see that some of them were carrying wounded infantry on the tops of the tanks, most of them on the engine covers. They were in a very exposed position, offering targets to any Jap sniper who might be near. Trooper Bacon, who was a member of the crew of Fox 6 Baker, Corporal Dodwell's tank, was actually sitting on the outside of the tank holding on to the wounded soldier to prevent him from falling off, when he, Bacon, was shot and killed. Corporal

---

a Appendix A87

Dodwell immediately climbed out to hold them both in position whilst the tank moved away as quickly as possible.

We all felt that we were letting the F.F.R. down by leaving them on their own for the night, facing an unknown number of Japs. It would soon be dark and we knew the importance of keeping the tanks ready for action for many more weeks. The infantry would be well dug-in in their positions, ready to defend themselves through the night. Anyway, it seemed that we would be back again to help them before the dawn stand-to. The Japs had had a rough day and would probably be too exhausted to fight through the night – as we were.

We went through the procedure of finding the scissors bridge again. It looked quite different going across it in the other direction in the dark. We counted the twelve tanks returning over it, waited for the Valentine to uplift the bridge and replace it on its own top, then we drove steadily back to Bishenpur, about ten miles to the north. It was pitch dark as we arrived, during stand-to, so we went straight to our own places, facing outwards, and jumped into our slit trenches.

On stand-down, we started to prepare our cold meal – no fires after dark – using tins of cold baked beans and bully beef and expecting to drink cold water. However, we were delighted to find that our friends in B Echelon, who had been in the box all day, had kept some hot sweet tea for the returning warriors. We had a quick wash followed by either sleep or guard duty. My turn on guard was from midnight to 0200 hrs. It was eerie alone at the side of the tank with the others grunting and snoring in their pits. My ears were still whistling, made worse by the day's explosions and gunfire from both sides.

The bedlam of tropical night life, insects, tree frogs etc., all added to the continual rifle and machine gun fire and exploding grenades in the nearby villages. It sounded as if the lads we had left in Pots were not getting much sleep either. The two hours spent on guard seemed to be endless and the hour of sleep that followed passed in a minute or two.

11th May 1944

The Major had ordered the Squadron to go to Pots and Pans to rejoin our friends from yesterday. We had a quick breakfast with a pialla [a] of garum char.[b] Ginger Whiteley had been the last man on guard and he had broken the rules by boiling water on the pressure stove at the bottom of a slit trench. It was good.

We drove off south, well before stand-to, and I could see the two Valentine Bridgers travelling with us. I had them on our 19 set net, but we still had no direct wireless link with the infantry. Would they still be there where we left them? With the dawn breaking as we reached Pots again, the first bridger repeated his performance of yesterday, in the same place.

0645 hrs. 6 Troop went over it first. We went next, followed by 5, 4 and 7 Troops. We all advanced to the second nullah, which had been yesterday's barrier. The infantry acknowledged our return, giving a cheerful 'thumbs up' from their slit trenches where they must have spent the night. A white officer jumped out of his trench, ran to the back of our tank and came on to our intercom. "Good morning, Major, good to see you again."

"What sort of night did you have?" from Huntley.

"Not much sleep but only the odd firing and grenades. They tried to 'jitter' us at 0300 but they spoke in Urdu and my chaps all speak Pushtu, so they had no effect. I think they were reinforced about an hour ago – lots of noise – so we can expect more resistance. Can you cross this nullah and proceed as per yesterday, we will keep close to you. They seem to be well dug-in under those bashas ahead of us."

"Will do," from the Major. As he said it there was a shower of mortar bombs around us together with machine gun fire and we heard no more from the officer.

The second scissors bridge was laid ahead of us. "Fox 6 followed by Fox 5, proceed across scissors 2 and open out, 6 to the left, 5 ahead. Out." We were all pleased to move away from the noise and the possibility of a direct hit from a mortar. All eight tanks were soon over the bridge and into the southern half of the village. Here

---

a Appendix A88
b Appendix A89

we had a very noisy two hours, blasting the foundations of the bashas where the Japs had built their reinforced bunkers. All crew members were looking out through their periscopes, identifying targets, giving the gunners plenty to do at ranges of only ten to twenty yards. As on Nunshigum, I couldn't see how any human being could survive this onslaught. The bamboo bashas were soon alight, making it even hotter for the Japs dug in below. Yet still they fired back at us with all their weapons.

At first, the Lees took this with very little damage. One tank went very quiet when its A set aerial was blown off. The commander was able to keep in touch with his troop leader using the very short wave B set and the lieutenant passed his orders that way. Fox 6 reported that Lieutenant Weir had dismounted to look for the infantry and had been absent for nearly an hour. He later admitted that he had wandered around, unable to make contact, and had spent most of the time dodging mortar bombs which seemed to follow him wherever he went. It had been raining heavily from before our arrival and everyone felt wet and miserable, mostly because of the lack of cohesion. The day really was a mess.

We were often out of contact with the infantry, who were not always available or ready to clear the few bunkers which we found and shelled. This lack of communication frustrated our attempts to push forward. Late in the afternoon we were advised from Bishenpur that an airstrike had been laid on for the next morning. In the meantime, B Squadron should make a harbour for the night in the north of Pots and Pans, ready for an early start tomorrow.

None of us fancied this but no one raised any serious objections. We made a roughly circular box, all tanks facing outwards, with the Grinders, and whatever infantry we could contact, dug in between the tanks. Huntley said we should sleep in our positions inside the tanks, ready for any night attacks from the Japs. Yes, we could dismount, one at a time, to relieve ourselves when necessary. Some of our crews had started with the 'runs', so this was essential.

Just after stand-to we had a visit from two members of our L.A.D. who had been out on foot during the afternoon trying to find the two tanks we had abandoned the previous day. They reported partial success and had found Lieutenant Kerridge's tank with the turret blown off. This must have been done later by the Japs, because we knew that all the crew had baled out safely and returned to Bishenpur, with the exception of the Lieutenant who had been wounded and sent to hospital. The night passed without any attacks but we all had very little sleep. The mosquitoes were very active despite the rains.

12th May 1944

When dawn came, after standing-to inside the tanks, we all dismounted, stretched our weary limbs and made some attempt to wash despite the shortage of water. I didn't see anyone shaving. Each tank had their pressure stoves going making tea and cooking our pseudo-sausages, called 'soya links' by some. They were called other names by most of the 14th Army. We managed to eat this breakfast and soon felt a little more human, despite the heavy rain.

The next thing was to await the airstrike, which had been delayed by the early fog.

The Hurribombers and Vengeances gave the Jap positions a steady plastering for twenty minutes only a few hundred yards to our south. Our tanks shook with every stick of bombs, which must have spoilt the Jap breakfasts – if they had any. This was a better day for B Squadron's activities despite some casualties. Perhaps we had closer contact with the infantry, now reinforced with the Gurkhas.

5 and 6 Troops moved up to the problem nullah, on the left front, despite heavy and continual shelling and mortaring. 4 and 7 Troops had similar experiences moving to the right front. The airstrike had made more deep craters, which caused hazards for the tanks. Corporal Dodwell found one of them and was unable to climb out of the now muddy bottom.

He ordered his crew to bale out, with their Brownings on tripods, and take cover. They did this despite having little practical infantry training, but the Gurkhas would be glad of two extra machine guns. Two of the crew were wounded – Corporal Dodwell twice and

Corporal Bean. Trooper Goulding had a near miss with a bullet going through his helmet without even parting his hair.

5 and 6 Troops spent the whole day under constant shelling – they could not even look out of their turrets without a sniper targeting them. The infantry suffered casualties every time they tried to cross the nullah and sometimes even when they tried to speak to the tank crews using the box on the rear of the tank.

4 and 7 Troops had more success in crossing the nullah on the right front after the Valentine bridge had been placed in a position selected by the sappers. Despite being heavily shelled, 4 Troop turned to the left and came up against strong Jap bunkers which they engaged at very close range. One Jap ran up to Sergeant Shuker's tank from behind it and stuck a magnetic mine on the rear. This one did explode but it merely blew away the tools which were strapped on the top of the engine compartment. He reported that there was a small petrol leak but no further damage.

"Fox 4 Able, slight damage from magnetic mine on rear. Still operative but footsloggers cannot keep up with us, Fox 4 Able, over."

"Fox 4 Able, roger. All Fox 4, pull back towards nullah, out."

The devastating machine gun fire from undisclosed Jap bunkers was causing heavy casualties amongst our Gurkha friends. 7 Troop were in a similar position. They shot up a number of bunker positions until Fox 7 Able, commanded by Sergeant Hilton, was hit by a Jap 75 mm shell on the rear. This ruined the engine and the tank was stopped. They were able to keep firing all guns for nearly two hours until the fighting moved away from them. They were then unable to fire without endangering our own side.

"Fox 7 Able, am leaving under smoke cover, over."

"Fox 7 Able, roger. You know the procedure, out."

When a tank crew evacuated under these sort of conditions they were expected to take their Brownings, with spare ammunition, grenades and side arms which included two Tommy guns. These were intended to be used for self defence, but there were few men who could resist the opportunity to 'have a go' at the enemy. The removal of parts of the breech blocks of the two heavier guns would prevent the enemy from using those guns against us in the future. This system worked well for the orderly withdrawal of a tank crew who were not under fire from the enemy, but in practice, after receiving a hit, and especially with casualties, many of these guide-lines were ignored – particularly if the tank was on fire.

When the 7th Hussars were forced to leave their tanks on the Burmese side of the Chindwin river in 1942, they had followed some procedures for immobilising their tanks, but the Japs had managed to juggle about with all the parts left and they produced some almost complete tanks to use in action against us near Bishenpur. The important thing in Pots was to save the crews for fighting another day. Experienced men were a sparse commodity. There was now quite a crowd of Carabiniers making their way on foot to the rear. Lieutenant Archie Weir and Sergeant Bunny Holmes had fixed a towrope to Corporal Dodwell's Fox 6 Baker and pulled it out of the crater, so that was a tank saved for tomorrow.

Just before dusk all the 'good' tanks were withdrawn and we were reunited with our dismounted crews and returned to Bishenpur – exhausted but exhilarated by the day's successes. We all had the greatest admiration for the Gurkhas and Indian infantry who had taken the brunt of the casualties on our side. As General Slim had said, the Japs were there to be slaughtered, but we had to admit that they had stuck it out in their strong bunkers and shown no sign of having had enough and wanting to run.

Once more we arrived back in the box after dark. The stand-to had just finished so we were able to do a quick maintenance job, replenishing the ammo, cleaning the guns, then ourselves, before cooking the first hot meal for what seemed like weeks. The Major came to speak to us just as we were trying to hide the light from our stove at the bottom of a trench. He ignored the breach of orders. "I want to thank you all for your efforts these past three days. B Squadron killed a lot of Japs. They are still being counted, and I want you to know that the Colonel and Brigadier Scoones are highly delighted with the results. You have had a long spell in action and I have reported to the C.O. that B Squadron will require at least twenty-four hours before they can be ordered into action again, so make the most of the rest. Guard duties will continue as usual and we can expect the Jap to try to keep us all awake. We are doing the same to him. Any questions?"

"Yes, sir. Have you any news of 17 Div. or 2 Div. breaking through to us?"

"Yes. 17 Division are only a few miles south of here at Ninthoukong. They are making progress and killing a lot of enemy on their way. We don't expect to see them for a few days at least. 33 Corps, coming from Dimapur, are also making progress and we hope to hear that the Royal West Kents at Kohima have been relieved any day now. There is still a big job for them to do before they will be through to Imphal – it will be weeks rather than days. I will see you all tomorrow. Goodnight."

A chorus of warm 'Goodnight, sirs' followed him into the darkness. That night I started with the 'runs'.

13th May 1944

It started during my two hours on stag.[a] The sudden sharp gripe in the guts brought perspiration to my face and an attack of the shivers. I still had fifteen minutes more on duty before I was due to be relieved but I could not wait as long as that. I awakened Joe Nussey, who was my relief, saying, "You're on now," and ran to the latrines.

I was on the trot for the rest of the night without getting a chance of any more sleep. Stand-to was a misery, and I was very glad to be able to visit the 'lats', where I found others with the same problem. "I'm reporting sick this morning," said one, "maybe they'll send me back to India."

"Not on your Nelly," replied another, "I went sick yesterday, was given a dose of white stuff and told to get back to duty before the Japs attacked us. There aren't enough reinforcements to replace all those with the shits."

"You need a bullet up the arse just to get back to the field hospital

---

a Appendix A90

at Imphal," said the third moaner, "the M.O. told me that I could work myself back to feeling better. It's no dice trying to work your ticket out of this lot." This proved to be very true.

The hospitals at Imphal were returning patients to their units long before they were really fit for duty, to give them the chance to fight the Japs amongst their friends, rather than remain lying in a hospital bed without any weapons. We had already heard many tales of Japanese atrocities in hospitals, including the bayoneting of patients and nurses, and we had no reason to disbelieve them.

That morning the Major sent Captain Murphy with four tanks, L.A.D. and some sappers to Pots in order to collect the ditched tanks left the previous day. The original drivers went with them and there was some rejoicing in B Squadron lines when they all came back safely with all but the burned-out tank. That one was a write-off and a replacement was sent from Imphal on a transporter. All the crews, who had been fighting for the past three days, got as much sleep as possible during the day. Some of our crew slept four or five hours without awakening, even when the artillery box sent hundreds of shells over our heads into the villages and on to the Japs in the hills. We were exhausted.

14th May 1944

Before stand-to we were off again down the road to Pots, but our numbers were reduced to the five tanks made up of 6 Troop, the Major and S.S.M. Craddock. We had been told that the Gurkhas had fought through the night and cleared the village to the east of the Tiddim Road – without our support – and had asked for our help to clear the Jap from the remaining bunkers to the west of the road. The sappers led the way searching for Jap mines which could have been laid during the darkness. Their Valentine Bridger was again used to cross a culvert blown up by the Japs and our tanks were soon into the centre of Pots, meeting up with Johnny Gurkha. It was good to see their cheerful smiles so soon after they had been involved in night fighting – they were eager to continue to sort out the 'Japani wallah'.

Communication was slow at first. The Gurkhas seemed to be

unaware of the infantry boxes on the rear of the tanks, so once again our officers dismounted in order to discover the possible targets. The Gurkha officers and V.C.O.s [a] were very keen to point them out to us. One of them took Archie Weir under his wing and they both crawled on their bellies through the mud and bamboos to within five yards of some of the bunkers before pulling back. They then gave our lieutenant a cup of sweet tea. He needed it.

We had all been waiting for nearly two hours before we heard the plan to attack at 1400 hrs. The Major rejoined us in the tank. "Right, men, tiffin here and then a busy afternoon. We should finish the job here before dusk. You'll be glad to know that reinforcements have arrived and they will be calling on our services as required. I'm told that they will be the West Yorkshires."

We wondered what it would be like to work closely with British troops. We had been very satisfied with the Indian, and especially the Gurkha, infantry in action so far. Perhaps they would be more inclined to use the I.C. boxes on the rear. Each of us had five minutes, in turn, outside the tank, smoking and relieving ourselves. Most of us went self-consciously into a cluster of bamboo for privacy from Jap snipers and our nearby infantry.

1400 hrs. 6 Troop went into the target area and we immediately heard the sound of 75s crashing out their challenge. Fox 6 Able and Fox 6 Baker were commanded by Corporals Sharp and Coram, their first action in that position. They performed as though they had done it before many times. The bunkers were quickly destroyed and flattened. Odd rifles, steel helmets and Jap bodies were mixed up with the timber and mud which had once been a stronghold. The procedure now seemed to have become commonplace.

Our infantry were beginning to spread over an ever larger part of Pots, mopping up as they went. Some of their kukris and bayonets were stained red as they carefully investigated all the damaged bunkers. In many of them they found dead and wounded Japs and the latter were aggressive even then, throwing grenades at our men.

---

a Appendix A91

Some held grenades to their own chests, preferring to kill themselves rather than submit to the shame of being taken prisoner.

It was here in Pots that I saw, for the first time, one of the most obscene sights of the war. Two Japanese bodies had been blown up by our shells, stripping their uniforms from their fronts and they lay on their backs exposing huge erections pointing uselessly to the sky. One witty trooper said he thought they must have seen the open doorway to their heaven. It was a strange phenomenon that we were to see many more times in the next twelve months.

Sergeant Major Craddock had no intention of missing out on the attack and the Major sent him to the outside of the wood, on the north west of Pots. He joined up with the infantry there and they soon got into the routine of identifying targets, letting the Sergeant Major blow them up and then moving on to the next one. Huntley made sure that we did not feel deprived either. Every tank was used to destroy bunkers and help the infantry to move forward. It was smooth and rapid, once the impetus was established. Smiling infantry, both Gurkhas and West Yorks, gave the thumbs up after every success. The result was not quite perfect because the two groups of infantry were acting independently and, at one stage, a large group of Japs squeezed between them and again became established in the middle of Pots. Corporal Sharp was the nearest to them and he was able to destroy many of this bunch before dusk.

An infantry officer came on to our intercom. "Hello. The failing light seems likely to beat us today but we have them pinned down and want to make an early start in the morning. Can you stay with us and give us some extra strength for the night?"

I didn't fancy the idea of another sleepless night inside the tank but it was not my decision.

Huntley gave it a thought for only a second. "Yes, I'll just let my number 9 know that I won't be back until tomorrow." He switched to 'send'.

"Fox 9 over."

"Fox 9 here, over."

"Fox 9, am staying with friends this evening, don't wait up for me, over."

"Fox 9, roger, out."

It was as easy as that. It sounded like a teenage daughter phoning home to Mummy. However, it was not easy for us. We all felt shattered after the last three days and 6 Troop must have felt even worse after leading the infantry all day today. The Major decided that they needed a break and replaced them with 4 Troop, who had been waiting in reserve outside the village all afternoon.

"All stations Fox 6, withdraw and return to box, all stations Fox 6, over."

The three tanks all answered cheerfully and promptly and were soon on their way north towards Bishenpur.

"Fox 4, advance to join us for the night, Fox 4, over."

"Fox 4, wilco, out."

4 Troop were with us and settled into their stand-to positions as the night fell. The 'Grinders' were digging in on each side of us and we started to eat some of the biscuits we had left over from the day's rations. The firing had dropped to only a sporadic rifle shot and the odd burst of machine gun fire.

There were two of us in our crew who had the 'runs' now, and neither of us fancied having to jump out of the tank to relieve ourselves. Urinating was a very simple matter, using the empty 75 shell cases, but these were not much use as a latrine, being only three inches in diameter. I suppose that we would have had to try to use them when we were trapped inside the tank, if I had not had a flash of brilliance. I spoke to the Major with all the crew listening. "You know, sir, that Holmes and I have the runs and will need to go a few times during the night. May I suggest that we lift the escape hatch in the 75 loader's corner and go there rather than climbing out under fire?" He never hesitated. "Of course. You will have to shunt your bodies around a bit and I think we will need the fan going more frequently. Yes," he chuckled, "a good idea."

It was not easy for our 75 loader, Joe Nussey. He normally stood in his well, next to the ammo, and would probably have rested during the night by sitting on the edge of the well and leaning against the hull door, which was welded shut. Every time any one wanted to use the hatch, Joe had to climb across behind the driver to allow them to pass. This would also disturb Paddy Ryan. The result was another night with little sleep for any of us.

Each hour at least, one of the tanks would find the battery output falling due to the use of the wireless and fan and we heard the Homelite charger motor start up. It shouted our position to the Japs and often brought the odd mortar shell in our direction. No doubt they knew where we were anyway but they wanted to let us know that they were not beaten by any means. The Grinders and the infantry dug in around us were also all on 100% stand-to all night.

Just after dawn, an infantry officer came to our tank and reported that all seemed quiet and that he was sending out patrols to contact the Jap. He would advise us of the result. When it came, forty minutes later, it was good news. The village was clear of live Japs. The few who had survived the past three days had slipped away during the night and our job was done. Our infantry had suffered heavy casualties but they had never wavered and had won through. The Japs had left some heavy equipment behind including two anti-tank guns, two 75 mm guns, a small tank and two huge 10½" mortars. Some of these had been put out of action by A Squadron during their actions in Pots before B Squadron became involved.

On the way back to Bishenpur, Paddy made a testing comment on the intercom. "I suppose that we'll all be on a fizzer this morning for not sleeping under our mossy nets for two nights." We were all too tired to comment and Huntley ignored it. The mosquitoes had drawn blood from us all and we looked to be in a poor condition when we dismounted with puffed, unwashed faces in need of a shave, and hands swollen up like a bunch of bananas.

It was sheer bliss to sleep stretched out in our slit trenches for most of that night. I went through my two hours on stag feeling like a zombie. I had to keep walking around in order to stay awake and was asleep again as soon as I was relieved.

Chapter 7

Bishenpur and the Mule Compound

16th May 1944

Much maintenance was required for both machines and men. Some of the rifling of the 75s had been worn nearly smooth by the number of shells fired during the past few days and these were promptly replaced with new guns. The ammunition lorry, a Dodge manned by Troopers 'Lakhri' Wood and Travers, visited each troop and replenished stocks – no question of rationing now. Nearly every tank had lost some, if not all, of its periscopes and many of the fishing rod aerials had been truncated – often by our own grenades, thrown from the turrets. Within a few hours the tanks were again ready for action. Not so, the crews.

Some replacements for our very few casualties had been supplied from within the Regiment, others from reinforcements flown in from India. In the Major's morning sitrep he told us that Lieutenant Kerridge was improving rapidly in an Imphal hospital and hoping to rejoin us soon. Of those remaining on duty, a few were having health problems. The growing number of men with diarrhoea highlighted the need for improved hygiene, especially the need for washing hands before preparing food.

The rains brought another new problem – leeches. We knew that they had been used in medicine for centuries, and that they had some benefit to the human race, but in the quantities that we saw they became a pest. The black, loathsome creatures multiplied rapidly in the rainy season, when they required animal or human blood in order to exist. They moved quietly and quickly, at any time of the day or night, by using a sucker at each end of their worm-like bodies. Rumour had it that they could squeeze through the lace-hole of a boot in order to reach the flesh of the leg. They would then latch on to the skin with small hooks and suck blood until they became bloated and fell off. No one liked touching them and the routine method of removing one was to touch it with a glowing cigarette end until it dropped of. Pulling it or cutting it off was no use as this would leave the sucking end still drawing blood from the victim until it developed into an ulcer.

The first time that I saw a leech in action was in the middle of Busty Bain's back as he was working, stripped to the waist, bent over a tank track. I was walking past and called out: "You've a leech on your back, Busty." He cursed and turned to his colleague. "Take it off me, will you." His pal, who was already smoking, sucked on his cigarette to make it glow more brightly, and then touched the leech with the hot end. It was not effective so he pressed harder. The cigarette slipped off the leech and into Busty's back. "You stupid twat," he screamed in pain, "What the effinell are you playing at?" His mate apologised and passed me the cigarette. "Here, you do it, Corp. I've never done it before." I put a piece of paper under the leech to hold it away from the flesh and let the creature rest on the cigarette. It soon dropped off, leaving a smear of blood to show where it had been.

My own experience was at night. Whilst on guard duty I needed to have a leak and went up to a tree to relieve myself. It seemed rather odd because I was splashing and spraying in the moonlight and I could see that I appeared to be much longer than normal. Slipping my hand lower, I realised that I really was much longer, only there was no feeling in the lower part. I knew then that I had been wounded, somehow, and that a strip of my penis had been torn and was hanging downwards. It was my worst nightmare. We all dreaded being damaged in our private parts. When I bent lower to have a closer look in the moonlight, I realised that I had a fat, black leech attached to the tip of my penis. Just at that moment it must have decided that it had taken its fill, or it objected to being washed in strong urine, because much to my relief it fell off.

To cure another problem, the open latrines, which could rapidly fill with flood water, were to be filled in and new ones dug in selected sites. A quantity of old oil should be poured into them to create a seal on the surface. Our M.O., Doc Griffiths, would be holding an inspection of the box during the next few days and we must correct these faults before his arrival.

"Bloody digging bloody slit trenches and now bloody latrines!" Paddy was at his best. "It's not bloody hygienic to wash in bloody rainwater from the bottom of one of his bloody slit trenches, is it?" And he had a point.

The water truck should have been available to supply us with fresh, clean water whenever we needed it but it was, in fact, only in the box for a few hours each day. The driver had to collect supplies from Imphal, because the local supplies were suspect. Water running from the hills was badly discoloured. It was the rain water, running down what had recently been dry nullahs, contaminated with animal and human droppings – some, no doubt, Japanese.

Those of us who had been in Pots and Pans for the past three days had not had any opportunity to replenish our water bottles and chaguls.[a] We had used our reserve supplies from the extra container on the tank, which proved to be a blessing, but it was not going to last very long without being refilled from a clean source.

The use of an oil seal on the revolting, seething mess in the latrines should have worked well, in theory, but it was cursed by the users who suffered some personal damage. An unidentified trooper had, on one occasion, been unable to find any old engine oil and had poured a quantity of high octane fuel into the large latrine used by the men near us. You can perhaps imagine the four-seater, fully occupied by four men who were in no hurry to return to the chores of the day. Sitting there, exchanging the gen from their own crews, and binding about their real and imagined problems, smoking and often scrounging a cigarette, when one of them dropped his lighted match into the space below, now filled with evaporating petrol. The

---

a Appendix A92

resulting explosion of flame, searing four backsides and eight thighs, was only exceeded by the language of the men involved. Their anger continued long after they had bent over in front of Trooper 'Doc' Armitage, our medical orderly, to receive treatment with a lotion and advice not to smoke near petrol. The nickname of 'smootharse' was quickly dropped after a few punches had been swung at the teasers. This notorious latrine faced the Silchar Track and was exposed to anyone using the Track. It also faced the 'neighbours'.

This was the artillery box, known as 'Gun Box', which seemed to grow in size daily. It started with a few 25 pounders, a welcome addition to the firepower of Bishenpur Box, and, as reinforcements were flown into Imphal, much heavier guns were added. Later, we saw some 'Priests'. These were R.A. weapons, heavy guns, like the 105 mm, mounted on the chassis of a tank. They provided some armoured protection for the gun crew. These 'neighbours' did a tremendous job, pouring shells on to known Jap positions, but they were also cursed for preventing anyone in Bishenpur from having more than half an hour's sleep before the guns fired again, or so it seemed. This morning they plastered the hills to our west, in between some bombing from Vengeances and Hurribombers which we could hear and see on the left of the Silchar Track.

I managed to reset the Squadron net on a new wavelength and call sign. These were sent each day to the squadron from the Regimental Signals Officer, Lieutenant Harry Blackburn. He was based with R.H.Q. and I only met him on his occasional visits to B Squadron. He was a wartime soldier who had been running the family business, wholesaling bakers' and grocers' sundries, in Bradford before the war – a very human person who was always prepared to listen to all the relevant points of any topic before making a decision. He had the respect of everyone, whatever their rank, and he achieved results with consummate ease.

"I noticed, Corporal, that B Squadron used the same call sign and wavelength for three days last week. Was that caused by my daily signals with the new ones not being received?"

"No, sir. I know that your signals came through to Squadron

Office, I read them this morning and we are now netted on the correct wavelength, but there were two reasons why I did not change either the call sign or the wavelength. Firstly, we were in Pots and Pans for five consecutive days and we slept in the tank for two nights, so I did not receive your signals until today. Secondly, we were within a few yards of the Japs all the time and liable to be attacked at any minute. In my view, it was not the time or place to make any changes in the net. Also, I kept the Major informed."

"Quite right, Corporal, quite right! I understand. Major Huntley-Wright told me you are doing an excellent job and we both want you to carry on doing so. Have you any problems?"

"Well, sir, I sometimes wonder about our security. If the Japs are listening to us they must be recognising some of our voices by now. Minor changes in wavelength and call sign would not fool anybody. Have we any 'I' [a] reports that they do listen in?"

"None that I've heard of. Let me know if you have any strange interference. I've listened to some of our squadron nets during actions and we all believe that it is better to speak openly, with only the occasional words in code, rather than to lose the meaning of the message. After all, our actions are comparatively small and very instant." He smiled. "The Welsh regiments tend to use Welsh, but we can't do that!"

I then told him of my problems with the tommy gun. "Carrying the tommy gun and these ten magazines of ammo makes it very difficult to move about inside the tank and it is a real struggle to carry the weight when I have to go to Squadron Office or to the latrines twenty or thirty times a day." "The first person to discuss this with is the M.O. He will be here tomorrow morning. Do what he says." Some of us managed to snatch the odd half an hour asleep at the side of the tank and we were all glad to stand down after dusk and either go on guard or bed down again.

---

a Appendix A93

17th May 1944

I started my stag at midnight and it was not easy to awaken my relief at 0200 hrs. He took over and I was immediately asleep. But only for five minutes.

I was awakened by an enormous bang and clatter. We jumped into our trenches, listening to small arms fire and grenades exploding in the village. The Major had joined us and ordered us all into the tank, as an attack on the box had started on the east side, near A Squadron lines. I made a check call on the 19 set and found all operators were on net although most of them sounded exhausted. The noise died down after thirty minutes and we stood down soon after dawn. The Major said he thought that the night attack had merely been a Jap patrol testing our alertness. They had certainly been effective in preventing the tired tank crews from having enough sleep.

Our crew decided to use the last tin of sliced bacon for breakfast. It was delicious when it followed a few spoonfuls of steaming hot burgoo, a porridge made from crushed biscuits and boiling water. A pialla of garum char put the finish to the first real breakfast for nearly a week.

We were just beginning to feel human again in the humid, overcast daylight when there was an enormous roll of thunder in the hills behind us. It seemed to last for ten minutes and then the clouds burst open and we were soaked in the deluge. We were a miserable bunch, wet through to the skin, sheltering under whatever cover we could find. There was a break in the downpour after half an hour, during which we started to dry out our equipment and reclean and oil our weapons. The monsoons were really with us – a time when all armies of the past used to stop fighting. But not us!

The morning sitrep told us of continuing situations. 17 Division, the Black Cats, were still fighting their way towards us from the south and were approximately ten miles away. The British 2 Division, part of 33 Corps, were fighting heavily around Kohima and making progress, but we could not expect them before the end of the month. General Wingate's body had been found, with others in the 'plane wreckage, four days after the crash in the Naga Hills. The Chindit operation was continuing successfully in northern Burma. Both 4 Corps and 33 Corps would continue fighting through the monsoon until the Japanese forces had been completely destroyed. We were winning but there were a lot more Japs to find and eliminate. During the next few days B Squadron would be having shoots on to enemy positions but these would be mostly carried out by one troop at a time. This would enable the troops not involved to rest after the heavy fighting of the past few days.

After this parade I reported sick at the M.I. Room.[a] This was not a building of any sort, it was the 15 cwt. truck, usually driven by Trooper Armitage, medical orderly, called 'Doc' by most of us. The M.O. had arrived to take the sick parade and Doc Armitage was sorting the crowd into some sort of order. N.C.O.s were to be first so that they could return to duty promptly and I was seen within half an hour. Most of the men were seen and out again in under two minutes. I quickly explained my problems. He looked at my tongue and said, "Keep taking the medicine, you may have sprue[b] and, if so, you will be much better keeping going on duty than lying in hospital and missing all your friends. If you can't carry the full ten magazines of ammunition then you should leave eight of them in the tank. That should lighten your load. Next."

That blew it. My hopes of being flown out to India, with a spell in a nice clean B.G.H.,[c] were dashed. So were the similar hopes of most of the sick parade. Doc Armitage had been right when he told us earlier that "you've had it".[d]

Each day brought some new faces into the lines, recruits to replace the casualties, both the wounded and a few sick. There was also a variety of 'visitors' from R.H.Q. and Brigade. One padre [e] drove up to near where I was standing just when a shell arrived from a Jap 105 mm up on the Silchar Track.

---

a Appendix A94
b Appendix A95
c Appendix A96
d appendix A97
e Appendix A98

"What was that, Corporal?" he asked.

"It's our local Jap 105, sir. He usually does it at this time of the morning."

Without any hesitation he spun his jeep around and shot off in a cloud of dust back to Imphal. We did not see him again for more than two months. Another, different padre arrived half an hour later and spent the rest of the day with us, despite frequent shelling and sniping. He was very supportive and men of different churches all spoke well of him.

That afternoon Paddy was wounded in the middle of his back. I had been on one of my visits to the lats when the shelling started. Looking up the Silchar Track, on the left hand side, I saw a puff of smoke on the top of the khud. Then I heard the sound of the gunfire followed by the screaming shell[a] and its immediate explosion in the middle of Bishenpur. Nothing unusual about that, and I continued with my occupation. "There'll be more," said my neighbour knowingly and we waited. The usual routine was for the Jap to send only three or four shells into the village at odd intervals but there were no more today.

When I returned to the tank I saw Sherley Holmes handing some kit over to Doc Armitage. He looked across to me. "Paddy was hit in the back and is going to Imphal. It is not too serious but we will be getting a new driver for a few days." Paddy had caught a splinter from the shell between the two buckles on the back of his belt. It had already lost most of its impetus and the belt had prevented serious damage to his spine, although the skin and muscle had been penetrated. We wished him well and awaited his replacement.

When the tall blond new driver arrived he was another Paddy – this time, Paddy Coffey, with a lovely broad accent from somewhere near Galway, certainly from western Ireland. He told me he was trained in the Irish Army and had been permitted, along with many more thousands of Irishmen, to join the British Army for the 'duration'. He soon fitted into our crew and was very proud to be with the Squadron Leader even on a temporary basis.

_____

a Appendix A99

During the past few months we had all been practising our Urdu, partly to help us communicate with the Indian soldiers with whom we were in frequent contact, but mainly, I suspect, to impress the newcomers that we were all old hands in the Indian Army. Urdu was the Hindi word for 'camp' and was applied to the Hindi spoken by British troops over the past two centuries. Most old soldiers had learned to use a vocabulary of up to only 400 words or so and, if there was any doubt about the correct word in Urdu, they would use the English word and would often mangle the relevant grammar without a thought or apology.

For example, one old Carabinier boasted that he could tell the tale of Goldilocks and the Three Bears in Urdu. It was his party piece and he could never resist a demand to perform during a relaxed few minutes. We all understood it and enjoyed it but no Indian would recognise the language as his own.

Ek upon a budghi teen bears hain,

Once upon a time there were three bears,

Ek barra bear, ek bibi bear aur ek chottha bear,

A Daddy bear, a Mummy bear and a baby bear,

Barra bear boltha, kia pukharro humara burgoo? (in a deep voice)

Daddy bear said, who's been stealing my porridge?

Bibi bear boltha, kia pukharro humara burgoo? (in a normal voice)

Mummy bear said, who's been stealing my porridge?

Aur chottha bear boltha, kia pukharro humara burgoo? (in a squeaky voice)

And Baby bear said, who's been stealing my porridge?

Aur sub bears oopha jantha.

And all the bears went upstairs.

Bibi bear boltha, kia pukharro humara charpoy? (normal voice)

Mummy bear said, who's been sleeping in my bed?

Chottha bear boltha, kia pukharro humara charpoy? (squeaky voice)

Baby bear said, who's been sleeping in my bed?

Barra bear boltha, dekkho humara charpoy, blanco bibi hai. (deep voice)

Daddy bear said, look in my bed, that must be Goldilocks!

The last line was always given with much rubbing of hands together and the lascivious smacking of lips.

After meeting Paddy Coffey, the call came from Norman Dimmock, imitating a well known charwallah at the Poona Depot: "Ho, sahibs, garum char hai. Taste and try, after buy, no good, throw it away." This same charwallah, a bewhiskered Punjabi, (some said he was a Pathani) told another story to all new arrivals at the Depot, whenever he saw an aeroplane flying overhead: "Dekho, sahib, ooper gharri kutchne gora!"

Look, sir, a cart in the sky without a horse!

When I heard the call for tea I looked around for my enamel pialla which I had left on the top of the tank when I had gone to the lats. It was not there. "Humara pialla kiddha hai?" I called. *Where is my mug?* Proving my fluency to our visitor.

"Kia pukharro humara pialla?" *Who has taken my mug?* The accusation had no result so I started to look for it. After a few minutes search I found it in the bushes behind the tank. It was a mangled mess of enamel and metal, with a small piece of shell splinter in the middle. The joke was on me. Dimmock then proved his skill in Urdu.

"Japani wallah makro tumara pialla." *The Jap has broken your mug.* It was fortunate that I had not been drinking from it at the time! When I took the wreckage to the Squadron Stores 3-Tonner, the clerk told me, "Sorry, Corp, kushne pialla." *I ain't got any.*

There was little I could do except fix a handle to an empty fruit tin and use that. I was quite proud of my new pialla, with a wire handle shaped like a pewter tankard, until the M.O. saw it on his next visit a few days later. He condemned it as unhygienic. By that time the stores had been replenished.

The few days of comparative peace helped us all to regain some strength. We slept at every opportunity, even if only for half an hour between the arrival of Jap shells and the heavy gunfire from Gun Box. Each troop was out on a shoot for one day in every two but there were no squadron actions like those we had had at the start on Pots. The Major and, we hoped, the C.O., had realised that too many tanks in an action could be counter-productive. They could get in each others' way, spoiling a shoot, and the crews could easily be exhausted by dehydration waiting inside the tank. An overnight stay inside, with the mosquitoes and Jap jitter parties, to say nothing of the fact that many of us were weakened with diarrhoea, could sap our strength very quickly. We were also feeling the shortage of some items of food and ammunition as all our supplies came from Imphal by road. Our transport was often delayed for a day or two because of the Japs shelling the roads.

I had reported to the Major that some of us had seen the gunsmoke at the top of the khud when the Jap gun shelled us and he had discussed this with the O.C. Gun Box. His reply had been to pass the can back to us. It was really too small a target for his big guns. We were the target, we had spotted it and we had the 75s – ideal for handling the problem.

The result was that each morning, after stand-down, one tank would be driven up the Silchar Track and parked at the ideal point to watch for the telltale puff of smoke when the Jap fired at us. Our 75 would then range on the target and stop it firing again. It became very testing for the commander of this tank to keep watch through binoculars for a long time, as well as boring for the rest of the crew, except the 75 gunner, who was hoping for a good shoot. After the first day the procedure was simplified to having a duty crew of only the 75 gunner and loader with a commander. The rest of the crew would rest outside behind the tank, reading or playing cards, unless it was raining. The three duty men would then change every hour, giving all the crew some extra experience. It worked well, even when the Jap gun targeted our tank. Sometimes their shell would land within thirty yards but they would stop firing immediately we replied. Over a period of days this duel became a test of nerve, especially when we occasionally fired one or two rounds just before we thought they might be going to fire at us.

Air observation told us that the gun was pulled back into a cutting in the khud for most of the time and that it was moved forward into the firing position only when about to be fired. This procedure was

carried out for at least three weeks and the tank was referred to as
'rota tank'. A half day duty in the crew was looked upon as 'cushy'
and there was no shortage of volunteers for it.

18th May 1944

6 Troop was ordered to have a shoot at a persistent cluster of Jap
positions to our east, strung along four peaks which had been named
Karachi, Fish, and Red Hill, 1st Pimple and 2nd Pimple. I went to
their position in the box, just before they left for the shoot, to discuss
the routine wireless calls that I would be expecting from them, as
they would be on a separate net from the rest of the squadron.
Wishing the three wireless ops good luck, I said, "You've got a good
troop leader now. Archie Weir has grown up a few years during the
past month and he won't do anything daft."

"Don't be so sure," replied one of them. "He's all set for an M.C.[a]
soon and he needs one to prove to his Dad that he's no longer a
little schoolboy. The C.O. is making sure that he gets his chance."
'Well,' I thought, 'there may be something in that.' However, I had
never heard before of anyone wanting to go into action hoping to
win a medal. Me, I'd rather survive!

On the way back to H.Q. A. Troop, I heard a 15 cwt. truck revving
past me, only to stop next to Trooper MacIlvenna, who was cleaning
his pistol at the side of his tank.

"Hey, Mac," called the driver, "you were a butcher in civvy
street?"

Mac hesitated, a canny Geordie, "Who wants to know?"

"We've got a bullock to collect from the paddy down the road
and the Q[b] says go ahead, we need the meat. Jump in." Which he did
and found another man sitting in the front holding a Lee Enfield .303.

I heard later that they had found the beast grazing at the edge of
the village. They shot it with the rifle and had just started to dis-
member it, ready for loading into the truck, when they were shot at

---

a Appendix A100
b Appendix A101

from further up the hillside. It was rifle fire and they dived for cover, unhurt. The shots came from our own box. They were our troops firing at them. They must have been Hindu soldiers who objected to seeing their sacred animals being butchered. Mac called to the nearest tank crew to pull forward to give cover whilst he and his mates finished chopping and loading the welcome meat. We all enjoyed a piece of fresh roast beef before stand-to that night. It was delicious.

6 Troop were back in the box in time to enjoy the feast. They had had a few long shoots at the four peaks and Lieutenant Weir suggested to Huntley that they should plan to get much closer next time. Perhaps a climb to the peaks would be necessary but the sappers would be required for a recce [a] and to help in the actual climb through the woods and over some of the nullahs they had seen. He and Lieutenant Ryman went on a foot recce the next day and both agreed that it would be possible to do the climb.

19th May 1944

17 Division had broken through from the south and were now assembling in Imphal. There was a growing feeling in the squadron that the war was moving in the right direction. It might have been merely the knowledge that we had been very successful in Pots and Pans, followed by some good shooting in the villages and on the hills, but there was an air of confidence which grew each day – until the small hours of this morning.

At about 0100 hrs the message was passed from tank to tank, from guards to sleepers – stand-to! It was all very quiet, except for the usual squeaking, rasping, creaking night life with the humming, pouncing mosquito. There was no sound of human life as we crept into our trenches and tanks. The commanders stood with their heads out of their turrets and those of us outside the tanks stood looking into the dark, listening for anything moving.

Then, it came. It was quite eerie and the hair on the back of my neck rippled with a cold shiver. "Sergeant, Sergeant," pause.

---

a Appendix A102

"Are you there, Sergeant?" Longer pause.

"Come and help me, Sergeant."

It seemed to be coming from a darker patch of bamboo about ten yards in front of me. No one answered or moved. Then, I heard a safety catch move with a click. The slight American accent told us all that he wasn't one of ours. A Jap had crept into our box and he was looking for a target, not caring whether he survived the night or not.

One of our grenades landed near where the voice came from, then another and then two more. There were flashes from our grenades and immediately we had small mortars landing around us with some rifle and tommy gun fire aimed at the flashes. A flare burst above us and we could see no movement, no Japs rushing us, and the firing stopped. It was only a jitter party, perhaps only two or three Japs looking for trouble. We stayed awake until after the dawn stand-down and then went in search of any bodies. We found nothing. They had got away and so had our night's rest. It made us realise that we were still vulnerable.

Our crew were on rota duty that morning so half of us bedded down behind the tank, a quarter of a mile up the Silchar Track, but we did not relax. The possibility of a sneaky Jap raid ensured that at least one man kept watch all around us. I was on guard duty early that evening when a truck drove up to the box from the north, deposited a passenger and some luggage, and spun around, heading back to Imphal.

I challenged the newcomer: "Halt, who goes there?"

His reply was a surprise, a voice from my early days in the Army: "Friend. Lieutenant S.R.B. Allen reporting for duty with B. Squadron, 3rd Carabiniers."

He had joined the Army with me on 11th September 1941 in 82A Squad, 56th Training Regiment, R.A.F., Catterick Camp.

"Advance Lieutenant Allen to be recognised by Alan Fenner of 82A Squad." [a] His surprise was a delight to see. "Good Heavens,

---

a Appendix A103

Fenner, after travelling all the way from England, across India and now arriving here in the dark, it's good to have such a welcome from an old friend!"

He wanted to ply me with questions but I had to call another guard to take him to the Officers' Mess.[a] "We are having night visits from the Jap now, so perhaps we can talk tomorrow?" I continued my patrolling.

20th May 1944

This was the last quiet day for a week. Two troops were out for a three-hour shoot on to the hills. Our crew had the afternoon in Rota Tank and we only fired three rounds – mainly to let the Jap know that we were watching him.

I listened to the News from Radio Seac and learned that the Russians were pressing the Allies even harder to start a Second Front by invading Europe. They had been demanding this for a long time, but now there seemed to be signs that it was imminent. Even the Germans were expecting it. The general comment from the lads was, "The sooner they start the sooner they'll finish and then we can expect some more help to wipe out the Japs."

Paddy Ryan came back from hospital, reporting for duty, so we said goodbye to Paddy Coffey, who stayed in the box in reserve. Paddy Ryan was proud to show us his belt with the hole in the back. "Saved my life, that did." He smiled. "Until next time!"

"You don't have to be so pessimistic," I told him after stand-down that night, "there's no reason why most of us shouldn't survive a few more weeks of action. After all, this lot will soon be over and we can count on being pulled out for leave and a long rest in India. We might never fire another shot – after this month. Most of the tanks and guns are finished anyway."

"Don't you believe it," he answered, "we are still effective and Bill Slim will go on using us to win his war. Besides, to cop it in action is a glorious end." He smiled as he said it. "Yes, who wants

---

a Appendix A104

to go back to civvy street and grow older and older, and perhaps, end up a crock?"

"I do for one," said Bob Greendale, who had come over to see us, "I want to go back to Hull and eat and eat until I've got a big paunch." We all laughed at Bob, who was normally very slender and wiry and who now looked painfully thin, like many of us. I said to Paddy: "It's all right, if that's your choice, but don't expect any of us to want to join you underground. What are we all fighting for if there's no chance of enjoying the peace when it comes?" This question was going to crop up quite a lot in the future. Paddy then showed us his wound which had healed well. It was a red blob, about the size of a shilling, in the middle of his back. That night was absolute bedlam.

21st May 1944

After 0200 hrs the entire box was wide awake with a variety of explosions and machine gun fire, tracers[a] curving all over the place. I was feeling safer in the trench, behind my Browning, than Huntley must have felt looking out of his turret. This was no jitter party. The Japs were attacking in strength and they were making progress. We could see a lot of activity about 50 yards down below us on the other side of the main road and there were many screams and shouts from both sides. It was the first time that I was able to recognise the word 'banzai'. It might sound harmless when it is spoken but it is a different matter when it is screamed, full of hate, by a Jap wielding a two-handed Samurai sword.[b]

We, in H.Q.A. Troop, couldn't see any targets so we did not fire. The fighting continued until near dawn, when it slowed down to the odd rifle shot, grenade or burst of machine gun fire. The Jap was still there inside the Bishenpur Box. They seemed to be digging in in the Mule Compound almost opposite our tank. Huntley ordered 4 Troop to move down there and remove them – no waiting to have any breakfast. At the same time, 6 Troop were ordered to leave the

---

a Appendix A105
b Appendix A106

box and drive north to Oinam, to join a 17 Division Box in the village, roughly halfway to Imphal. The Japs had cut the road there, blowing up a culvert to prevent our transport using the road to bring our supplies. They intended to isolate the troops at Bishenpur and then destroy them. We had to stop this.

This was to be the first time that B Squadron had been divided into two groups for more than a day. Half H.Q.A. Troop, the Major and the S.S.M., drove north with 5 Troop to join up with 6 Troop. This left Captain Murphy, with 4 and 7 Troops, to clear the Japs from Bishenpur. This was a separate action and it took a few days to achieve it. 4 Troop were firstly told to meet an infantry officer at the start of the Silchar Track. They looked for him for nearly two hours before learning that he had been killed. Captain Murphy then decided on a plan, sending 4 Troop into the box from the paddy fields from the north. The infantry were to attack the Japs from inside the Box, from the south. This resulted in the tanks having no infantry to consolidate the bunkers as they were destroyed. The infantry had no tanks to support their efforts. Another disadvantage of this plan was that both groups were firing towards each other and any over-shoots were likely to endanger our own side.

The Japs had attacked some Bofors anti-aircraft guns in Gun Box and had built very strong bunker positions within only a few hours of entering the village. They were spread from just below our large latrine, through the mule compound and into the north east wood, which 4 Troop tried to enter but failed. They were able to shoot up the bunker positions around the edge of the wood, spraying the trees with Brown-ings and killing some snipers. They also knocked out some Japs who were running across the mule compound, but by that time it was getting dark so the tanks returned to their box positions for the night.

22nd May 1944

7 Troop, with Captain Murphy, moved to the start of the Silchar Track and spent the morning blasting the Japs in their bunkers. They had cleared that area before tiffin. 4 Troop had more of a problem with the Japs across the road inside the mule compound. It was

surrounded by a high bund on all four sides, preventing a clear view of the inside; at the same time it gave the Japs the material and place in which to build a mass of firing points. The compound contained nearly 160 of our own mules, some of which were already dead and bloating in the heat, but the bawling live mules deterred our tanks from the usual carefree spreading of H.E. shells.

23rd May 1944

The half squadron were harrassed for most of the night by the Japs who were trying to infiltrate, and they were anxious to finish them off as soon as possible. Captain Murphy had a new plan for crushing the enemy between the two troops of tanks. This time he had 7 Troop facing the mule compound from the Silchar Track. The heavy night rain had added to the soft boggy ground and none of the three tanks were able to get into the ideal position for covering the west side. One tank actually became stuck in the morass and had to be pulled out later.

4 Troop had moved south of the compound and blasted the full length of the bund on that side. This was already riddled with Jap bunkers which were soon demolished. The tanks then gave the same treatment to the rest of the surrounding bund. Captain Murphy's tank joined in by shooting up a nullah which ran through the middle of the compound and which was also lined with bunkers. The half squadron spent two hours shooting an area of less than 100 yards square and nothing could live. Nothing did.

The tanks of 4 Troop moved into this compound of carnage, together with the infantry, and settled in for the night – another with little sleep. The stench of putrefying flesh, both animal and human, was appalling. No one envied the twenty-one men of the tanks commanded by Lieutenant Turner, Sergeant Hannam and Corporal Lewis. The men used their field dressings as face masks but these were of no real benefit. They were all very relieved to move out the next morning and return to their own patch on the west of the village, but the whole of Bishenpur was covered with the stench.

24th May 1944

The infantry patrol, which moved in to replace them counted more than 100 dead Japs and found many documents which were of interest to our intelligence officers. There were still some enemy dug in in the north east wood and near Gun Box. They awaited similar attention whilst the sappers did sterling work clearing mines and bridging a nullah to help to give the tanks access to these targets.

25th May 1944

The eight tanks of this half squadron lined up outside the wood and gave it twenty minutes of H.E. and machine gun fire, clearing it of the 40 Japs dug in there.

Chapter 8

The Villages and the Gentle Sex

21st May 1944

The general commanding the Japanese 33 Division must have been exasperated with the Carabiniers. His major task of stopping 17th Indian Division from joining up with the remainder of 4 Corps at Imphal was being frustrated by our heavy and effective fire-power. His wireless repeatedly reported that the Black Cats had been wiped out, but in fact they were pressing north and attacking every obstacle he could put in their way. His strongest road blocks on the Tiddim Road at Pots and Pans, Ninthoukong and near Bishenpur were constantly being eliminated by the onslaught from the Carabiniers' tanks with their 75s supporting the mixed Indian, Gurkha and British troops. He was frequently pounded by our artillery and R.A.F. bombers, which he appeared to survive, but the close contact with the Lee tanks, at only a few yards distance, inevitably resulted in the destruction of some of his crack imperial troops.

He had had enough and had decided to set a trap for this bane of his life. By cutting the road between Imphal and Bishenpur, the base for the Carbs, he could expect some of their tanks to rush north from Bishenpur to attack the road block. He would be waiting there with his artillery, ready for the point-blank firing of H.E. and anti-tank shells. His guns would have to fire quickly and accurately, before the tanks had a chance to spot their positions.

The fact of blowing up a culvert, to cut the supply route to Bishenpur, had the expected result of bringing tanks to the spot, but they were not the Carabiniers' Lees. They were the light Stuart tanks of 7th Indian Cavalry, our sister regiment in 254 Tank Brigade – not what he wanted. The Stuart crews, mostly Sikhs, had arrived to find the road disrupted and they immediately drove on to the paddy field to check the position. They were only 200 yards outside the village of Oinam, which was to the east of the main road where it bent around some tree-covered high ground. It was an ideal spot for an ambush. There seemed to be no Japs around so they took the normal human action under the circumstances. They had been ordered to Oinam immediately after stand-to and, having missed their breakfast, they started to make tea, with water on the boil at the side of their tanks. They had no idea that the Japs were awaiting the arrival of the big Lee tanks. The Sikhs gave a cheerful wave to 6 troop of B Squadron, when they roared up, beckoning our three tanks to join them in the paddy. The Carbs' hopes of a drop of garum char were soon dispelled.

Shell after shell exploded in and around the group of tanks. All three Lees were put out of action, although they were able to rotate their turrets and plaster the edge of the village with 37 mm and Browning. The three 75s were damaged and useless. Lieutenant Weir reported the chaos back to Bishenpur, that Sergeant Shuker was stuck in a nullah and that all crews were replacing their damaged periscopes. At least their 37s were able to put the Japs off their aim for a few minutes.

The Troop Leader's 75 gunner, Trooper Haigh, spotted a flash amongst the trees in the village and told the driver sitting next to him to slew the tank a little to the left in order to bring the 75 within traverse range of the Jap gun. As his own periscope and gun-sight were smashed, he couldn't aim his big gun until he had a bright idea. He opened the breech and looked out through the barrel. A few adjustments to the elevation and traverse put the gun 'spot on target'. Two quick rounds of H.E. resulted in a terrific explosion. The Jap gun, of a similar gauge, was eliminated, together with the gun crew, when their ammunition pile blew up.

Whilst the three Stuarts of 7th Cavalry appeared to be unharmed, 6 Troop of B Squadron were in a poor state and they remained where they were until they were joined by the Major, the S.S.M. and

5 Troop in the early afternoon. A fire in one tank had been extinguished by Trooper Jeffries, who had been burned whilst performing this task. Two of the crew, Lance-Corporal Charles and Trooper Thompson, had been hit with splash – small fragments of shells or bullets which had ricocheted after striking the tank.

'Nut-Nut' Thompson was a happy extrovert who was noted for keeping his hair very short. His head was almost shaven except for the small Gurkha pigtail on his crown. He always had a cheerful, often cheeky, reply to any word of greeting, but I never heard his reason for the lack of hair. Most of us struggled to find a volunteer napphi wallah [a] from amongst our own troop during a spell of maintenance but at that time we were all wearing a few days growth of beard and hair that was much longer than the required 'short back and sides'.

Before Captain Murphy had started his own battle of the mule compound, Major Huntley-Wright had had a number of R/T discussions with the C.O. who was at Imphal. The decision had been made for 5 Troop to join up with 6 Troop, now stuck at Oinam, and for Huntley, accompanied by the S.S.M., to control that operation.

We had a surprise delivery of American K-rations which we loaded on to the tanks, including some for 6 Troop. These were quite novel, being concentrated foods, hygienically packed in cartons, each a complete day's rations for one man. They even included a few sheets of toilet paper – a luxury – and we enjoyed the new tastes, especially the jam, for the first few days. After that we longed for fresh meat and vegetables which we had seen only rarely during the past month.

When we arrived at Oinam, together with 5 Troop, the Stuarts returned to their base near Imphal and we made a show of force outside the village. During tiffin, which was really our breakfast, a plan was made to search for any Japs remaining in the Oinam area and we were to give supporting fire to the Gurkhas. They sent out their patrols in all directions where we could see possible cover for the enemy, but no contacts were reported. At dusk an attempt was made to pull Sergeant Shuker's tank from the nullah but it was completely bogged

---

a Appendix A107

down and would require the help of the heavy lifting gear from the Divisional Workshops. This was done the next day.

22nd May 1944

The three damaged tanks of 6 Troop were sent on transporters to Oyster Box at Imphal, together with their crews. The efficiency of the Workshops was amazing. Within twenty-four hours the damage to the guns and turrets had all been repaired and the troop was returned to Oinam, ready for action. Whether the crews were ready for more trouble was another question. At least, they had been able to have a good wash and shave, whereas the remainder of us were suffering from the lack of water for drinking or washing. We were becoming rather malodorous, not only to each other but also to ourselves. We suffered from flatulence, bad breath and unwashed clothing. In simple fact, we stank from a variety of body odours. Huntley always looked immaculate but he had a batman who could spend the entire day finding water for his bath and laundry when he was in the box.

The Major had requested a water truck to join us on the main road but it had not been able to leave Imphal because of another Jap road block between us and the 4 Corps perimeter near Buri Bazaar. We had to face the fact that we were cut off from both Imphal in the north and Bishenpur to the south and we were glad to find any monsoon water in ponds or ditches in order to wash. This particular week none of us shaved. That included the Major, and we must have looked a pretty villainous bunch by the end of it.

23rd May 1944

Our half squadron spent the next few days in a seemingly endless series of attacks on the small villages to the north of Logtak Lake, where the monsoon waters gathered to flow into the Manipur River. They were dotted about in the paddy fields, which should have been planted with rice but which were now lying idle, since the villagers had been removed from the fighting. Most of the locals had been flown out to India.

All the villages looked very similar from the paddy – groups of well made bamboo bashas dotted amongst the clusters of growing bamboo and other larger trees. They all looked quiet and empty and each one had to be approached warily and then thoroughly searched before we could be sure that there were no Japs. Some of the empty villages were booby-trapped and the patrols suffered casualties from that problem. When we heard any firing we moved nearer to the spot and contacted the infantry. The procedure of identifying bunker positions and then blowing them to matchwood became very routine. We had some long spells of waiting outside a village whilst the footsloggers combed it and chased out any Japs they found.

We all had good shoots with Brownings at groups of beaten Japs trying to move in the open across to the next clump of bamboos and bashas. I caught a glimpse of one bunch of a dozen men being urged across the paddy with either an N.C.O. or an officer behind them prodding some of them with his sword.[a] They were having a hard time. They simply would not accept the fact that they were being beaten every time they came up against our heavier firepower. We thought that we were having a rough time with the shortages of food and water but the Japs were in a far worse position for supplies. Their artillery seemed to be fewer than before. They were certainly short of ammunition, whilst we had no hesitation in using our stocks. We had the occasional visit from the ammo truck to replenish before we ran short of stock. Worn guns were replaced – sometimes under the eyes of the enemy.

The half squadron had a shoot on to the four peaks of Karachi, Red Hill and the two Pimples, previously handled by Archie Weir's 6 Troop, but it was proved that he had been right. Close contact was the only answer. The village on the side of these hills was infested with Japs. Lieutenant Kerridge with 5 Troop forced a way into the west side and helped the infantry to consolidate, before they moved back into the paddy fields to try from the north. They met a Jap

---

a Appendix A108

anti-tank gun there but it was put out of action with little damage
to their tanks.

24th/25th May 1944

We had two full days attacking Jap bunkers in the village, supporting 9th/12th Frontier Force Rifles – a repeat of Pots and Pans.
In the afternoon of 25th May, the Major placed our tank in the paddy,
waiting to catch any running Japs, when I spotted a body in front
of us. An arm was raised and held upright waving about and I told
Huntley on the intercom.

"Driver, advance slowly to see who it is." Paddy Ryan did as he
was told. As we approached I reported, "It's an Indian and he looks
in a bad way. Have you heard of any Jifs around here, sir?"

"No," Huntley replied, "but we need to be alert. Jump out, Fenner,
and take your sidearm with you. See if you can help the chap." I
squeezed behind Paddy, past Ginger and raised the hatch. It was good
to have my head in the fresh air and I looked down to the ground.
The sepoy was wounded, with a blood soaked blouse to prove it, and
I could see no weapons near him. His helmet or puggari was missing.

As the tank was between me and the village I felt quite safe as I
climbed down.

"Abhi tikh hai?" I spoke to the sepoy. "Nai, sahib, bahout
kharab," [a] he groaned, putting his hand to his shoulder.

"Ooper jantha?" I asked him pointing to the top of the tank. He
muttered something that I couldn't understand when there was a
spray of machine gun fire from the village on to the other side of
our exposed tank accompanied with the shrieking of charging Japs.
I cocked my tommy gun and looked round the front of the 75 sponson
to see seven or eight small Japs, led by a sword-wielding, outsize
officer, obviously bent on spoiling our day. I raised my gun, aimed
and squeezed the trigger in the same movement and, bloody hell, it
fired one round and jammed! I was now unarmed, in the open, and
feeling very lonely and naked.

---

a Appendix A109

Fortunately for me, the turret had already been aimed towards the village and Sherley Holmes' Browning opened up very quickly. The 'kami kaze' [a] Japs had their wish. They died in action and would, no doubt, be happily received into their heaven, despite the fact that they had not killed any of us. "We'll wait five minutes to see if there are any more coming out," Huntley called down to me. "Can you get that man up on the tank without any help? If not, Nussey can join you out there and give a hand." Joe Nussey was soon outside and we both helped the sepoy to climb up the front of the tank and seated him on the engine cover, just behind the turret, where I held him in position. Huntley then ordered Paddy to drive the half mile back to the road where there were some medics with a jeep ambulance. We helped him down and returned to our position outside the village.

The tommy gun worried me and I suspected that I had again bulged the barrel, but I was wrong. Stripping it down as we drove across the paddy field, I looked down the barrel and found it clear of any obstruction. The cocking lever would not move forward to take the next round from the full magazine and the problem was cured merely by changing the magazine. A closer look at the faulty one showed that the front lip, over which each round must slide, was turned upwards, creating a catch which stopped the movement of the next round. This damage must have arisen during the past few weeks of carrying and handling the weapon without testing it. I had learned another lesson, when I could easily have been killed. That stoppage had not been taught us on the tommy gun, although I remembered hearing something about changing magazines on the Bren gun.

The Armourer Sergeant told me later that I should never have assumed that the second stoppage was the same as the first one at 108 milestone. "Never assume, Corporal, it makes an ASS out of U and ME!" I never forgot that one.

During the mid-afternoon of 25th May we had some really good news. The water wagon had come through from Imphal and each tank

---

a appendix A110

was pulled back to the road for supplies of clean fresh water. Then the message came to us. Only water bottles and chaguls will be filled – we couldn't have any for our reserve container on the tank. This limited the ration to about a gallon per man – only enough for drinking for two days – none for washing or for laundry purposes. Huntley expressed his views very forcefully. "My men have been in continuous action for the last five days without enough water to drink, let alone to wash, and they are needed in action for another few days at least. I shall expect you back with more supplies tomorrow."

The sergeant stuck his ground. "Sorry, sir, I have to supply the Bishenpur Box as well and understand that they are in the same fix as you. I'll try to be back here tomorrow." He was really running the gauntlet[a] as the roads, both north to Imphal and south to Bishenpur, were being cut by Japanese ambushes nearly every day. I felt much safer inside a tank and was not confident that he would make it with fresh supplies for us the next day.

26th May 1944

Our attacks on the village below Karachi continued. Archie Weir's troop shot up some bunkers, but the Japs were experts at having machine guns positioned to cover each strongpoint and creating heavy casualties amongst our infantry when they followed up after our shelling. The impetus of our advance could easily be lost when communication between the infantry and tanks broke down. When this happened, it probably arose from the fact that we were working with three different Indian regiments, the Mahrattas, the Baluchis and the Frontier Force Rifles, all excellent soldiers but from three different divisions, with no single officer in charge of the operation. At one stage, when our tanks were a hundred and fifty yards ahead of the infantry, a Japanese counter attack pushed them back and the Baluchis suffered fifty per cent casualties. This lack of cohesion cost lives and delayed our real progress.

----

a Appendix A111

27th May 1944

This morning a company of Baluchis started their advance at 0430 hrs and 6 Troop met them an hour later. Similar slow progress to yesterday was made for nearly 300 yards before a halt was caused by unseen machine guns. At least six strong bunkers were destroyed during the day before we consolidated for the night, securing the western half of the village. We were up against a very strong enemy force and the decision was made at Brigade H.Q. that the only way to resolve things was to gain control of the four peaks already identified.

28th May 1944

It was understood in B Squadron that Lieutenant Weir had volunteered for the attack on the peaks and that he had got his wish. He did a few foot recces with Lieutenant Ryman and it was decided that they could get one tank up on to the peak of Fish, and that the firepower of one 75 mm would be sufficient for close action bunker-busting there. His two other tanks were to climb on either side of him, as far as possible, and to give covering fire when the opportunity arose.

It had not rained that morning and the hot sun had partly dried out the surface when the climb started at 1500 hrs. Some artillery and tank shelling had been applied to soften up the Jap bunkers and all seemed to be well. The 3rd/1st Gurkhas were leading the climb. Lieutenant Weir couldn't have asked for better infantry as his tank struggled up to the top of Fish, then to Red Hill via Karachi. He found a very strong group of bunkers on 2nd and 1st Pimples. His good shooting with 75 and Browning helped the Gurkhas to capture the nearside and top of 1st Pimple.

Unfortunately, he had crested 2nd Pimple, running over the top of the Jap bunkers and had slithered down the soft slope on the other side. He found that there was a deep cutting between his position and the 1st Pimple, preventing his advance to this last peak. Worse still, he found that he could not reverse back to the peak of 2nd Pimple. He was stuck. He spent the next hour shooting at the surrounding Japs with his turret guns. The Japs had had enough by that time and they ran, being shot up in the process. The Gurkhas had, by now, cleared both Pimples on their west slopes, but they were badly shot when they went over the ridge on to the east slopes.

Archie Weir accepted that he could do little more to help the infantry and he ordered the tank to be abandoned. The crew evacuated under fire and moved back to be under cover. A Gurkha officer met them and discussed the various problems, thanking them for all their help so far. "We are very short of automatic fire, is it possible to dismount your machine guns for us to use?" Eager beaver Archie Weir immediately volunteered himself and Trooper Jimmy Leach to fetch the Brownings. This was neither easy nor comfortable. Firstly, the sheer weight of two Browning machine guns, the belts of 200 rounds and the two tripods, called for two journeys each man, struggling over rough ground with some slopes of one in one. Secondly, they were under fire from rifles and light machine guns for part of the journey, and also whilst climbing in and out of the tank. It seemed to be rather unwise, but they managed it with the welcome support of covering fire from the Gurkhas.

29th May 1944

The infantry were not only awake all night but they were also very active in night patrols, giving the Japs a return jitter party. Bursts of small arms fire and grenades kept us all awake but it was effective. The enemy could not take it any more and they slipped away before the dawn stand-to – they were the live ones. We found many dead Japs and a lot of weapons and equipment.

It was probably the previous day's activity that won Archie Weir his M.C., and it was the opinion of his troop, and most of the squadron, that he had earned one a few times before then.

Our half squadron continued to have daily shoots on to Jap positions on the hills on both sides of the valley until 5th June. The routines were well established. Sometimes we felt like zombies, snatching the odd thirty minutes of sleep whilst the tanks were being driven from one point to another, sometimes during a shoot, where even the 75 did not awaken me every time it was fired. We were always pleased to keep a rendezvous with the supply trucks of water, food or ammo, in that order, and we were occasionally let down by their non-arrival. Sometimes their road to us was blocked by the Japs. Washing seemed to depend on having a rain storm, during the lulls between actions, when half of the crew would strip down, enjoying a refreshing shower with a soapy lather and plenty of rinsing water. Nowhere did we find any nimbu pahni. That had to come to us by truck.

We continued to have casualties, mostly caused by disease such as dengue fever, amoebic and other dysentries, with a few men getting malaria despite the preventative treatment.

31st May 1944

Lieutenant Kerridge took his 5 Troop up a small ridge near Wainen and all three tanks were knocked out by shellfire as they crested the ridge. They all abandoned their tanks and five men were slightly wounded – Corporal Coram, Corporal Sharp, Troopers Warrilow, Kirby and Jackson. They remained near the tanks, hoping to recover them, but they were stuck there with the infantry for the next two nights before succeeding. They were short of food, until their hopes were raised when Lieutenant Kerridge saw a deer. He shot at it – and missed. They were then even more hungry and they let their troop leader know that he had let them down in no uncertain terms. One comment was "We're bloody cheesed off not having our venison stew, sir." In fact all the Squadron were browned off [a] with the continuing shortage of food and water.

4th June 1944

Things looked more promising when Huntley ordered the eight tanks of our half squadron to return to Bishenpur Box to rejoin Captain Murphy and his half. We should have been back with them during the afternoon but the infantry offered us some targets to the west of the road. These turned out to be a waste of time, because the Japs fled when they heard our tank engines. The result of this delay was that

a Appendix A112

we did not arrive back in Bishenpur until well after midnight. Our old spot on the hillside was unoccupied and the squadron cooks had a welcome hot meal of bully stew awaiting our return. We even had a restricted ration of fresh water for drinking, but not enough for a good stripped wash. That had to wait until the morning.

5th June 1944

It was the Major himself who walked around the squadron at the end of stand-to that morning. He looked slightly better than we did as he had obviously had a wash and change of battledress, but he had not yet had a shave. Like all of us he had a week's beard and he was aware of it. "As soon as you stand-down, I want you all to have a good clean-up, yourselves first, with a wash, shave and change of clothes, then the tanks, and then your breakfast. We can expect Colonel Younger to visit us today."

None of us expected the C.O. to be on his way from Imphal so early, but I had my first experience of his very strong personality only a few minutes later. Two of us went, in different directions, looking for water for washing. I was just crossing the main road carrying a canvas bucket by its rope handle, when a jeep roared up and stopped behind me. Colonel Younger was driving, with a sergeant sitting beside him.

"Corporal!" I jumped to attention in my ragged battledress and without my cap.

"Sir!" I didn't wait long. He was scarlet-faced. "Whatever is happening here, Corporal? You are a disgrace!" I felt a disgrace. I had done so for the past two weeks.

"We returned to this box during the night, sir, after two weeks in the villages without enough water to drink, let alone wash, and I'm now looking for some water for a wash and shave." I pointed to the pond at the roadside. It was covered with evil green scum which bubbled with escaping methane gas as we looked at it. That shook him. "Where is Major Huntley-Wright?" he snapped. "I believe you will find him in either the tank lines or in the officers' mess." This latter was merely the area of bushes where the officers slept and ate when in the box. The Colonel grunted and drove off.

I couldn't fancy washing in the green soup so I walked up the Silchar Track for nearly half a mile until I found a running stream. I filled the bucket and returned to the tank, where I found that Huntley had called us all together.

"This morning Colonel Younger came here to inspect the squadron and to express his appreciation of all that we have achieved during the past few weeks. He was surprised to find officers, N.C.O.'s and men who were unwashed, unshaven and wearing filthy rags of battledress. I can assure you that he expressed his view that it is unacceptable. His final comment was that he would go away and return this afternoon. You now have two hours in which to prepare yourselves for the C.O.'s inspection."

"Excuse me, sir," came from the ranks, "is the C.O. not aware that we have been in action, non-stop, for two weeks?"

"Yes, he is, and I will have the opportunity this afternoon to explain the effect of the shortage of water, you may be sure. I was as surprised by his early arrival as you all were."

This was the nearest thing to an apology that I have ever heard from one officer for another senior officer's unwarranted anger. The C.O. must have left his Oyster Box in Imphal before or during the stand-to, and taken the risk of a Jap ambush in order to be with us so early.

We pressed on with the big clean-up. Bishenpur Box still stank of rotting flesh, especially near the mule lines, which had been bulldozed to bury the Jap casualties. I was still suffering from the runs, fifteen to twenty times a day, and had lost about a third of my weight. To help to reduce the weight of my tommy gun, I had removed the butt and left it in the tank. It had now become an automatic pistol in a sling and could only be fired in my hands and not aimed, using the shoulder. It was still too heavy to carry far and I had got into the habit of changing it for Paddy Ryan's pistol and belt when I had to walk to the latrines or to visit the other tanks. This created a problem later.

The C.O.'s comments during his visit at 1300 hrs were not as critical as we had expected. Perhaps he had given some thought to the effect of his early morning arrival. I had explained to Huntley that I had been the first to be bollocked and he told me not to worry about it any more. The C.O. had told him that he would have arrested any one other than me, as he had grown to respect me for the work I had done and was still doing. I was amazed at this, as the only time that I had spoken to the Colonel was on the wireless when up on the peaks of Nunshigum.

The C.O. ordered us all to stand at ease and he let us know how successful we had been during the past fortnight. Both half squadrons had performed extremely well and had been responsible for eliminating some hundreds of the enemy. We had continued in action, despite severe shortages of food and water (at this there were some glances around with raised eyebrows) and had now reunited for the final effort before a period of rest with leave. There were cheers at this point.

The three Japanese divisions, which had started their invasion of India so confidently, were now weakened to the point of being incapable of continuing their advance. Their generals must have realised this fact some weeks earlier but they would not admit it. When ordered to capture a village or a hill top, they would continue to send more troops into the fight, until they were either successful or completely eliminated. This was happening on the Tiddim Road – our road. They had attacked Ninthoukong, about ten miles south of Bishenpur, only this morning.

7 Troop were ordered to support the infantry that afternoon as five Japanese tanks were reported to have entered the village.

This was an opportunity for Lieutenant Allen, one of the few subalterns who had recently joined B Squadron as potential troop leaders under training. He did not even reach the village.

As he led the three Lee tanks towards Ninthoukong, his tank was hit five times by a 47 mm A.P. shell on the left front, near the wireless operator, Trooper Laurie Marshall. The first shell hit the heads of some of the rivets, shearing off the tops, resulting in one of the rivets hitting Marshall in the left elbow and the rib cage. Another rivet ricocheted around the inside of the tank before striking

a fire extinguisher, which hit Lieutenant Allen in the buttocks. The
two seriously wounded men were eventually returned to Imphal for
hospital treatment.

The other two tanks of 7 Troop entered the village and were soon
in sight of the Jap tanks. This was our first tank-versus-tank action
and the excitement came across on the wireless. One of the crew
members gripped his microphone too hard, switching to send, and
we all heard his reaction.

"Look, Jock, there's one of the bastards ahead, can you see it?"
We heard his 75 fire. "You've hit it, you've got the sod!" He must
then have released his pressel switch, as the air became clear, so I
let him know the error of his ways.

"Baker 7 Able, you were transmitting, then. Remember procedure.
Congrats on your shooting, Baker 7 Able, over."

He replied, still very excited, "Baker 7 Able, thank you, sorry.
We knocked out a tank, over." The Major had listened to all this
and he butted in. "Baker 7 Able. Excellent. Keep up the good work,
out." They soon reported a second Jap tank knocked out.

Huntley ordered 4 Troop to accompany us down the road to
Ninthoukong, where we joined up with the 7 Troop sergeant and
corporal ready for a planned attack at 1500 hrs. By this time the
Gurkha officer who met us was gleefully reporting that all five Jap
tanks were out of action – two hit by our 75s and two knocked out
by one of his men using a PIAT. That man was later awarded a V.C.
for the day's effort. All five Jap tanks were bogged down in the
mud, useless and no longer a threat. During the afternoon Sergeant
Treves dismounted from Baker 4 Able to do a foot recce with his
troop leader when he was hit by a sniper. He was evacuated but he
died later that day.

We were all very committed inside the village and, when darkness fell, there seemed to be no respite for either side. The Japs
were just as determined to win as we were. It was unlike any other
night spent inside the tank, when we had waited for dawn before
having another go. Small arms, mortars and grenades were heard
throughout the night. Our own Bombay Grenadiers used their rifles

at least twice to deter the creeping approach of Japs bent on trouble. It was perhaps the worst night I had ever had in the villages.

At 2000 hrs. Sergeant Bunny Holmes tried to cross a nullah in the pitch dark and, as might be expected, he became bogged down. He and his crew had to wait until 0600 hrs before they could see to remove their breech blocks and Brownings and creep back, in a torrential downpour of over two inches or rain, towards the rest of the half squadron.

6th June 1944

This date must be etched in the minds of everyone over the age of fifty. D Day in Europe, involving millions of people on both sides of the War, was a far bigger job than ours in Assam and Burma. For us, this day was similar to any other in the past few weeks, only it was raining more heavily than usual. In that part of the world it was normal to have 140 inches of rain each year, most of it falling from June to September – July being the worst month with nearly 50 inches. The rain was bad that day, with worse to come later.

Perhaps it was the rain, or it might have been sheer exhaustion on both sides, but we made little progress on 6th June. I switched over to Radio Seac for a quick flash of news early in the afternoon and heard the momentous announcement: 'Combined Allied Forces landed on the coast of Northern France this morning'. I told Huntley, and the crew on the intercom and their comments showed little excitement. "Good," from Huntley.

"Perhaps we will get some equipment when they are finished with it," from Paddy.

"They've taken their time," from Sherley.

"They'll be up against bigger tanks than we are," from Ginger.

"It's raining again," from Dimmock.

We must have been feeling the effects of never having more than one hour's sleep during the past month without being awakened. Our promised rest at Bishenpur had not even started before we were in action again here in Ninthoukong. The memories of the C.O.'s pep talk yesterday had faded rapidly and we continued with what was our normal activity – waiting too long, shooting sporadically and crapping too often. We were back on to K Rations again and we were beginning to hate the sight of the hygienically sealed packets of 'plastic' food.

During the afternoon Bunny Holmes and his crew volunteered to go and collect their tank and rejoin the action with the rest of us. They took spades and axes and followed another troop tank to the spot where they had left their own. Whilst their comrades made a lot of noise with their engine and all the weapons, the dismounted crew dug at the bund, hacked at some trees for logs and built a path for their own tank to reverse out of the bog. It was sheer hard labour, sometimes waist deep in water and sludge, but the simple plan worked and the tank was recovered. As one of them said later, "We had some tins of bacon and jam in the lockers and we weren't going to let the Japs swipe those." Also the tank was their 'home' as well as their means of fighting.

The Major was well aware of the way the long days and nights in the tanks were sapping our strength, and he planned to give each troop one day in every three resting in Bishenpur. It was a good idea but it was often disrupted by the uncooperative enemy . At least he got the C.O.'s agreement. They both knew of the toll taken by exhaustion – costly mistakes leading to loss of life, equipment and opportunities to kill the Japs. Any man could fall asleep on his feet if he were deprived of food and rest for long enough. During the next four weeks each troop spent two or three days and nights at a time in and around Ninthoukong or Awang Khunou, a nearby village.

The Japs had become more likely to move from one point to another when our pressure on them was too effective. This happened frequently and it became routine to place one tank outside each village or clump of woodland, waiting to shoot at the running enemy. This tank often became a target itself to the Jap artillery, making it wise to move about in the paddy fields.

Whilst a second troop would be enjoying its 'day off' in Bishenpur, washing, cleaning and maintaining, mostly, and sleeping for an extra hour or two, the other two troops would be having a more clean and wholesome day shooting at the hill tops at identified bunkers or gun emplacements. Favourite targets were known as 'Dog Picquet', 'Sapper' and 'R.K. Ridge'. The Jap 75s really were a pest, dropping shells near any moving vehicle, whether wheeled or tracked. Our base in Bishenpur was another favourite target and their shells landed amongst us most days. If they had the opportunity to range on a target they seemed to be able to hit within a few yards of the spot. In order to spoil their aim we resumed the practice of having a tank from the resting troop placed half a mile up the Track, waiting to spot the gun flash.

It was during this period of controlled action that I had a few experiences which stick in my mind. They all occurred whilst I was engaged on the latrines, looking up to the khud side.

On the first occasion I was enjoying the rest from my chores with Paddy's pistol and belt at my side. The belt was, unfortunately, the famous 'souvenir' with the hole between the back buckles where he had been hit earlier. I heard the instantaneous shriek and explosion of a Jap shell which landed only twenty yards to my right. Fortunately, it had passed over the latrine and all its shrapnel continued to travel away from me. The bad news was that I had jumped with shock and knocked Paddy's belt, pistol and holster into the vacant hole next to me. I looked down into the mess and saw it all disappear below the surface. Oh dear! No one was going to delve for that.

I returned to the tank and confessed to Paddy what had happened. "Bloody hell, man, that was my souvenir! I was going to show that off for the rest of my life – how I was saved by my belt." He pulled a face. "Oh well, it could have happened to me anyway, I suppose."

"Sorry," I said, "I'll go draw another one for you." Which I did. The armourer sergeant wrinkled his nose when I told him of the mishap and he issued the replacement. "Don't bring the old one back here, I don't want to handle it. Sign this, Corporal, there you go." It was as easy as that.

The next incident was only a few days later, as I sat on my throne. Looking up the track, I saw a movement of something grey coming down towards me. It dropped below a fold in the ground before reappearing as it got nearer. It was grey and it was big. I looked again, rubbed my eyes and – yes, I was not seeing things. It was an elephant coming down the Track – only a small one – and it was walking so very quietly, with its trunk raised, looking rather disturbed. So was I. I quickly tidied up and pulled my trousers up, by which time the jumbo had arrived and halted in front of me, holding out its trunk. It was only a youngster, standing as high as my shoulder, and it had a piece of chain locked round one of its hind legs. I could only think that it had broken away from the Japs, who, we knew, used elephants, as we did, for some of the heavier chores in the jungle. This one had probably helped to pull the Jap 75 mm or 105 mm guns into position on the top of the hills.

I spoke to the creature and held out one hand. Not knowing any elephantese, I tried the Yorkshire farmer's way of addressing cattle: "Here, cush, come over, cush, whatsamatter, cush, ista gan yam?"[a] But it didn't understand plain Yorkshire. I had by now spotted that I had a baby she elephant and I tried Urdu.

"Tikh hai, bibi, abbhi bahout achcha hai?" [b] She liked that and curled her trunk round my wrist, so very gently. After letting her caress me for a few minutes whilst I talked to her, I turned towards the village, leading her down the hillside. She followed me all the way to the Squadron Orderly Room where I was met by Sergeant Major Craddock.

"What have you there, Corporal?" I couldn't resist the opportunity. "I believe it's an elephant, sir, I mean, a Japanese elephant. I found her on the Silchar Track."

"Then you'd better keep her, hadn't you, Corporal?" We all had a good laugh. "Can I draw rations for her?"

"If you go down to the mule lines you should be able to indent for some," he replied. He was quite serious about 'finders keepers'. I suppose he didn't want to be responsible for keeping her until we could find another home for her. The chain did not seem to be

a Appendix A113
b Appendix A114

causing any discomfort so I fixed a rope to it and tied her to a tree
whilst I went to the mule compound to explain my needs. The
havildar [a] in charge said he had no experience of elephants, but he
thought that they needed plenty of water and green fodder. They
were noted for their hard work, affection sometimes, and for long
memories if upset. He also told me that there was a British officer-
sahib, named Williams or 'Elephant Bill', who looked after all our
elephants in Assam and northern Burma. He would send a message
back to Imphal asking for help from him.

He did this, but I had to look after the creature for a week before
Major Williams came to Bishenpur with a mahout. He was delighted
to have another elephant on his strength and guessed that she was
about seven years old. Lucy, as we called her, became very affec-
tionate, especially to me. She almost smiled when I spoke to her at
feeding times. On the odd days when our tank was away from the
box I had arranged for our B Echelon to ensure that she was fed
and watered. I learned, during that week with her, that female
elephants have their two breasts, each with a single nipple, placed
side by side between their forelegs – in a similar position to the
human race. She was given a warm welcome by all the troops in the
box – British, Indian and Gurkha – and some of the more sex-starved
soldiery liked to talk to her and at the same time caress her chest
and bosom. She never objected and often curled her trunk round
their necks. I warned them that she would trample on them if they
made any further advances, but I thought she would grow up to be
a flirt. We were all very sorry to see Lucy led off to Imphal where
she would earn her keep helping in the war effort. She is still
probably working in Assam or Burma to this day.

The third experience on the latrines happened a few days after
Lucy was taken from me. I saw a human figure, about half a mile
away, walking towards me in the light rain.

As usual, during one of my visits, I was contemplating life in general
and thinking what a delightful companion Lucy had been. The cama-

---

a Appendix A115

raderie in each tank was something outstanding, but there was not the warm affection that I had received for such a short time from this elephant. I'm sure that I would have had reason to worry if any of the others had caressed me like she did! Living so closely together, sometimes for twenty-four hours a day inside a tank, could test relationships to breaking point, but that very rarely occurred. If it did, a man could ask for a transfer to another crew where there was a vacancy, which might be caused by a casualty or promotion. Such requests were refused only occasionally, perhaps if it would cause an imbalance of N.C.O.'s in the crew or in the troop, but every consideration was given to them. A wise squadron leader wanted happy and co-operative teams of men in his tanks. If a tank commander acted foolishly at any time, by an action such as putting his crew to unnecessary risk, he could be embarrassed by having six simultaneous requests for transfer out of his tank. This was never looked upon as being mutinous, which it probably really was, but it usually resulted in the tank commander himself being transferred out of the tank. He could be moved out of the troop and, on very rare occasions, out of the squadron or even out of the regiment. I know of only one officer who was sacked in this way. He had a nervous breakdown, after nearly a year of action, and fired his turret Browning at the dismounted crew of the Squadron Leader's tank, including me, thinking we were Japs.

Whilst thinking on these matters, the approaching figure had come near enough for me to see that it was female – not another elephant but a young woman.

She was a well shaped girl, aged about twenty, dressed in a dark European skirt and tight fitting fawn jumper. Her brown skin and round face made me think that she was a local lass who had been lost in the mists. Her black hair was bedraggled and wet from the rain, which was still falling, but apart from that, she looked quite wholesome and attractive.

"Good morning, young lady, can I help you?" I smiled and put on the charm. Then I realised that this was the first female human I had seen for nearly three months. The Imphal plain had been almost cleared of them in the evacuation, when the Japs invaded.

"Sahib, sahib," she whispered, pointing up the hill from where she had walked. "Japani wallah bahout mila hai, kushnai khana," [a] rubbing her stomach and looking forlorn, "Japani jig-jig bahout mila hai."

"Kitna Japani ooder hai?" [b] I pointed up the khud. This was a daft question for me to ask, because I could only count up to twelve, in Urdu, at that time. Her reply in rapid, fluent Urdu was completely lost on me, but I did get a message. She was a Jap comforts girl, and they had kept her short of food but not short of men. She would probably be riddled with all sorts of the horrible diseases described to us by the M.O. in his V.D. talks. No doubt she would have plenty of information for our Intelligence people. She was not for me, or any of the squadron.

"Idher aow," [c] I pointed down into the box and started to walk slowly down the hill. She followed behind, just like Lucy did, and just like the Indian bibis walking behind their husbands. I led her along to the Squadron Office. Once again, the S.S.M. saw me approach and he moved towards us.

"Not again, Corporal, what do you call this one?"

He had a twinkle in his eye.

"I haven't given her a name yet, sir, but I'll work on it. Do I have the same arrangements as with Lucy?"

"What do you mean?"

"Well, sir, am I responsible for feeding her, and the other arrangements?"

"Not on your life, Corporal, if you are thinking what I think you are, she might lead you and your crew astray."

I explained that she appeared to be an escaped comforts girl, that she was hungry and that I thought she might have some information about the Jap strengths and guns, etc. She had probably come from near the Jap 105 mm, which was such a pest to us.

---

a Appendix A116
b Appendix A117
c Appendix A118

"I see what you mean, Corporal. I'll get our I.O.[a] involved. Leave her here and return to duty."

My abrupt dismissal was rather disappointing and I never heard any more about the girl. I don't even know where she had originated. We found out later that the Japanese army took a number of such unfortunate young women along with them throughout their campaigns. They were recruited, often forcedly, from every place that they captured. Married women were usually treated with respect, but single ones were used, abused and eventually rejected when they had lost their attraction. Apart from satisfying the soldiers' sexual demands, they were required to do the mundane chores of an army on the move, including cooking and nursing the sick and wounded. When food was in short supply, as it was in this campaign, they were the first to be starved. It is a sorry tale that is a permanent blot on the history of the Japanese.

---

a Appendix A119

Chapter 9

Our First Leave

End of June 1944

During my routine visits to the other troops, when in the box, I noticed a subtle changing of attitudes. We had now spent three months in close contact with the enemy and there had been a tremendous drawing together of every member of each tank crew, each troop, and B Squadron as an entity. Each casualty had been a loss to all of us; we welcomed their replacements and quickly absorbed them into this dynamic unit. The sense of humour had not only remained with us throughout the privations but had grown in sharpness and accuracy. Nicknames were earned and lost. Archie Weir had become a troop leader who was defended by his men against all criticism. His accolade was the name of 'Zumper'. I don't know the reasons for it, but he was proud enough to write a poem for the Squadron magazine and sign it as such.

One of the new subalterns to be given a troop was Lieutenant Swan. He was a dark, well-built young man of strong personality, with whom everyone felt a rapport. His twenty men were very pleased to be led by such an assertive character and they cheerfully went off into action with him, until they realised that he had one trait that they did not like. He was not only brave but he was also ambitious – in his early days. I learned this when I was asking his operator how things had gone on their day of close action on Banana Ridge, overlooking the Silchar Track. It had started on the night of 7th July, when 5 and 7 Troops had gone out to prepare for an early attack which would be supported by 4 and 6 Troops firing from the paddy fields outside Bishenpur.

8th July 1944

5 and 7 Troops had a good close shoot at bunkers on the Ridge and Lieutenant Swan had half his body exposed to the Japs whilst he potted at them with his pistol. Some of these young men never learn! Corporal Sharp's tank lost a track when it ran over a mine and the crew had to evacuate it. Lieutenant Ridge moved nearer in support and the two troops helped the infantry to kill another 80 Japs. Once again they were unable to move over the crest of Banana Ridge and they all withdrew for the night.

9th July 1944

The same action was continued, but little progress made. Corporal Sharp's tank was found to have been blown up when they reached it late that day. Whilst having a cold meal during a lull in the fighting, Lieutenant Swan's crew took the opportunity to try to probe his mind. "Don't you think you are risking your life, standing out of the turret like you do, sir?" asked one of them.

"We are all taking risks being here, anyway," he replied, "you don't get a V.C. for sitting inside with the hatch closed." The crew were horrified. "You mean, sir, you are setting out to get a V.C.? They are mostly posthumous!"

"Of course, a V.C. would be very welcome. There will be quite a few awarded for the fighting around Imphal and I wouldn't refuse one," he laughed. "The important thing is to be seen and recommended for one."

His men went very quiet, until he got out of the tank for some reason. Then, it came out.

"I think I'll apply for a transfer," said one.

"Me too," said another.

Within a minute, the six men had all agreed to submit applications for transfer out of his tank – the letters to be given to Lieutenant Swan in the first place. They waited a few days before approaching him on the subject. During those days, he led them, accompanied by other troops, in a number of actions in which he excelled, often being exposed to danger from snipers and Jap artillery. They made steady progress along the hills and ridges from which the Japs had controlled their infiltration of the villages.

———————————

Some of the other comments heard during my wandering around the lines were more political. In the very mixed bag of soldiers in the squadron we had the rare extreme left wing and right wing agitators from civvy street. They only caused trouble from the clash of their views when they were affected by alcohol or thrown together for long periods. They were rarely left in the same troop together, never in the same tank. On the odd occasion one of them would try to involve me in political debate.

"What do you think caused the War, Corporal?"

"Have you read 'Guilty Men'?", etc.

I used to laugh it off with a half-hearted salute, either the communist clenched fist or the Hitler 'Sieg Heil', and say, "Joe for King!" or, "When we get our horses back, we'll sort 'em all out." That type couldn't stand much banter and they usually shut up, after giving a mouthful of latrine language. I did hear the occasional comment that might have indicated a deeper feeling of hate for the establishment, and, sometimes, for the anti-establishment. "We will have to sort 'them' out after the War." "'They' don't deserve to live after all 'they've' done." "Why should 'they' live in luxury while we're out here starving, stinking like shit, and being shot at all day and night?" The mysterious 'they' were listed, by various voices over many months, to include war-profiteers, politicians, civilians of call-up age, anyone in authority, and all those 'shagging' the wives of men in the Forces.

Nobody took this chatter at all seriously. It was accepted as normal 'binding', getting it off the chest, and it probably gave a healthy release of pent-up frustrations. Anyone intending to kill someone in that list would surely keep it a close secret, if he wanted to avoid the rope for his efforts.

Perhaps your man did keep such a secret and let it fester in his mind until after the war, before planning and carrying out a series of murders. The conditions for developing such a warped mind could have been created during the long days of deprivation, filth, lack of sufficient water or nourishment, with a variety of illnesses to weaken the body. Furthermore, there was plenty more fighting to come, during the next twelve months, before the regiment was sent to India to prepare for the invasion of Malaya.

As I look back on the fighting in Imphal, there had been many chances to kill off any hated character. For instance, there had been many threats to the S.S.M. but no one had harmed him and he had grown into quite a hero, starting from Nunshigum. Admittedly, some of his crew had requested a transfer out of his tank, but that could be explained by their wanting to stay with friends who had been moved out on promotion. For example, Pete Phillis wanted to stay with his friend Ben Galli when he was made corporal and given a tank in 4 Troop.

14th July 1944

B Squadron were, once again, ordered to support a strong infantry attack on Ninthoukong, which had been recaptured by the Japs. The continual rains had created bogs in the paddy fields and inside the village, so that our tanks were frequently stuck in the mud. The infantry cleared half the village with only a little support from our tanks. Most of the time we were sitting waiting in the rain.

15th July 1944

Sergeant Bob Greendale and Sergeant Bill Shuker, of 6 Troop, were able to penetrate to the occupied bunkers and knock out five of them, killing thirty Japs. They returned to Bishenpur for the night and shared in a ration of beer, the first for four months. The road from Dimapur had finally been opened and the first convoy through to Imphal had carried some urgent essentials, such as ammunition and medical supplies, but also some non-essentials like crates of beer which would not have been much of a loss to the war effort if the Japs had destroyed it. Many of us, with digestive problems, were quite ill after drinking our one bottle, and felt rather flat after the experience.

16th July 1944

After stand-to that morning we were warned that the heavily
reinforced Gun Box would be firing its biggest barrage of the campaign during the next hour and that we could expect a lot of noise.
The targets were the Jap positions in and around Ninthoukong. We
had heard them many times before now and did not pay much
attention until it occurred. I suppose that the new supplies of ammo
had reduced the need for rationing and the artillery command had
decided to be really effective.

Suddenly, there was the most hellish explosion which went on
and on. The ground literally shook, and continued to shake for an
hour, as every piece fired steadily, over our heads, towards the
Ninthoukong area. My 'whistling' ears acquired a new variety of
howls and screams, which I still have twenty-four hours a day, and
which is now diagnosed as tinnitus. The bombardment was the last
straw for the Japanese. They ran from the villages, from the hilltop
bunkers and fled to the south and east.

C Squadron of the Carabiniers, who had been fighting to the north
of Imphal, now drove south through Bishenpur down the Tiddim
Road in pursuit of the running, demoralised enemy. We cheered them
on their way and suddenly realised that the war was over for us.

18th July 1944

Huntley was a happy man when he gave the morning sitrep. "You
have had a long, tough period in very close contact with the enemy,
and now you can look forward to a period of rest, with leave in
India, spread over the next three months. The Jap has been beaten
in Assam and northern Burma, as forecast by General Slim, and is
now trying to escape complete annihilation, as our troops chase him
away from here.

"Our future role will depend upon circumstances when the situation is reappraised, but the main thing now, for B Squadron, is to
enjoy the leave which is due to you and then get our tanks, crews,
weapons and supplies all in good order, ready for anything. Some of
you are going to be repatriated under Python, so there will be plenty

of work to do reorganising and retraining the crews." He said a lot more and we were feeling a surge of relief and excitement.

Lieutenant Swan's crew had offered him their requests for transfer, but the circumstances had changed. He had experienced a few near misses when he had been exposed to enemy fire and he had also heard that he had been recommended for an M.C. He had let his crew know that he would prefer to be a live M.C. than a dead V.C. They accepted this and decided to stay with him.

24th July 1944

B Squadron moved from Bishenpur, home for so long, and now the burial ground of so many Japs who had been such fanatical foes. We drove north on transporters back to our old base at Yaripok.

It was refreshing to walk again around this delightful village. Although it had been occupied by other troops during the siege of Imphal and occasionally attacked by Jap jitter parties, it was as clean, tidy and wholesome as when we left it three months earlier. We were once more living in bashas, although we still slept on the ground. There were no charpoys and no locals to make them, but it was sheer bliss to sleep under a mosquito net again with a guard duty on only one night in three. Rations improved, with a few fresh vegetables and fruit such as pineapples and mangoes. Fresh water was plentiful and we had regular swimming parties in the river. Each of us was issued with two new battledresses and the old, tattered rags were simply dumped in a pile to be burnt. We began to feel human again.

1st August 1944

"What do you think?" burst out Norman Dimmock, "I've just passed the Squadron Office. They have white stones along the path and crossed lances outside the guardroom!"

"Back to bull, I suppose," commented Paddy Ryan, "you can't keep the donkey-wallopers down. They've opened the Sergeants' Mess [a] and they're already talking of 'when we had horses'." [b]

---

a Appendix A120
b Appendix A121

A notice on Squadron Orders informed us that a Field Dental Officer would be available during the next few days and that all ranks requiring dental treatment should report that fact. Many of us did so. When my turn for treatment came, I was intrigued with the mobile equipment supplied to the young lieutenant who saw me. There was no dentist's chair. I sat on a small stool in the open watched by a queue of waiting patients. The drill was operated by a foot treadle, so that the dentist was really standing on one leg only, pounding away with the other leg whilst he tried to drill a tooth in a shaking patient, sitting on a rocking stool. I was not too happy about my treatment.

Firstly, he took an x-ray of an aching tooth in my front, upper jaw and told me there was no sign of any problem. "But I will extract it for you." He did that quite painlessly and looked at the root of the tooth. "I can't see anything wrong there," he mused. "Then, put it back, quick," I told him. "Too late," was his reply, as he threw the tooth into a waste bin. "Next?"

Other signs of peace and civilisation included a weekly visit from a WASBI[a] truck, with supplies of comforts such as soap, razor blades, toothpaste and brushes. The best part of buying such items, with newly drawn pay, was the sight and smile of the uniformed lady selling these luxuries. Many of them were Anglo-Indian, with a few British memsahibs. All of them were a treat for sore eyes and some of us felt rather strange talking straight English without the usual seasoning of Urdu and swear words.

One excited trooper, when asked what she could do for him, replied to the Wasbi: "You could do me a lot of good with something you have not got on display." She blushed, knowing what he meant, and sent him away. Sadly, she reported him to Huntley, so the man was put on a charge. I heard afterwards that Huntley told him not to be such an idiot; in future he should control his tongue. 'Admonished' was written on his records. Leave and repat became the buzz words of the month.

---

a Appendix A122

6th August 1944

This was a day of immense joy. I was on a 3-ton truck, with a party of twenty men of B Squadron, being driven to the airstrip near Imphal to go on 14 days' war leave in Darjeeling. We were full of the holiday spirit and looking forward to the first leave for two years – in my case, the first leave in India. We looked like a collection of scarecrows, as thin as laths, with sunken eyes, but all chattering excitedly about what we would do when we arrived in Nepal. The journey involved a flight in a Dakota, D.C.3, – the 'maid of all work' which had helped to keep us supplied throughout the monsoons.

As I was in charge of the group, I had been briefed to take them from Dum Dum aerodrome, near Calcutta, to spend a night in a transit camp in the city before joining a train going north. The leave was due to start on our arrival in Darjeeling, but this was delayed for 24 hours. Our party became split into two groups – one going shopping and the other having an extra meal. This resulted in the second group having an extra night in the transit camp and resuming the journey the next day.

We spent our two weeks in a leave camp, where I remember the joy of seeing clean, fresh water coming out of a tap and sitting on a seat at table instead of squatting on my heels like an Indian peasant, as I had done for the past three months. Many of us were unable either to enjoy or digest the quantity of food and I spent the first eleven days in bed under the eye of a resident doctor. Happy young Nepalese girls kept the rooms tidy and brought the meals to my bed. It seemed strange not to hear constant gunfire and not to have to carry weapons at all times. During the last three days I was able to go for short walks in the beautiful hillsides and into the town of Darjeeling, where I bought a Gurkha kukri.

The return journey, down the quaint, narrow gauge rack-and-pinion railway, passed too quickly and we were soon on a quick flight from Dum Dum to rejoin the Squadron at Yaripok.

We found them involved in a full programme of training, including N.C.O. cadres for drill on the airstrip, man management techniques and the making and dismantling of booby traps. I found this last course to be very interesting. A sapper N.C.O. showed us a variety of ways of deterring and killing strangers. He demonstrated how to cut green bamboo and make a range of weapons including daggers, bows and arrows and especially punjis, the sharpened, pointed stakes which could be set in the ground as a method of defence. We were all surprised how the green skin of the bamboo would become even sharper as the wood dried out over a period of days or weeks.

He also showed us how to make bombs which could be detonated by trip wires or by anyone interfering with them. He had a number of gadgets which had obviously been made in a factory which produced metal hinges. Some of these would release a spring to fire a detonator when pressed and some when the pressure was released. If we used both types in the same trap it made the dismantling of a bomb a very dangerous job. I have had the greatest respect for bomb disposal officers ever since that course. Fortunately, I never had to do any sort of bomb disposal, although I made and installed a few hundred punjis when fighting through the jungles.

The beginning of September came, and the Major gave the weekly sitrep which had surprising news. "Now that we have all had our leave and the Regiment is up to full strength again, we can look to the future with every confidence. You will be pleased to know that General Slim is so delighted with the Carabiniers, he has told Colonel Younger that he will not go into northern Burma without us! We have helped to kill in excess of 40,000 enemy since they invaded Assam, and we estimate that some 60,000 have escaped over the Chindwin. They are now preparing to meet us and fight on. They have had a severe pounding but they are still a force to be reckoned with. The 14th Army must chase them, find them and destroy them before we can say we have beaten them. That is our task. We shall not be setting off for a few weeks yet, but we need that time for us to complete our training of reinforcements, practise our techniques with our new infantry colleagues and to reach the Chindwin.

"I am pleased to tell you that B Squadron will be leading the advance across the Chindwin, together with the British 2nd Division. As you know, they successfully led 33 Corps from Dimapur, fought to recapture Kohima and helped to drive the demoralised 15th and 31st Japanese divisions back into Burma. Each of their three Brigades [a] of three battalions will take a turn in the lead, and B Squadron will be there with them at the sharp end.

"A Squadron will be following us until we break out of the jungle into more open country where they will operate separately from us. C Squadron is even now continuing to chase the retreating Jap 33 division down to Tiddim. They will advance into Burma from there."

There were a few moans after this sitrep. The main one was the regret that we would not be fighting alongside our Gurkha friends, who had set the highest of standards. "Well," said a Geordie in his strong accent, "at least they'll be able to talk to us and be understood!" "Maybe," came a comment from a Jock, "but I bet they'll never be able to understand you!"

After the parade Pete Phillis came over to our tank. "Don't you wish you were me, honest now?" He was going home on Python, together with Corporal Galli – two lads from Leeds who had been together for six years in India. "If you give me your home address I'll go and see your folks for you and tell them how you are. Have you anything you want me to take for you?"

As my parents lived near Hull at that time, I thought this a good idea. "Thanks, Pete, I'd like to get my kukri home safe and sound. Will you take that?"

It was agreed and I heard, three months later, that they had kept their promise.

These 'repat-wallahs', waiting to go on Python, became something of a disruptive influence with their 'How long now?' and 'It won't be long now'. They were talking of going home and to whatever comforts might by available in Blighty whilst the rest of us were planning more months in action, well aware of the risks that were involved. Admittedly, the weather was improving but we would be fighting against time as well as the Jap, if we were to finish it before the next monsoon rains in April 1945.

---

a Appendix A123

During these months of preparation we tried to amuse ourselves with a Squadron Show. The rehearsals were used as an excuse for missing other parades, but we had a lot of fun. The latent talent was brought out by some slight management skills and occasional heavy persuasion. I still had the heavy, dark moustache which I had grown in Bishenpur, but I was pressed into taking the part of a village maiden. "No, no, a thousand times, no. I'd rather die than say yes." This was my one and only line, but it raised a roar of approval from the audience every time they heard it. A willing Wasbi had loaned me a skirt and girls' pullover which I filled out with two oranges. They soon lost their shape and juice after some frantic squeezing by sex-starved squaddies. The show was presented to the officers and men of R.H.Q., A and B Squadrons, and it was an uproar. The vocalists, including Norman Dimmock, brought a sense of reality with memories of home and loved ones. Nostalgia was never quite like that.

Another of our highlights was a football match versus A Squadron. Corporal Jimmy Leach made it look easy by scoring three of our six goals against only two from A Squadron. We also sent squadron parties to two E.N.S.A. concerts in Imphal. The first one included Marie Burke, who sang the old favourite Ciri, Ciri Bim, and was warmly applauded. The second show, a few weeks later, was a surprise for most of us. Noel Coward, hero actor of 'In which we Serve', well known by us all for his stage plays as 'the maestro', was actually booed off the stage halfway through the show. He made the mistake of assuming that the ignorant British soldiery wanted non-stop sex and foul language – and he gave it, undiluted, from the start of the show. He was well into the epic 'Eskimo Nell', which he claimed to have written, whilst he caressed his male pianist, when half the audience stood up and walked out. We had heard enough.

A notice appeared on the Squadron notice board asking for volunteers to be trained as glider pilots to fly Chindits into Burma. 'Only men with experience need apply.' This was the opportunity we had been waiting for. There would be six weeks training followed by two weeks leave. The only snag that we could envisage was that the planned flight for the gliders would be going east, with no return ticket. The pilots were to be trained to fight as infantry and, after landing safely, would take their chances with the rest of the Chindit column. This raised a few doubts. More than forty men volunteered from B Squadron, including me. Huntley called me into the Squadron Office and gave me back my application. "I don't know whether you are being serious, Fenner, but this is not for you. You are not fit enough to march five or six hundred miles carrying a 60lb pack, that is, if you complete the training and land your glider safely. Anyway, I need you with me." And that was that.

We were all given the negative within B Squadron and I heard later that no Carabiniers were permitted to go to Imphal for an interview.

Our Commanding Officer, Lieutenant-Colonel Ralph Younger M.C., was awarded the D.S.O. and promoted away from the Regiment. He was succeeded by his second-in-command, Major F.J.S. Whetstone – an awesome sight, at least six feet six inches tall with a moustache joined to his sideboards by hairy cheeks. He used to walk around the lines using a very long stick, like a bishop's crozier.

The list of awards for gallantry included the D.C.M. for Sergeant-Major Craddock, whose activities had been outstanding. His tank, like ours, had been in nearly every action involving any of B Squadron's tanks, from Nunshigum onwards. His award was welcomed by all. He was already on his way back to Blighty on L.I.L.O.P.[a] This meant that he would be returning to the Regiment in two or three months' time. He was succeeded by the newly promoted 'Bunny' Holmes, a slightly less aggressive man, who had also excelled himself many times in action.

At a much higher level, the four generals responsible for the success at Imphal were knighted in September's gazette. The ceremony took place in Imphal on 15th December 1944 when they were dubbed by the Viceroy of India:

General Sir William Slim, 14th Army

---

a Appendix A124

General Sir Geoffrey Scoones, 4 Corps.

Lt. General Sir Montagu Stopford, 33 Corps.

Lt. General Sir Philip Christison, 15 Corps.

The 14th Army Commander continued to be called 'Uncle Bill' by his troops even after he became Lord Slim.

Whilst this was happening, B Squadron were on their way down the Kabaw Valley on transporters, still part of 254 Tank Brigade commanded by Brigadier 'Cully' Scoones, brother of the General of 4 Corps. This time, however, we were with British 2 Division of 33 Corps.

The Squadron Leader's tank crew had been reorganised, with two of them going into other tanks. They would strengthen the experience of new crews made up from reinforcements who had no battle experience. Sherley Holmes, Norman Dimmock and I were the only members of our crew remaining after Bishenpur. Paddy Ryan had gone into hospital, and he was replaced by our old friend Paddy Coffey, who was delighted to rejoin the tank. George Kerr from Glasgow was the new 75 Gunner, with Dimmock as his loader. Sherley's loader was Charlie Woodward. The two new men had joined us from the training depot.

"Two Troops 'B' Squadron Will Move . . ."

Around the Imphal plain there was fought a grim campaign,
It flared up in the March of Forty-Four.
And the Lee and Stuart tanks with the growling, plodding ranks
Helped foil the steel-ringed clutch on Manipur.

The Jap was full of tricks – like those unseen 'punji' sticks –
He was cunning with his booby traps and mines.
The British had the Lees, which could mow down eight-inch trees,
The Jap had One-O-Fives . . . and One-Four-Nines.

And he, to give him credit, had his cold hard nerve (you've said it)
He carried out his orders . . . knew no "Buts" . . .
A single-purposed fellow, whose skin alone was yellow . . .
Fanatic, he was called . . . but he had guts.

Still, he didn't stick his mug out of his deeply sunken dug-out

When a troop or two of Lees was on the prowl.
That stub-nosed Seventy Five made him scared to be alive,
But he wasn't trained at throwing in the towel.

"How-Easy" . . . "Able-Peter" . . . Whilst the Three-Seven Millimeter
Was spewing out its screaming havoc fore and aft . . .
Whilst Browning muzzles spat, with urgent rat-tat-tat
The Jap had need of all his jungle craft.

But his deadly bullets sang at Shenam and Potsangbam . . . .
Men played, with Death, a solemn game of Dice . . . . . .
And more than one brave head drooped riddled through with lead
At Nunshigum. For them . . . the Supreme Price.

And at Ukhrul . . . Silchar Track . . . was heard guns' thudding
crack . . .
Again at Kanglatongbi . . . Bishenpore . . .
But Nippon's hopes were shattered when the Squadrons, widely
scattered,
Came up and closed each partly opened door.

In besieged Kohima too . . . then later at Tamu . . .
The Tiddim Road . . . at Shwebo and beyond . . .
Those men who breathed their last, so that others might go past,
Live on, bound to us by deathless bond.

Life has its rallentandos for the "Oyster Box Commandos"
But these poor devils had to keep their nerve . . .
For them no crazy thrill of shooting men to kill . . .
For them to wait . . . and, waiting, also serve.

The story is not finished, but glory, undiminished,
Will linger in the mind in after years.
There are battles still not fought, but there'll always be that
thought . . .
A proud one . . . "I was in the Carabiniers."

January 1945
Charles Warren.

Chapter 10

Crossing the Chindwin

The Legend of Loka-natha, The God Of Peace

The king lion, having got out of his golden cave bedecked with jewels, met a flying elephant. He disputed with the elephant on the territorial sovereignty and grazing rights over the sky and its silvery sprouts, and there ensued a fierce and bloody battle. The lion got upon the elephant's head and was sucking the blood from its trunk when Loka-natha, the god of peace, appeared, striking his tiny cymbals, which he held between his toes, sang and danced. Entranced by the divine arts of music, dance and poetry, the lion and the elephant forgot their quarrel and made their peace.

The Burmese Kings of old had the figures of Loka-natha, the king lion and the flying elephant sculptured on their thrones to allude to their mission of peace.

(Translated from the Burmese in the Shwebon-nidann by Zeyasankha, circa 1783)

Information supplied by Duya Cigarillos, the Foodstuffs Industries Corporation, Rangoon, Burma.

Mid December 1944

We set off down the Kabaw Valley feeling very well prepared for any contact with the enemy. We were accompanied by our staunch friends, the Bombay Grenadiers, who rode with us on the transporters. These Punjabi Muslims were very pleased to be the responsible 'minders' of the Carabiniers' tanks and I've had the greatest respect for their abilities and loyalty every since. They would ride the tanks until fired upon and then would jump off and ensure that the Japs did not get near enough to be able to mine the tank.

One lesson we had learned from our experience around Bishenpur was that the intercom box on the rear of the tank had not been used as it had been intended. The infantry had either not known what it was to be used for or they had chosen not to expose themselves to the risk of being shot by snipers. In order to get over this problem, we had had a No. 38 Set fitted inside the tank. This could be netted on to the infantry wavelength and would enable the tank and infantry commanders to speak to each other during combat without having to take any unnecessary risks. It would be a real improvement in our communication systems.

The Valley had been described to us as a death trap, full of Japs, disease, mosquitoes and leeches. That must have been during the wet season. We found it dark, heavily wooded, with a sprinkling of chattering monkeys, and a poor road. Each night we camped at the roadside and dug in as before. On one occasion we were next to an empty Japanese camp, which must have been built for the smallest of them. Huts, furnished with tables and chairs, were made out of bamboo and they looked like dolls' houses. I was too big to sit on their chairs and put my feet under the table, and I realised that many of the Japs had been well under five feet in height. They were all now gone and we were not fired upon until we reached Kalewa. This was an empty village on the western side of the Chindwin at a point where a ferry used to operate connecting with the road to Ye-u, our objective in central Burma. We camped for the night, expecting to be crossing the wide river in the morning.

16th December 1944

After a quiet night and a peaceful stand-to I walked down the road to see one of my troop operators about a technical problem. I must admit that I was not very tidy that morning. During the night on guard duty I had torn a V-shaped hole in my battledress trousers and my cap was still in the tank, together with the butt of my tommy gun. Then I saw them in front of me walking from the river. A group of ten or more red-tabbed army officers preceded by the unmistakable Lord Louis Mountbatten in his gleaming white naval officer's uniform, fruit salad of medal ribbons and gold braided cap. They were walking quickly, talking loudly and I just wanted to disappear. I felt really ashamed of my appearance. I couldn't salute without a cap, and I couldn't slap the butt of my weapon. Then a disruption saved the situation.

A Jap Zero fighter plane must have spotted the shiny white target offered by Lord Louis and he dived at us firing his machine guns. The first man into the muddy ditch at the side of the road was our Supremo – and I was the second. We were about a yard apart and I waited to see what his reaction would be. The plane flew off and did not return. Lord Louis jumped up, laughed and nodded to me, then his retinue stood up and joined him back on the road. Fortunately, no one was hurt, but the entire crowd of field rank officers [a] were coated with mud. I crept away and visited the tank crew as originally intended.

At the morning sitrep, Huntley told us that Lord Louis had stated that he was pleased with our preparations for the advance into Burma and he was confident that the column of British 2 Division, with B Squadron leading, would make rapid progress to Shwebo. The leading group would include one battalion of infantry, changed each day, one battery of R.A. Priests, less one troop, one section of Sappers,

---

a   Appendix A125

with Lieutenant Ryman in charge, and a detachment of Group Work-shops and Recovery Company. It all seemed to be well planned, except for the fact that we were to be in the lead every day until we reached Shwebo – a greater distance than the 100 miles to Ye-u, which we had previously been told was to be our objective. We were to go as fast as we could drive on our own tracks, clearing any major road blocks in our stride, but pressing on and leaving any odd pockets of Japs to be handled by those following us. If supplies did not reach us by road, we could rely on air drops as before. When we reached and captured Shwebo we would have a rest.

Our own crew quickly realised that we would be with the leading troop of B Squadron, together with the Sergeant Major's tank, every single day of the advance. That meant that we would have to be alert for any sign of Jap defensive positions every minute of every day. There were a few cynical cheers at the promise of a rest at Shwebo but, in the main, we had a holiday feeling, due to the improving weather and the recent few weeks of good food and relaxation. I was running to the latrines only six or seven times a day, which was a great improvement.

20th December 1944

The rafting of the tanks across the Chindwin took longer than we expected for a number of reasons. The raft was made from a section of Bailey Bridge resting on four pontoons, and it could take only one tank at a time. There was a possibility of being shot at by the Japs as we floated downstream, although we were assured that the landing at the other side would be safe. Loading and unloading was a straightforward job of simply driving on or off, using prepared jetties at Kalewa and, lower down the half mile wide river, at Shwegyin, on the Burmese side. The raft was attached to a motor boat or a DUKW, which supplied the power to take it across the fast current. After having waited for three days, we started to cross and assemble ready for our spearhead through the jungle. Our crew made the journey riding on the raft, but sitting outside the tank and keeping it between ourselves and the eastern bank of the river. As Paddy Coffey said, "If it tips over we won't have time to get out if we ride inside." He sounded just like his predecessor. It took all day for the transfer of the tanks and Priests and it was dark before we were all positioned for a short night's sleep, including two hours of guard duty each man.

21st December 1944

Reveille 0400 hrs. A quick brew of char with cold bacon sandwiches before setting off at 0600 hrs. It was still dark when the Major called me across to a 15 cwt. truck which had just come over on a raft.

"Fenner, we've had a late delivery of extra supplies. Here are the six bottles of whisky for the officers and the rum ration for the Other Ranks. For Christmas, you understand? I'm putting you in charge of them until Christmas Day, so make sure that nobody gets their hands on them. Right?"

This was good news. We weren't forgotten and could look forward to a tot of rum to celebrate. I thought that a whole bottle of whisky might be a bit much for some of our young officers. Perhaps they would share [a] them around their troop? Anyway, I had to find space to carry them on our tank. The bottles were soon stored in odd corners of the food bins and behind the wireless set where I could keep an eye on them. The rum, in a small wooden barrel, was packed on the rear engine cover under some tarpaulin. It would ride all right there.

After some last minute juggling for position, the column of 6th Infantry Brigade set off due east along a very poor dirt road, aiming for the next village of Pyingaing – immediately renamed Pink Gin by Huntley. We were leading the way through jungle into a teak forest. Some sunlight reached us on the ground and it was pleasantly warm without the direct, hot sun making things uncomfortable. We were carrying an extra forty gallons of drinking water in the old petrol tank above the engine and four five-gallon containers in various bins, plus our own water bottles and chaguls hanging on odd pegs on the outside of the tank.

---

a Appendix A126

All spare corners inside the bins and in the hull were packed with tins of meat, fish and milk so we had no worries about any possible food shortages such as we had experienced at Bishenpur. The other lads were aware that their rum was in safe hands. All was plain sailing.

The occasional bridge over the dried river bed at the side of the road (the nullah in Assam became the 'chaung' in Burma) was unable to take our weight, but we soon mastered the art of driving down the bank at the side of the bridge, across the chaung and up the other side, rejoining the road. Sometimes, when we could see another bridge ahead, we would stay in the chaung and drive along the river bed until we decided to climb out and rejoin the road. The decision was up to the commander of the leading tank, usually Huntley himself.

Sometimes, when we found that the side of the chaung was too steep for us to drive down it, we called Lieutenant Ryman forward to give his help. This often required the use of explosives and/or a bulldozer. This Sapper officer was always available with his expert knowledge whenever we asked for him over a period of at least twelve months. I believe that he was awarded an M.C. for some of his activities but he must have earned it, or something even better, many dozens of times when he exposed himself to enemy fire during his engineering work, enabling our tanks to move over obstacles during actions. He still carried his cut-down Jap rifle for defence and I saw him fire it on more than one occasion.

On one of these excursions along the chaung I spotted a bamboo table and chairs against the side of the river bed, close to a steep bank which overhung the position. They were just the same size and design as those that I had seen in the huts in the Kabaw Valley. I could also see that the ashes in the fire place were undisturbed by any breeze.

"There have been Japs here, sir," I told Huntley.

"We can expect that," he said, with his head out of the turret, "they have been retreating along here for a month or more."

Just before we halted for the night I noticed another similar camp

site, and this time the fire was still burning! It was dark when we
dismounted. The Major ordered slit trenches to be dug as usual and
this time he had rolls of Dannert wire opened on the perimeter of
our camp. I again raised the question of the nearness of the Japs and
suggested "Don't you think we should now be netted to the infantry
on the 38 Set, sir?"

"No hurry," he replied, "I'll tell you when to do it. You see, they
are changing the battalion every day, to give them a rest, and I am
told each morning who it will be." At that point I stuck my neck
out and took a chance. "Then, may I ask if we are going to be
changed with A Squadron from time to time, so that we have a rest
occasionally?"

He could have exploded but he was not that sort of man. He took
the time to explain it quietly, with a smile. "You see, Fenner, it is
quite an honour for B Squadron to be chosen to lead this advance
for the first month, and I shall see to it that the leading troop is
changed every day. This will reduce the tension on the tank commanders, so that they are following the others for three days out of
every four. Until we actually come into contact with the Japs, I plan
to be near the front of the column and I hope that my crew will
appreciate the reasons for that. I can tell you now that I have
recommended that your name is put forward for L.I.A.P.[a] as soon
as possible, so you can look forward to having a long break in the
U.K. If you find that any of the others in my crew are feeling the
effects of being in the lead every day, and they would like to transfer
to one of the troops, I will arrange it. I am well aware of the extra
hours and stress that you have all had, and I appreciate the support.
Let me know if any problem is likely to arise."

I thanked him and told him that I would keep him informed if I
thought there might be any such problem. "I am delighted to hear
about the possibility of L.I.A.P., sir. What would happen if the O.K.
came through when we were on this advance?"

---

a Appendix A127

He smiled again. "I will release you whenever that happens, Fenner. No one is indispensable — none of us!"

I kept this news to myself but I felt very much cheered by the hope of being sent back to Blighty for at least two weeks leave at home.

22nd December 1944

We had a good run through the teak forest all day. We had no contact with the enemy and we saw no signs of their presence, although we all knew that they were somewhere near us. There were the usual delays when crossing the chaung, which frequently changed from one side of the road to the other. This chaung was becoming narrower and deeper as we moved further east, away from its outlet into the Chindwin and nearer to its source in the range of hills ahead of us. By this time it had become mostly too narrow to be used as a substitute for the road, which we now had to use as much as possible. For this reason we missed the Jap camp sites which were hidden in the chaung.

That night we made camp under a huge teak tree and I removed the keg of rum from the tank in order to use the Dannert wire for the perimeter and the tarpaulin sheet for a cover in case of rain. The rum was put under a bush at the side of my sleeping trench and that was the last time that I saw it.

23rd December 1944

During my guard duty from 0200 – 0400 hrs. I had to patrol the perimeter. The night was dry and pleasantly warm. The strong moonlight created shadows which tended to change in shape as the leaves moved in the gentle breeze. I didn't need to have an imagination to see possible Japs on all sides, creeping towards the wire, walking between the tanks dotted around me. The night noises were as loud as usual and did not help to relieve my apprehension.

I was looking over the coils of wire when I first saw the creature padding towards the camp. The striped camouflage of its coat blended easily with the shadows, but I instantly recognised the tiger as it came up to the wire and, without hesitating, walked straight through the coils! The wire did not move and therefore the tin cans containing pebbles did not rattle. I knew then that I must have been hallucinating, because nothing of that size could get through the Dannert coils without disturbing them and rattling the cans.

This worried me. I knew that I was wide awake. The tiger was still there, only by now it was on my side of the barrier, some ten yards away from me, and I recalled stories from the 'Boys Own Paper' about man-eating tigers in Bengal.

I had to do something so I decided to throw a pebble at it to test its reality and, at the same time, prepare to fire a burst from my tommy gun if it attacked me. Keeping my eyes on the tiger, I slowly bent down to pick up a stone which I then threw at the big cat.

Instantly, it spun around, leapt over the wire and ran off into the jungle. This time it did touch the wire and the tin cans rattled all along my side of the camp.

"Stand-to!"

An alert sentry about twenty yards to my right did not hesitate to arouse the camp and, for a minute, there was the sound of a hundred men sliding into slit trenches or clambering up the side of a tank and into the turrets.

After twenty minutes silence, broken only by the night noises of insects, frogs and monkeys, Huntley asked me what had caused the alarm. "A tiger, sir, jumping out of the camp when I frightened it!" "I should keep that story to yourself, Corporal. If you tell the others they will accuse you of starting on their rum too soon. Stand down."

And so we returned to bed or guard duty, whichever applied.

0730 hrs. I went to the perimeter wire, where I had seen the tiger jump out of the camp. Sure enough, there was a tuft of coarse white fur where its belly had caught on one of the barbs. It had not been imagination.

We were all washed, shaved and dressed, cooking a hot breakfast of soya links, baked beans, burgoo and tea, when Huntley came back to the tank. "Mount, start up, there's a road block ahead." I looked at the pans of hot food, then at him, and he knew what I was thinking.

"Take the pans into the tank with you. You can eat on the hoof."

"But, the wire and the rum, sir.?"

"Leave all that, we'll be back before tiffin."

Chapter 11

Christmas 1944

23rd December 1944

As we drove east, eating our breakfast from a communal pot with spoons, Huntley told us that he had spoken to the O.C. Infantry who had asked for our help with a road block a few miles ahead. Patrols had been sent out during the night and they had bumped into a large party of Japs at a point where the road went through a gorge. They appeared to be well dug in, both on the road and on the high ground on each side. We had expected this and I knew that we should have been locked on to the infantry net with the 38 Set, but it was too late now.

One troop of tanks, with ours leading, drove on until we met the infantry, pinned down at the road side with snipers picking them off and an odd burst of light machine gun fire. There was nothing we could see except trees rising to 200 feet above us and fairly thick undergrowth. Huntley said, "I'm just going to see their No. 9," as he climbed out of the turret. We waited, for half an hour until Lieutenant Swan called us from the next tank. "Queen 4, what is happening? Over."

I answered, "Queen 4, No. 9 with footsloggers more than 30 minutes. No news, over."

"Queen 4, will investigate, out."

Another 30 minutes passed before he came on again. "Queen 4, your No. 9 has been knocked out and will be taken back. I am in charge, over."

"Queen 4, is he dead? Over."

"Queen 4, yes, out."

All our crew had heard this, as well as the other tanks, and we were shattered. If only I had disobeyed orders, and netted to the infantry, this wouldn't have happened. I climbed out of my seat in the hull, and up into the turret, to take Huntley's place as tank commander. His headset was fixed in a thin cloth helmet like Dizzy's up Nunshigum, and very different from my usual rigid head protector. I put it on and looked out of the turret to see if I could spot any snipers in the surrounding trees. I could see no possible targets but one of them must have seen me.

There was a tremendous hammer blow on the top right of my skull and I woke up lying on the floor of the turret. Sherley Holmes was looking down at me. "What happened?" he said. I realised that I had been hit on the head and tore off the helmet, expecting to find a hole in it, and perhaps some blood stains. There was no hole or mark that I could see. "The buggers shot me," I said, feeling my head again. There was a growing lump which was very tender. "They must have hit the turret ring and the splash hit me and raised this lump." It was the only explanation. With a splitting headache, I gingerly climbed back into the commander's position and lowered the two flaps to stop anything more coming into the tank.

"Co-ax traverse right and scan the trees for snipers. Fire the odd burst into the trees, even if you can't see him." "Roger," from Sherley and he kept the turret moving, with the guns pointing upwards, firing occasional short bursts.

Lieutenant Swan called to ask what we were firing at, so I told him what had happened.

"Roger, Queen 4, only fire if you see a target now. We are moving forward. Wait there for orders, out." It was not a happy position for us. We could only wait and keep our eyes open. There was support from a few Grinders dug in on either side of us as we waited, slowly rotating the turret to scan the trees.

Lieutenant Swan quickly found plenty of targets in the steeply wooded slopes of the gorge and his troop fired all their guns frequently for nearly an hour. He soon realised that he was not going to succeed in clearing the road, mainly due to the lack of communication with the infantry, and he reported this fact back to Brigade

H.Q. We were all pulled back half a mile just before dusk and we spent a miserable night wondering what would happen now.

I saw Mr Swan return to the box and asked him about Huntley. "How did it happen, sir?" He quietly told me that the Major and the infantry C.O. had walked forward together to have a quick recce, when a sniper hit him. "It was a mortal wound and he didn't have a chance." "Did he say anything?" I asked. "Only that he wished it was all over – and it soon was. I was with him until he died."

24th December 1944

Lieutenant Swan gave us his sitrep after stand-down and breakfast. We were all saddened to know that Major Michael Huntley-Wright, known to all ranks as 'Huntley', had been killed in action the previous day. This was after leading the Squadron so successfully during the eight months since Nunshigum. The Commanding Officer had informed him that our new Squadron Leader was Major E.S.P. Dorman, who would take command during the next 48 hours. Our answer to the Japs would be to attack them and continue to attack them until they were all destroyed.

We were now up against a major Japanese defensive position, which we could not bypass due to the terrain, and plans were now being made to attack it with very heavy fire from tanks, artillery and, if necessary, airstrikes. This would take a day or so to lay on but in the meantime we would build a strong defensive box where we were standing, and this would be the base for our attack. We now had plenty to do, digging, reinforcing and, as ever, maintenance of our vehicles, weapons and equipment.

I told Mr Swan later of our loss of the Squadron rum ration and he laughed. "We'll not be celebrating this year anyway – perhaps in a week or two, by which time we'll find some more rum for you." Infantry patrols were sent out to keep a check on the Jap positions and also to let them think that we were about to attack them at any time.

25th December 1944

The tanks were all netted smoothly, both on the two wavelengths of our own No. 19 Sets and also on the No. 38 Sets to the infantry wavelength of the Company H.Q. No. 48 Set. This worked well and was to become the biggest help and time-saver from now on.

During the afternoon 5 Troop went out to attack a bunker position which had been reported by the morning's patrols, and their 75 mm fire drove the Japs out before our men from the Royal Berkshires occupied the position. This success raised morale throughout the group. We had forgotten Christmas.

26th December 1944

Another fighting patrol went out with 4 and 7 Troops in close communication on the new net. An artillery barrage was cancelled when they found only light opposition, but it was another example of British infantry and tanks working hand-in-glove. The team moved from one bunker to another destroying each in turn. Smoke grenades were used to identify any targets which could not be easily seen. The confident tank commanders all returned to the box saying that we should have had these extra wireless sets in the Imphal plain, where they would have saved many lives.

Late that afternoon we met our new Squadron Leader and tank commander. Major Dorman was an Irishman with a cultured English accent – very different from Paddy Coffey. He had been promoted from one of the other squadrons and was now thrown in to the thick of a fight before he could get to know his officers and men. He had met Archie Weir before, in the Officers' Mess in India, but all our other officers were recent replacements of casualties, and probably less experienced than he was. He did well. He had obviously lived with a tank crew before but he was not at all like his two predecessors. I told him of the success of the 38 Sets for speaking with the infantry and said that I hoped he would never feel the need to climb outside the tank when near any Japs.

"Don't worry about that, Corporal, I'll watch that problem" – and he did. He had obviously been told by his superiors that B Squadron could not afford to lose a third Squadron Leader, that it would be considered as carelessness, and he regularly closed his turret flaps when in action. That night he completed his plan to lead an armoured column, including the Durham Light Infantry, to advance quickly to Wainggyo, starting the next morning.

27th December 1944

0530 hrs. We had worked through the night, loading food, water and ammunition, which had been delivered by truck after dark, and we were all ready for some sleep when we heard the order "Mount, start up, advance", and off we set, half a squadron with the Major and S.S.M. Bunny Holmes. This time we really were going to apply the orders given before we left Shwegyin – to brush aside any opposition and press on towards Shwebo.

The other half squadron was to remain with the main group and complete the clearing of the road block after we were well on the way going east. Under the command of our new 2 i/c Squadron, Captain L.O. Pearce M.C., they did their usual successful job of destroying Japs and their weapons, despite the occasional setback. Sergeant Elliott became stuck in a boggy patch, but he was eventually pulled out by two D 8s, heavy units from the Recovery Section. Whilst in this fix, he had seen a Jap tank, possibly one of the old Stuarts from the 7th Hussars, and it was later found to have been abandoned. Lieutenant Barrow and the recently promoted Sergeant Bob Greendale had some excellent shoots up the hillsides.

At the same time, Major Dorman led our column at speed through the chaungs in the jungle until we reached Wainggyo early the next morning. It was near Pink Gin that we drove through the centre of a large Jap H.Q. I don't know who were the most surprised.

The ground had become much flatter and the undergrowth thin enough for us to ignore it when we burst into a clearing dotted with huts and tents. It was undefended and Paddy Coffey simply carried on driving. He went through the open cookhouse, where the fires were blazing under cauldrons of rice, and the front of our tank was covered with hot boiled rice. It smelled beautiful and we all fancied a plateful, but there was no order to halt, or even to slow down.

One of the Jap cooks must have been hiding nearby, because he appeared to jump out from under our tracks just before we could flatten him. He was a long streak of a man, perhaps 5 feet 10 inches tall, and he ran very quickly away from us, jumping from side to side to avoid any bullets which might be aimed at him. He escaped into the jungle before anyone could fire a shot at him.

We continued to press on all afternoon, crossing some chaungs, which always slowed us down, until we formed a small box for the night in the jungle. Drivers were excused guard duty so that they could have a few hours of unbroken sleep. Some of us had managed to doze in our seats in the tanks during the day despite the noise, movement and frequent bumps into trees and chaungs.

28th December 1944

Reveille 0530 hrs. Mount, start up, advance and eat anything available as we drive. The orders were simple and we carried them out.

We reached Wainggyo by mid-morning without any problems. It was a small hutted village on the edge of the jungle and there were a few residents still there. These were the first Burmese that I had seen, and they seemed to be small, quiet, nervous people, who had very few possessions. We had brought a young Karen with us to act as interpreter [a] and he repeated what he had learned from them. Their headman had been killed by the Japs only two days ago. He had told them that the village had no store of rice and could only offer a few fruits and vegetables, but the Japs had tortured him and eventually hung him from a tree, using barbed wire as a rope. He had died the same night, unable to disclose where the Japs would find any non-existent rice. The enemy force had numbered over 100 men, with a few mules carrying guns, and they had left the village, going east, only the day before.

5 Troop were immediately sent after them accompanied by a company of the Royal Welch Fusiliers, the leading infantry for that day. They soon reached Tawgin, another small hamlet, where they found it occupied by some of the 4th/10th Gurkha Rifles before the R.W.F. had arrived. These Gurkhas had been operating separately from our column and we were glad to see their uniforms and smiling faces again. They had been sent through the jungle to meet us near

---

a Appendix A128

Kaduma in order to prepare a dropping site for our first air drop of supplies. I was most impressed by this planning from Divisional H.Q., especially when it was announced that the Gurkhas had orders to shoot anyone from our side or the Japs' who attempted to pick up any of the supplies which would come from heaven by courtesy of the old workhorse, the D.C.3 Dakota. We had been warned. The other half of the squadron caught up with us so we had a strong box for the night. Most of us had some sleep.

29th December 1944

0730 hrs. Major Dorman led the half squadron of 4 and 5 Troops, with two platoons of the Royal Berkshires and some Priests, heading for Kaduma. This was the first time that most of us had seen a Sherman tank – the modern version of our own Lees. It was with us, acting as O.P.[a] to the Priests, and we were all pleased with its appearance. The hull was all welded, not riveted, and the 75 mm gun was mounted in the turret, giving it 360° traverse like our 37 mm, but so much of an improvement. One day we hoped to be issued with Shermans!

That day had a few highlights. We were sniped, had a few grenades fired at us and, for our first time in Burma, we met mines laid in the road. We had just slowed down to fire at possible targets, when we found that we had driven over at least a dozen mines, with more ahead of us. Lieutenant Ryman and his sappers soon cleared them all and we set of again leaving a few dead Japs on the way.

30th December 1944

0730 hrs. After a quiet night we set off again, with 4 Troop in the lead and the Royal Berkshires in support. The first obstacle was a weak bridge, so we tried to cross the stream, only to find that 5 Troop had problems. One tank lost a track and became bogged whilst another got water inside the engine and was stopped beside it. They were pulled out later, whilst our tank, the S.S.M. and 4 Troop all pressed on into more difficulties. We ran into another mined road,

---

a Appendix A129

this time covered by snipers. 4 Troop had all three tanks put out of action by the mines.

The surviving 5 Troop tank, with our two from H.Q.A. Troop, moved forward into the jungle at the side of the road, where we could see Japs squatting in shallow foxholes and slit trenches. They had not been there for very long, and some of them were still digging to deepen their holes, using the little heart-shaped Jap spade with the spyhole drilled through it. The three tanks rumbled on, shooting them in penny numbers until the survivors couldn't take any more. They ran in panic. As the ground was very uneven, the Major told the R.B.s that we would withdraw to make it easier for their men to clean up the area. More than thirty bodies were counted and it was assessed that the position had been held by a full company of Japs. We reported our success back to Brigade and were told to 'Press on'.

As the country had now become much more open, we increased speed and arrived before dusk at a point about two miles from Kaduma, a small town. The only disturbances during the night were caused by the arrivals of the 4 and 5 Troops tanks which had been knocked out earlier. Rapid repairs and replacement of their tracks by B Echelon had helped them drive through the dark to complete our numbers.

I can quote a letter sent to the C.O. from Major-General Nicholson that night:

> Please convey to all ranks B Squadron Carabiniers my admiration of their efforts during the last nine days. That we have covered 80 miles and broken through at least four enemy positions in this time has been largely due to the action of the tanks. I appreciate fully the determination with which you have driven on in the lead in the face of mines and the constant threat of anti-tank guns. By doing so, you have already saved many infantry casualties, and I am glad that so far damage to the tanks has not been great. I was particularly impressed by this morning's action near Thaunggyaung, where for the first time on this trip you were able to assault the Jap position and rout him. May you get many other such opportunities, and may they be equally successful.

I should also like to pay tribute to the fitters and others responsible for maintenance. I was told that you were mounted on old crocks – they have turned out to be thoroughbred hunters.

The Major read this to us the next morning.

31st December 1944

0730 hrs. Our column moved eight miles to a concentration point where we had expected to remain for two days, waiting for the remainder of our main group to be assembled. This was not good enough for our Irish Squadron Leader. He told the C.O., in the true cavalry spirit, that we had the 'bit between our teeth' and felt 'full of oats' and he requested permission to continue the advance towards Ye-u. He was soon given the order to advance as far as the Kabo Weir, a possible hazard for tanks, on the outskirts of the town.

On our way there we were strafed by a few Zero fighters, and suffered casualties amongst the soft vehicles and the Grinders, who were riding on the outside of the tanks and Priests. We learned on the wireless that our other half squadron was also attacked from the air that afternoon.

1915 hrs. As it was getting dark, we decided to halt about two miles short of the Kabo Weir and harbour for the night. The Royal Welch then sent out patrols which crossed the weir and bumped into some Jap defences. They pulled back and rejoined us in the box.

I was on guard duty at midnight and saw the New Year in in full moonlight, thinking that we would soon be through Ye-u and on to Shwebo, followed by a long rest in India. I had already given up any hope of going home on L.I.A.P. since Huntley had been killed,

1st January 1945

0800 hrs. Major Dorman and Lieutenant Ken Ryman made a foot recce of the weir and the local canals, but they could see no obvious way across for the tanks. The Kabo Weir controlled the flow of water to the whole of the central plain of Burma and it was fed by the River Mu, which flowed from the mountains in the north, parallel to the giant Irrawaddy, before joining it near Myinmu, in the Sagaing bend. The Mu was nearly a quarter of a mile wide in some places near Ye-u, and the depth varied with the width as well as the season.

1300 hrs. Lieutenant Ryman joined the Major, who ordered our tank to go on a solo recce upstream of the Weir. We drove nearly three miles along the river bank, stopping every now and again for the two officers to dismount and test the depth and the current. It was a beautiful, warm, sunlit day and we all fancied a swim, but the officers were the only ones who had a dip. They were fully clothed and armed when we saw them swimming frantically, being swept downstream. They soon made it to our shore and we presumed that their swim was a mistake. Their only comment was that they had not found a place for the tanks to ford the river.

Our armoured column was temporarily stymied and Brigade accepted the fact that the tanks could not advance for the time being. Brigadier Smith ordered his infantry to cross without tank support and to capture the town. We were glad to have three days rest as we had lost a lot of sleep during the past week. Messages of congratulation were received from 33 Corps, 2 Division and the 6 Brigade Commanders, on the advance of 110 miles in ten days and the capture of the Kabo Weir.

Major Dorman told me that he had a job for me to do the next day. He wanted me to take the tank, with the others of the crew, and go with the Sergeant Major's tank to a dropping zone three miles into the country, where we would meet a company of Gurkhas. We were to strengthen the defence of the area in order to prevent any stray party of the now desperate Japs from collecting any of our supplies as they dropped. There would be both freefall and parachuted parcels of valuable stores.

"Watch your heads if you get out of the tank. I don't want to hear that you have been knocked out by a hundredweight of spam. There is no cure for that!" He added, "And, also, I am changing some of my crew. Coffey is sick and needs a break for a couple of weeks. Whiteley, Holmes and Nussey are going to strengthen some of the other troops, which have had casualties. This will give you time to weld the new crew together before we go on to Shwebo in a few days' time."

This was not really a surprise as I suspected that he had heard some of them talking about our crew always being at the head of the column, whichever of the other four troops was leading in their turn. It had certainly been a bit of a strain, knowing each day that you could be hit by a Jap gun. I had felt it myself and had wondered about asking for a transfer but I didn't want to give up the position I had held for eight months.

2nd January 1945

The airdrop was a restful exercise. The S.S.M. was told by the Gurkha officer to go to the other side of the dropping zone whilst I stayed where we met. About thirty Gurkhas were dotted around the area between the two tanks. This was marked, in the centre, with strips of white canvas and it was at least 400 yards away from us where we waited. We could see clear country, dotted with the odd bush, for more than a mile in any direction and didn't think that any Japs could get near us without being spotted. We waited.

I stayed in the tank commander's seat, with Sherley Holmes and Norman Dimmock also in the turret, lazily scanning the horizon. The rest of the crew I permitted to dismount and stretch out in the sun. A balmy breeze made it all very restful.

Half an hour later we heard the drone of the aero engines. A string of Dakotas approached us, circled, and then each took its turn to fly low across the dropping mark. We could see the handlers pushing piles of hessian-covered bundles out of the open hatchway before circling again for another turn to drop more supplies. "I hope they remember to let go of the pile, before it's too late," [a] commented Joe Nussey with a chuckle.

The freefall loads were still moving forwards at over 100 m.p.h. when they hit the ground and they tended to bounce forward before stopping. The more delicate loads of ammunition, engines, etc., were dropped by parachute, which opened automatically as they left the plane. These came down much more sedately and did not bounce around, although they did land with a thump. The whole routine was

---

a Appendix A130

carried out very smoothly and it was obviously well practised. The Gurkhas were standing near their group of 3-tonners, watching the loads coming down. It was all over in half an hour.

The last plane to fly over missed the marked target, with its last drop, and we saw a large object coming down at great speed in our direction. I shouted, "Look out," but the lads outside had no time to move. It bounced from about twenty yards away and then came to a halt within two yards of Joe, who had jumped up whitefaced. We had had a lucky escape.

"Don't touch it!" I shouted from the turret, watching for any Gurkha reaction from the distance. There was none. I could see them labouring away, manhandling the bundles into the trucks. They would not be able to see 'our' parcel from there. We all jumped down to examine it. The hessian cover had been torn at the corner and we could see the contents – white sugar and about one cwt. of it.

"This was meant for us," said one of the crew.

"Manna from heaven," said another.

"Don't leave it for the Japs. Put it on the tank," from the third.

"Don't be daft," said the first, "put it inside the tank so the rain won't spoil it."

"You mean, so that the Gurkhas can't see it," said the other.

I said, "Inside with it and we'll share it around the squadron."

This we did.

Today, I wouldn't like to justify our actions, but, at that time survival was a strong force, and ethics were not a leading topic for debate. On a later, similar occasion, when we received a 56lb. tin of hard tack biscuits which had been dropped from heaven, we found that they had been badly broken and were also full of weevils. We started to use them for making burgoo, simply by pouring boiling water over a plateful but we were soon fed-up with 'seed-cake-bur-goo' as it was called. We got rid of the remaining half tin of the broken biscuits by putting it on the side of the road when the infantry were trudging past.

"Help yourselves to a handful of biscuit" I said, and the tin was eagerly cleared within minutes by the passing soldiers. None of them came back to complain about the weevil – we had all eaten more than our share of them in recent months. During the afternoon, Captain Pearce's half of the squadron moved from Kaduma to Wetpo with 5 Brigade and they harboured there to await our half joining them.

Chapter 12

Shwebo and Ywathetgyi

3rd January 1945

After three days of so-called 'resting', we were transferred from 6 Brigade. The three battalions of Durham Light Infantry, Royal Welch Fusiliers and the Royal Berkshires all sent messages of thanks and good wishes. They had each been in action with us, and we had never envied their job of walking into trouble without the benefit of our protective armour, even if it had been a different battalion leading each day.

Our half squadron was now put under the command of 5 Brigade, so we would be working with the three battalions of the Worcesters, Dorsets and Cameronians. Once more our 'final objective' had been extended. This time it was not just Shwebo but all the land west of the Irrawaddy, known as the Sagaing Bend. This included some 3000 square miles of open country, bounded by the Chindwin and the Irrawaddy. It was riddled with canals and streams which would be continual hazards for vehicles and would keep the sappers very busy. We would be on the opposite side of the river from Mandalay, and go up to the famous Ava Bridge. Built by British engineers, it had been the only bridge [a] over the river in its one thousand miles of wandering from China, through the length of Burma and on to Rangoon, some 300 miles to the south. Our retreating army in 1942 had blown up some of the sections of the bridge, and it was not repaired until more than twenty-five years later. The only communication between the land on the two sides of the Irrawaddy was by ferry, a hazardous journey through sandbanks and islands in difficult currents.

---

a Appendix A131

Part of General Slim's strategy was intended to make the Jap think that we were going to cross the river near Mandalay and encourage him to prepare his defences facing across the river near there. As the weeks rolled by, it became obvious that the bluff had succeeded.

Whilst the Japs were looking west for our attack, the 14th Army prepared a giant hammer and anvil with which to crush and destroy the entire Japanese army in Burma. 4 Corps were sent secretly south through the Chin Hills before they turned east to cross the Irrawaddy and capture Meiktila, a town about eighty miles south of Mandalay. They were the 'anvil'. Strict wireless silence was observed throughout.

At the same time, 36 Division continued to march south from northern Burma, along the east side of the Irrawaddy towards Mandalay, to become the 'hammer'.

The job of 33 Corps, which included the British 2 Division with the R.H.Q., A and B Squadrons of the Carabiniers, was to mop up all the Jap forces on our side of the river with as much noise and activity as possible. We were to appear to be preparing to cross the river and attack Mandalay.

C Squadron of the Carabiniers helped to lead 4 Corps in the headlong dash across the plain from Pakokku to Meiktila. Their successes make another story, which included having one of their tanks climb to 9800 feet above sea level on Kennedy Peak.

The urgency behind all this activity arose from our need to capture a southern port, preferably Rangoon, before the monsoon rains stopped the air supply for this large army of ours. Failure to do so would lead to disaster.

═══════════════

During the three days rest we prepared our vehicles to be driven and worked over a few hundred miles on our tracks. Engines were replaced by our B Echelon and R.E.M.E.[a] Worn gun barrels were pulled out and exchanged with new. Crews were adjusted, promoted

---

a Appendix A132

or demoted, and we were soon ready for setting off across the River Mu.

Our new 75 gunner was a slightly-built lad from Glasgow, George Kerr. He was supported by Dimmock. In the turret we had Ted Dyer,[a] an 'old man' of 42 from Bournemouth, with his loader, 'happy' Charlie Woodward. The two half squadrons continued to operate separately – Captain Pearce's half with 4 Brigade and ours with 5 Brigade. Major Dorman's half squadron found two possible crossing places south of Ye-u and all our tanks were eventually waterproofed, ready to drive through four feet of flowing water.

5th January 1945

0830 hrs. on a lovely sunny day. We were all safely across the River Mu, where we met little resistance and harboured ready for the drive to Shwebo.

6th January 1945

0700 hrs. 6 Troop led us to the point, just north of Shwebo, where the canal crossed the road. A small road block was soon cleared by the tanks but we were shelled frequently for the next 48 hours, which we spent in our harbour preparing to enter the town. One tank was hit by a 75 mm shell but it suffered no damage.

8th January 1945

We were all mounted and ready to go when we acquired a new extra passenger. Alfred Wagg, special correspondent to the *Daily Mail*, was the first and only war correspondent that I met. He gave me an entirely new view of journalists and their work. Apparently, he had been one of the last to leave Shwebo during the retreat of 1942 and he wanted to be the first to re-enter the town. He squatted just behind the driver's seat and questioned me about living in and around a tank for months on end. I explained how we had more comforts than the infantry as we could carry more food and water, that the armourplating gave us more protection so that we could

---

a Appendix A133

happily drive up to a machine gun without much risk, but that we were always the obvious target for the bigger guns and suicide bombers. There were plenty of things about which we could complain, but if it was necessary to fight a war against the Jap, this was the way that most of us would choose.

As we approached the moat surrounding the town, Wagg asked our driver to open his visor so that he could see ahead of us. "Not on," said Fred Wood, "unless you want your bloody head shot off as well as mine!" I let him look through my periscope occasionally, but I needed to use it myself for most of the time.

Machine gun fire, from bunkers on the other side of the causeway, was soon quietened by our 75 and the first tank went across. As the second tank was moving over behind it, the crew noticed that the road surface was uneven and we soon had Lieutenant Ryman called forward to examine it. He found that the road was heavily mined with 500 lbs. aerial bombs, ready to be exploded by wires from the bunkers. Luckily we had killed the Japs before they could do us any damage.

The Worcesters then went into the town ahead of us and Alfred Wagg joined Ken Ryman in his jeep so that he could keep up with them. There was very little trouble from Japs, as only a few had been left behind by the retreating enemy. The only living things that we found were a few hens scratching in the dust, and we had them in the pot that evening as we harboured near the moat. Wagg showed me his four-page report of the day's efforts and the only things I could recognise were the name of the town of Shwebo and the names of our crew. I read his printed article after the war, and found that it had been severely edited. My parents had been very pleased to read my name and whereabouts.

9th January 1945

Whilst we rested for three days, the other half of the squadron reached Shwebo from the south-west and found another aerial bomb booby trap at the entrance to the town. This was safely defused. They had been in action with the Lancashire Fusiliers and the Royal Scots of 4 Brigade the previous day, when Lieutenant Barrow's tank was hit by a 47 mm anti-tank gun, killing the operator. Sergeant Baverstock had then knocked out the Jap gun.

10th January 1945

Captain Pearce led his half to Chiba, about three miles south of Shwebo and he found that the Japs had retreated from there.

11th January 1945

Our half squadron joined up with them to be ready for our Christmas break.

12th January 1945

Squadron Orders were quite specific:-

'Christmas Day 1944 will be 12th January 1945.

0600 hrs. Reveille.

0730 hrs. Breakfast.

1000 hrs. Church Parade C of E.

1230 hrs. Tiffin Noel served by Squadron Officers.[a]

1400 hrs. Internal Economy. Volunteers for a Squadron football match will be nominated.'

It was all very refreshing. The missing rum was neither mentioned nor replaced, and the Major presented each officer with a bottle of the whisky which I had guarded for so long. Each man had a bottle of beer with the roast chicken lunch which had been prepared by the squadron cooks. The unreal atmosphere was enjoyed as a taste of another life which might soon return.

There was one rumour running through the squadron that was never proved true or false. We heard that one of our men had gone into a nearby village and demanded the services of one of the young women whilst threatening the life of the headman. There were plenty of things which happened to distract us from pursuing the matter.

The next three days, officially designated for the maintenance of our well-worn tanks, did not give us much peace. Reports were coming in, at odd intervals, of small parties of Japs scavenging for food. Major Dorman took a troop to investigate one of these stories

---

a Appendix A134

from a village near some jungle. We were driving steadily through a wooded area with our tank in the lead. I was smoking a cigarette when Paddy Coffey, who was back in the crew, asked the Major to clarify the route. "Keep going ahead, Coffey." Immediately ahead was a large tree, which we would normally avoid.

"What about this tree, Sorr?"

"Avoid it and carry on," replied the Major, rather testily.

Coffey swerved to the right of the tree and kept moving, at which point the ground opened up in front of us and we went down into a pit – or so it seemed. We were stuck in what was possibly a tank trap. The rear of the tank was above us all and the Major was livid.

"What the bloody hell are you playing at, Coffey?" came over the intercom.

Paddy was also livid. "The curse of the Blue Saints on ye, sorr. What do you think I'm doing? I'm trying to get us out of the mess you got us into, sorr."

"Bale out," was the Major's reply. Within thirty seconds the other six had clambered out and were on the bank, looking down at the tank wedged into this hole.

I could not move from my place. All the racked 75 ammunition had fallen forward, because there was nothing to hold it in the racks above my head. Some 120 rounds of 75 H.E. and A.P. ammo, each weighing about 24 lbs. was now in the well where I kept my legs during the drive. They reached up to my waist and were wedged by their own weight, making it impossible for me to move. I had dropped my cigarette and I only began to worry about that when I heard and smelled the 100 octane petrol pouring from the engine compartment, now above my head. It filled the well and I was soon knee deep in petrol. I remembered the crew of the C Squadron tank on the Manipur Road, when they had turned their tank over and lost a man in the petrol fumes.

"Help me out," I called, "I'm stuck and can't move."

"We'll soon have you out," said the Major, safely outside.

I didn't realise that he was talking to the tank and not to me. He quickly had two other tanks positioned in line behind us. They fixed two towing cables, one to the rear of our tank and the other to join themselves together. They then tried to pull us out. No luck. "Get back into your seat, Coffey, and help by trying to reverse out when I tell you," from the Major. I was going to have company if the tank brewed up. It only needed our tracks to strike flint and create a spark, to ignite the heavy petrol vapours. The Major then had a third tank, linked up by cable to the other two, and the combined power from four aero engines, in low gear, pulled us out. By now, I was waist deep in petrol and Dyer and Dimmock pulled the 75 ammo away from me and put it back into the racks. Somehow, they cleared the petrol from the well whilst I was breathing fresh air outside and rubbing my bruised legs. After that experience, none of us ever smoked inside a tank again.

16th January 1945

We harboured at Chiba and prepared to move to the Sadaung area.

18th January 1945

We transferred to the command of 4 Brigade at 2 Division, consisting of 1/8 Lancashire Fusiliers, 1 Royal Scots and 2 Norfolks, and prepared to move south, nearer the Irrawaddy. The next eight weeks were spent obeying orders to support these infantry units in their mopping-up operations in the Sagaing Bend. There seemed to be no end to the procedure of recce, attack and then harbouring in a new box, before starting all over again. A few highlights remain vividly in my memory – being machine-gunned by our own tanks, a so-called earthquake bombing of a Jap position only 400 yards away from us, a real earthquake, followed by a few days rest near Monywa on the Chindwin, where I first met a Burmese girl, and, the continuing list of casualties.

22nd–26th January 1945

We attacked strong Jap positions in and around Ondaw to give the impression that we intended to cross the Irrawaddy to the north of Mandalay. Supporting each of the three battalions in turn, we helped with the continuing slaughter of the Jap army. Intelligence reports, based on captured documents, showed that the Jap high command were aware that the morale of their troops was falling steadily with defeat. One included the order, 'Soldiers of the Imperial Japanese Army, make your foxhole your grave.' I can imagine the reply from the average British Tommy if he were given such an order.

News of the Jap suicide bombers committing hara kiri in the Pacific had filtered through to us, but we saw very few Jap planes in central Burma. They must have had a few surplus aerial bombs because these were used against us later in the form of booby traps.

It was near Ondaw that we found a Lancashire Fusilier and a Burmese prisoner hanging upside down by the ankles. They were both alive after three days in that position without any food or water. They had both been shot and bayoneted – a not infrequent Japanese practice with prisoners. It only made us more determined than ever to make sure that none of them escaped our attention.

During this period we cleared many villages, such as Ywathit, Kyaukse (a common village name), and we saw Wasps used for the first time. These were tracked vehicles carrying flame-throwers – diabolical weapons which usually sprayed burning fluids on to the target, rather like using a garden hose but with devastating results. On some occasions they were used firstly to spray unignited fluid on to the huts at the edge of a village and then to fire a burst of flame. Using this method, the village was suddenly turned into a circle of fire, burning inwards and destroying any trapped occupants without any chance to escape.

30th January 1945

We prepared for an attack on the town of Ywathetgyi where we would support the Royal Scots. Major Dorman[a] was his usual calm self when he told us of the plan. It was simply another attack on a Jap-held position, this time on the banks of the Irrawaddy. They could not escape to the south because of the mile-wide river. We would be attacking from the east, driving any survivors into an ambush at the west of the town. Our first objective was a windmill on the high ground, from where we would see the river and the

---

a Appendix A135

railway line running from Sagaing and on to Monywa and Ye-u to the north.

31st January 1945

After an early reveille and a good breakfast we joined up with the Royal Scots and approached the outskirts of Ywathetgyi. Then we waited. At 1130 hrs. we heard the drone of a large number of planes and the Major spotted a formation of Mitchells heading in our direction. A total of four squadrons of them bombed the eastern end of the town, about half a mile ahead of us. Clouds of dust and debris shot upwards with each explosion and we could not imagine that anyone could live through it. But, we knew from past experience that most of the Japs would survive in a condition to fight us until each individual was killed. The Mitchells were soon followed by two squadrons of Hurribombers, and one of Thunderbolts, bombing the western end of the town.

Before the dust had settled, we moved forward towards our objective. 4 and 5 Troops were leading and they took their usual share of machine gun fire and grenade attacks from the dug-in enemy. They made steady progress, sorting out the strong points and erasing them, moving slowly uphill towards the mill. We were about thirty yards behind them when I spotted two Japs running from some bushes and then stopping, hesitating, looking after the tanks ahead of us.

"Major, two Japs have just jumped into a slit trench ahead of us." I told him.

"Are you sure, Fenner?"

"As sure as I sit here, sir," I confirmed.

"Then guide Coffey until we are next to them."

This I did. I told Paddy to halt when I judged that the Japs were just below my visor and then I opened it. There they were, just five feet below me, I could see the two Japs, squatting in the bottom of their foxhole. Each had a rifle, but was not trying to use it. The shape of their steel helmets left no doubt that they were Japs. "Definitely Japs, sir," I told the Major on the intercom. He did not answer me. I merely saw a Mills grenade land on the ground at the side of the foxhole, obviously dropped by the Major. As I looked at it, there was no time to close my visor, the thing exploded just five feet from my face. I would have been killed if any part of it had entered the tank through my visor but yet again I was lucky. Not so the Japs who were now slumped in the bottom of their hole. "You got them, sir, but, hasn't it gone quiet?"

The wireless was very subdued. There had been some traffic between the other troops ahead of us but I could only hear them faintly now. At the first lull in the R/T, the Major called the 4 and 5 Troop Leaders. "Able 4 and 5, report progress, 4 and 5 over." They did not reply. Instead, they started to talk to each other again, still very faintly. "Fenner, what have you done with this set? they're not hearing me." I quickly switched to send and tested the variometer reading, which was nil – a sure sign of physical damage to the aerial. A quick look out of my visor confirmed that the fishing rod aerial [a] was in position and unharmed. "It must be the grenade, sir. It has not damaged the aerial but it might have got the lead under the front wing." "Then get it mended, Fenner, and quickly."

I did a rapid check of my kit, put a roll of black insulating tape into my map pocket and checked my army-issue Swiss knife, full of gadgets. Then, I slipped out of my webbing equipment and ammo pouches and left them, with the Tommy gun, on my seat.

"Could we move the tank so that the left side is facing away from any Japs and I'll get out through your cupola, sir?"

"Carry on."

Paddy moved the tank a few yards and slewed it across our line of approach whilst I wriggled into the turret, which was filled with the three crew members, and squeezed upwards, past the Major and out of the top.

It was a bright warm day outside as I climbed down to the ground. A section of the Royal Scots were lying down looking relaxed as they rested. I couldn't resist giving them a greeting, which was supposed to be friendly. "Och, are ye orright the noo, Jock?" The

---

a Appendix A136

immediate reply came in broad Yorkshire. "Get stuffed, tanky," with a grin on his face. Never assume that a Royal Scot is from north of the Border.

When I looked under the left wing of the tank I saw what I had expected. The rubber-covered cable, running from a small hole in the armour plating to connect with the aerial base had been cut cleanly by the grenade blast. The procedure was simple. I bared the two cable ends with my knife, ready to twist them together to make a firm connection. As soon as I held the two bared ends, one in each hand, I completed the aerial circuit and the Major could then hear at full strength again, and he could also transmit at full strength. He didn't wait for me to complete the job, but switched to send, putting 400 volts pressure through my body and into the aerial. The strong surge of electric current knocked me over. I ran up the side of the tank as he was speaking into the mike and tapped him on the head. "I can't mend the fault if you're giving me electric shocks. Will you please wait until I tell you it is mended!" He could tell that I was annoyed and nodded. I then completed the joint and added a few inches of tape, before climbing back into my seat using the same route that I had used to get out. The battle continued sporadically until late afternoon.

We had cleared the area around the windmill and seen the river about a mile away. It looked like a huge lake running across the country as far as we could see. The town was not yet cleared and the Major was ordered to pull back ready to harbour for the night.

"Before we do that, I want to check whether those really were two Japs you saw, Fenner. It would be awful if they were our own men, wouldn't it?" he said to me. "I can assure you that they are two dead Japs, Sir, but I would like to see what your grenades really did to them." He told Paddy Coffey to pull back the three or four hundred yards to the edge of the field, where we had left the Jap foxhole. "Right, let's all go and see what we did," he said. "Can I come, too?" I asked. "There doesn't seem to be any activity on the set." "Right," he answered and all seven of us climbed out of the tank and walked the hundred yards or so to find the position. It was exactly as I had described it. The two dead Japs lay at the bottom of their hole. Pulling one up by his shoulder straps showed the damage done by a grenade at close quarters. He had been cut in half. His battledress pocket revealed a few pathetic papers and photographs of his family. The Major grunted with disgust. "Let's get back to the tank," and he started to return.

The burst of machine gun fire was a shock to us all as we threw ourselves flat on the earth. We had no cover. Another long burst was kicking the ground up only a few feet in front of us, when I realised what it was. "That's a Browning," I shouted to the Major, "I'm sure of it."

"You're right. Get back to the tank and stop it," he said with his face biting the soil like all of us.

I could see our unoccupied tank waiting at the other side of the field and I upped and ran. Being a cross-country runner, I have rarely tried to sprint quickly, but that was the first time that 100 yards had been covered in less than ten seconds. Roger Bannister came later. I even accelerated when another burst of Browning followed me across the ground up to our tank. I was breathless, to say the least, as I ran up the side of the tank and crawled into my seat. My chest was heaving as I listened to the 5 Troop Leader talking to his sergeant on the wireless.

"Able 5 Able, I'm sure you got him with that last burst. There is no activity now that I can see, keep watching, out." I butted in before anyone else could speak.

"Able 5, cease firing, Able 5, over." I was still gasping for a normal breath.

"Able 5," he replied icily, obviously not liking to receive an order from a corporal, "roger, I have just done so, over."

"Able 5, you have just been firing at Number 9 and all his crew. I will dismount again to see if they are O.K., Able 5, out."

He and his troop must have been shocked by my announcement, and our conversation would have been heard by all the other tanks, as well as by R.H.Q. They would all be awaiting news of whether Major Dorman and his crew had been shot. As I climbed down to the ground I saw the other six walking back, apparently safe. The Major was very calm as he looked at me.

"Who was the bloody idiot who shot us?"

"5 Troop, sir, they stopped immediately I told them."

"Thank you, Fenner, you certainly moved quickly."

That was not the end of it. The new young lieutenant from 5 Troop reported sick the next day and he was quietly replaced. I met him again in May, at the 3 B.G.H. Poona, where he was a patient in the psychiatric ward and I was being discharged from hospital, to return to the Regiment via the R.A.C. Depot. He told me that he had been very stressed throughout the Burma campaign, and that his mistaking our crew for a bunch of Japs had been the last straw. He asked me to meet his specialist to describe the conditions under which we had fought. I did this and soon decided that I did not like 'trick cyclists', as they were known. He seemed to think that we had both imagined the war.

2nd February 1945

After resting for a day, we returned to Ywathetgyi in order to complete the job of clearing the town. The centre was a mass of tank obstacles, caused by craters from the heavy bombing of two days earlier, but we were able to find plenty of targets during the day. The most interesting were two sampans loaded to the gunwales with Jap soldiers trying to escape across the Irrawaddy. 5 Troop, with a new troop leader, shot them both to pieces and estimated 50 Japs drowned in the muddy waters. The town was completely in our hands by dusk.

It was near Kyaukse, during a days' rest from action, that we had a big delivery of mail from home. Everyone seemed to receive a few letters and, as usual, individuals disappeared into quiet spots in and around the tanks to read them in peace. I had walked a little way outside the box and was sitting reading my letters for the second time, looking for any new angle on the items of news. I leaned back against the trunk of a large tree when I felt the pressure on my back. I was definitely being pushed heavily forwards and I moved more than twelve inches, pushed by the tree. The tree and I then moved backwards and rocked from side to side. It was weird and the movement lasted for nearly a minute. It had gone very quiet. The birds had stopped their chatter and I suddenly felt very isolated. There was no one else near me as I stood up to look at the tree.

It appeared to be perfectly normal until another movement of the earth made me realise that I was in the middle of an earthquake. This second quake threw me to the ground and I decided that it was time to get back to the others near the tanks. They had all had a similar experience and the men and the birds all started to chatter again. Within half an hour we had pushed the excitement into the back of our minds and resumed our chores, preparing for yet another attack on a Jap-occupied village near Saye.

This was intended to be more of a diversion, to try to draw the fire from the Jap artillery so that their gun flashes could be spotted. Identifying such targets would give our higher command the opportunity to use the growing numbers of bomber squadrons in massed heavy raids on Japanese strongpoints.

We had become aware of the increasing use being made of the wireless wavelengths by the greater number of units of the 14th Army and it was sometimes a problem to find a spot on the dial where there was no interference. Each morning I used to listen on our allotted wavelength, to see if there were others using it and, if so, I would move the dial slightly up or down to try for a quiet spot.

On this particular morning I had netted the group successfully on two separate wavelengths, and we were advancing on the target village. There were a few messages being passed to adjust the formation of the leading tanks when a very strong carrier wave butted into our wavelength. There was a full minute of this, preventing any of our group from using their sets and then we heard the voice.

"Three King Tare Three, Three King Tare Three, Howareyoureceivingme, over?"

The American voice gave a clear callsign, but his message was just one long garbled word.

The Major said on the intercom "The bloody man! What can you do about it, Fenner?"

"I can try to flick the group over to the other wavelength, but that Yank could drown any transmission, and we might lose half the group."

"Don't try, I will deal with him." He switched to send.

"All stations Easy, report signals, all stations Easy, over."

The troop leaders replied, mostly complaining of the Three King Tare Three interference, when the American station came on again.

"Three King Tare Three to the Easy Group – get off my wavelength, over."

This was just the message for Major Dorman to answer, which he did, in his most cutting British Officer's accent. "Hello Three King Tare Three, this is the Number Nine of Easy Group. You are on our, repeat our, wavelength. I am leading an action with the enemy and will not change until the action is completed. Please stop your interference. Out."

It did the trick. There was no answer from what was obviously an extremely powerful U.S. Air Force transmitter and we had no more problems that day.

We reached the edge of the village and waited whilst the Lancashire Fusilier patrols entered, probed and returned to report. They had found a few Japs with machine guns, which we had heard, but there appeared to be many more men and some vehicles clustered at the other side of the village – a good target for our usual, heavy-handed attention. Was this a brigade or divisional H.Q.? There was a second similar village only half a mile south of this one, which might also be occupied.

The plan was quickly made for two troops of tanks to lead the Lancashire Fusiliers in and to proceed as far as the southern edge of the first village, if this was possible. It became another long day which resulted in the destruction of many of the Japs and the capture of a wide variety of mortars, guns and wrecked vehicles, including many documents. These were quickly loaded on to a jeep and sent back to 4th Brigade Intelligence, where they were scanned through the night. Major Dorman was told to harbour where we were for the night and await further orders. Despatch riders were coming and going throughout the hours of darkness and the Major told us that he had received hearty congratulations for the day's results and for the useful information gleaned from the documents. We had destroyed a large part of a Japanese Divisional H.Q., the remainder of which was in the second village, to our south. We had orders to be ready to clear that at 1000 hrs. that morning, after it had received an 'earthquake' bombing.

This was a 'first' for us. It sounded ominous. We had all seen some bombing of villages but we were told that this new system would obliterate the village and we would have little to do afterwards.

1000 hrs. We were all mounted in our tanks. The infantry were well dug in and had been told to be 'heads three feet below the surface' when the bombing started. Then they came.

Squadron after squadron of heavy bombers, about 10,000 feet above us, flying in square formation even when dropping their loads. It was my most frightening experience of the war. We had no direct line of communication with the bomber crews, who were looking down on at least two small villages of bashas surrounded by bamboo thickets, trees and fields. And we were in one of them.

The bombs fell in large clusters and it was the first time that I heard the expression 'the earth moved'. There was no pleasure or satisfaction in it. The whole of No. 2 village moved – upwards and in pieces. Our tanks in No. 1 village jumped and rocked with the vibration and I felt the tremendous air pressure on my eardrums. Most of us felt an immediate urge to visit the latrines, but we dared not go outside the protection of our tanks as we could hear debris falling on and around us. It lasted perhaps for only fifteen minutes but I could hear the noise in my head for a few weeks afterwards. Truly, it was an earthquake, but, this time, man-made.

We were not needed to help to clear up. We simply could not get the tanks anywhere near the second village which had craters in craters, in craters. The Lancashire Fusiliers went in on foot with fixed bayonets, but these were also not needed. There were no Jap bodies or weapons to count, only hundreds of pieces of both. Talking about it afterwards, we all marvelled that we had survived and that the Yanks had been able to hit the small target so accurately.

Chapter 13

In the Sagaing Bend

End of February 1945

During this time we learned that both Lieutenants Swan M.C. and Weir M.C. had been promoted to Captain. This met with the approval of the entire squadron and one cynic said that they deserved it for surviving so long under fire. If he were right, there were many of us who had survived more than a year and who could look for a promotion.

The C.O. must, by now, have seen a few signs of exhaustion in B Squadron, both in men and vehicles, as he knew that we had been moving and fighting steadily for more than eight weeks. He ordered us to go to a quiet area for four days' rest and relaxation.

We arrived at an unspoilt village on the banks of the Chindwin, only a few miles south of Monywa. The headman welcomed us and we were allotted space in some well-built empty bashas. Guards were minimal and it was sheer bliss to swim in the river and complete our laundry and running repairs without the possibility of a Jap attack.

On the second day I took a group of eight men on a fishing expedition. We set off, on foot, following a tributary of the Chindwin, and were carrying our sidearms as usual, but we also were carrying two Mills grenades each, drawn from a suspect batch in the stores truck. I understood that they were another supply left over from the 1914/18 War, similar to those used on Nunshigum. Officially, we were testing a sample.

After walking three miles, we reached a bend in the river where there was a deep pool. The surrounding trees gave plenty of shade and we all voted for a swim. It was idyllic. With one of us standing guard with a tommy gun, the other seven were soon diving in and swimming around in the nude. It was enough to drive any fish away for a long time, but one of us relieved the guard so that he had a splash, and then we all lay in the sun to dry.

After a snack tiffin we got down to the serious business of testing the grenades – and fishing. Four of us stood on the bank and each threw one grenade into the pool. We waited the required seven seconds and then saw the four underwater explosions. The grenades had all performed as expected. As the water surface heaved, we saw a dozen fish float to the surface, and the four naked men dived in and quickly caught them and threw them on to the bank. It was a great success. One or two of the fish escaped as they appeared to revive on touch, but we were learning.

We decided to try again, further upstream, and we soon found a similar pool. This time Ginger Whiteley and I were amongst the 'anglers'. Four more grenades were thrown into the pool but this time there were only three explosions.

"One must be a dud," said Ginger and the four of us dived in. As I came to the surface there was a fourth submarine explosion and I felt a hammer blow all over my body, which was below the surface. It knocked the air from my lungs. Ginger Whiteley had been completely submerged at the time, and he came to the surface, bottom up. Two of us swam up to him, turned him face upwards and swam with him to the bank. He was coming back to his senses as he was hauled up by his arms, and was soon feeling normal again. The others had not let the fish escape and we had a good haul to take back to the village. The armourer was not very interested in my report and merely commented, "You must have had one with a delayed fuse mixed with the others. It happens." We enjoyed grilled fresh fish that night.

On the morning of the next day I was sitting on my haunches, in the true Indian Army fashion, stripping and cleaning my tommy gun, when I heard a delightful girl's voice behind me.

"Excuse me, sir, may I speak with you?"

I turned and saw a little brown Burmese girl, dressed like all the others that I had seen, in a long skirt to the ground and a little sleeveless jacket. The accent was so British that I could hardly believe that a villager could have acquired it, so far to the north of the country.

"Of course," I smiled, putting down the oily mainspring, "who are you?"

"My name is Ma Tin Mying. I am living here, with my brother, in the house of my uncle, who is the headman of this village. I was wondering if you have recent copies of *The Tatler*."

I regret that I laughed at this as I shook my head. *The Tatler*, last seen in a dentist's waiting room before I joined the Army, was not the sort of reading matter to be found in a cavalry regiment, well, not amongst the Other Ranks in the middle of Burma.

"I'm sorry I can't help you there. You see we have been chasing the Japanese for a year now and most of our supplies are brought in by air. Tell me, how have you learned to speak English so well?"

It was her turn to laugh – a happy, tinkling sound, from behind some very white and even teeth. "I am a B.A., Rangoon University, where we talk in English all the time. After I graduated, we came up here to avoid the Japanese. They were causing trouble for some of my friends – they are not very nice people at all. Up here we have very little news."

The Major was walking past at that point, looking rather quizzical, so I introduced the young lady to him. After greeting her he looked at me.

"Is it all going well, Corporal?" There was a sparkle in his eye as he walked away.

The result of my meeting with Ma Tin Mying was that we had supplies of locally grown fresh vegetables organised for the next day. I gave her some Lifebuoy soap which she accepted with glee. They had not seen soap of any kind for more than a year and, in return, I was invited to take refreshments at the headman's basha that evening.

It was the first time that I had been invited into someone's home in the three and a half years since arriving in India and I found it a pleasing prospect. The other crew members agreed that I should take two cans of fruit and milk from our stores, and I arrived with these just after dusk. I was welcomed by Ma Tin Mying and her younger brother, who was the proud owner of an old 'wind-up' gramophone, and only one record. This might have been an old pre-war favourite, 'Blaze Away', but it was so badly worn and the needle so useless, that it was impossible to be sure. The evening was spoilt by the brother playing this one useless record continuously. It was not possible to have any real conversation with his sister. She told me that there had been no Japs in the village for more than three months, and then they had only been marching through on their way south.

The 'refreshments' consisted of a ripe mango, served on a plate – a real treat after months of army rations, but the gramophone drove me away after an hour when I thanked them both, hoping to meet them again. My farewell included the comment, "Isn't it a beautiful moon, tonight?" To this, Tina (as I thought of her) laughed again and explained:

"That expression is used in Burma when a young man wishes to indicate his admiration for a young lady."

I think I blushed at that, as I had only been stating a fact. The Burmese moon was simply huge. I was brought down to earth by the comments of a sergeant I passed on my way back to the tank. "That was a nice bit of crumpet you found, Corporal, don't miss your chance there!"

I did miss it. We were ordered back to the Sagaing Bend area for more action. We were soon back into the routine and I was feeling the need for a change from always being involved in every squadron attack.

23rd February 1945

I took the opportunity when the Major was talking with me about our plans for the next day. "I've been thinking, sir, and would like to apply for a transfer to 4 Troop."

"Whatever for, Fenner?" He seemed to be rather surprised.

"It's nothing personal, only that I've been doing this job for more than a year and it is becoming more difficult because of the 'runs', and yet I'm expected to put in more hours in the tank than anyone else. If I could be with my friends in the 4 Troop Corporal's tank then I would be able to cope better with the medical problem. I might also be in line for promotion to troop sergeant because I have had plenty of experience of commanding a tank in action."

He gave it a few seconds thought. "I see what you mean. I'll chase up that recommendation for L.I.A.P. for you, but you want to go into Corporal Moore's tank, do you? I already have two corporals in that crew. I'll let you know." That was that.

24th February 1945

We had another shoot at some Jap artillery dug into some woodland across a deep chaung, but we were not able to get close to it. An early return to our box gave us news of an intelligence report, gleaned from some more captured documents. Low-ranking Japanese officers had sent many reports to their various H.Q.s that the tanks (Carabiniers were mentioned) were the biggest cause of their problems. They were unbeatable and were causing the rapid decline in infantry morale. Fighting patrols, sent out at night, were unable, and possibly unwilling, to attack British boxes, which were strengthened with tank support. Our Lees were the scourge of the Imperial Japanese Army. To counter this, orders had been sent to all formations to make the destruction of our tanks the first priority. All soldiers must be prepared and willing to die, by taking the initiative and destroying one tank at the same time. Explosives and weapons were to be supplied for this purpose and each successful soldier would receive his reward (in heaven?).

We were rather quiet after reading this report. We really should not have been surprised by it because we had done the enemy a lot of harm over a long period and we were continuing to do so. It was the old story – every action creates a reaction. We shrugged our shoulders and soldiered on, with more driving around the villages, crossing roads we had passed down a few days or weeks earlier, shooting, repairing broken tracks, replacing worn guns and forever loading ammo for more shoots.

2nd March 1945

Major Dorman had not come back to me about my transfer request when 4 Troop were ordered to drive south, down the road leading to Sagaing. They were about twenty miles north of the Ava Bridge, in open country, moving along the dirt road. 4A, the troop sergeant, was leading and had just crossed a culvert when the second tank in line 4B, commanded by Corporal 'Dinty' Moore, blew up. It had not simply blown a track with a mine, it had literally been blown upwards into pieces and scattered around the now missing culvert. The crews of the other two tanks were very shocked when they realised what had happened. Seven of their pals, the crew that I had applied to join only a few days earlier, were dead and their tank was now an unrecognisable spread of pieces of engineering.

On receiving the wireless report from the troop leader, Major Dorman ordered the two remaining tanks of 4 Troop to return to the box. Once again I realised how lucky I had been. If the Major had agreed to my transfer to that tank, I would not be here.

3rd March 1945

Major Dorman called me across to his jeep. "Fenner, you and I are going to have a look at yesterday's disaster. Bring your sidearm."

He drove the two of us the ten miles south to the blown culvert, where we dismounted. We could see the huge gap in the road which had been blown by at least one 500 lb. aerial bomb. The place was surrounded by odd bogey wheels, pieces of tank track and armour-plating, spread up to 400 yards away from the point of the explosion.

"See if you can find any bodies." said the grim-faced Major, "None have been buried so far."

After walking around the area for half an hour, I had found only one, pathetic left hand, severed at the wrist. It was small and delicate and I immediately thought that it had belonged to Trooper Norris, a twenty-one-year-old from Hull. He was a brilliant artist, only recently having joined the squadron from the Depot, and we all admired his cartoons of various characters we knew.

I nearly cried. Despite having spent a year killing Japs, and seeing friends and officers killed in a variety of ways, finding that hand really hit me. I showed it to the Major.

"This is all I can find of the entire crew, sir."

"Then we must bury it here and mark the spot. I'll report it and there will be another search of the area."

"May I suggest that you say we have buried some of the remains of the seven men in your report. We don't want the relatives to be told that they are missing, do we sir?"

"Of course – then, let's get back to the box."

There was another grim message when we arrived back. Another Carabiniers tank had been blown up on the same day in exactly the same way. A Jap soldier with a large stone in his hand had been sitting on an aerial bomb under a culvert, waiting for a tank to be driven over before striking the detonator to blow himself and the tank to smithereens. The mind boggles at the thought of such a human booby-trap. This time it was the tank of Captain Cornaby, a twenty-four-year-old officer of – I think it was – A Squadron, who were operating in the same area.

In the Htauk-Kyan War Cemetery, Rangoon, there are now two neat rows of head stones, dated 2nd March, 1945. Corporal L. Moore with his six crew members and Captain H.P. Cornaby with five men lie in beautifully kept gardens containing hundreds of large butterflies fluttering around in the sunshine. They died together and they are now remembered together.

Too late to help those two crews, an order came from R.H.Q. that any tank approaching a culvert should be very wary and take any necessary steps to avoid a similar disaster. We hardly needed to be told this. Leading tanks would often try to approach a culvert from the side and occasionally fire a 37 mm H.E. shell to clear any suicidal Jap out of the way. There was no similar loss after that day.

During the next two weeks we swept along the north bank of the Irrawaddy finding odd lots of disorganised and demoralised Japs trying to cross the river and escape our attentions. There were many occasions when the infantry of 2 Division were in action without our support. They sent parties across the river at various points in order to find and identify any Jap strongholds and we heard a variety of reports of successes and the occasional disaster. I was told that one battalion commander (it could have been the Norfolks, but I'm not sure) had led a foot patrol into the night and they had all disappeared. Why a lieutenant-colonel was leading such a patrol was never explained, but similar tales were told over the evening meals as we waited to cross the river with our still-effective tanks.

We all looked forward to helping to take Mandalay – best known for the flying fish of the song. As it was more than 400 miles from the sea, we didn't expect to see these fish, but Mandalay was an ancient capital of Burma, as also were five or six other towns dotted across the country. It was also famous for the large Fort Dufferin, which we hoped to see.

Mandalay was still our final objective before we were to be pulled out of action and rested in India – or so we thought. We had heard it all before. Firstly, it was to clear the Imphal plain, then to reach Ye-u, then Shwebo, then the Irrawaddy, and now Mandalay. One squadron wag said, "A pound to a penny, in rupees, that we will be given another 'final objective', further south, before we finish," and no one took the bet.

We were all cynics when it came to promises of leave. The real question was whether the tanks would be able to keep going. Time after time the rifling of our 75 mm guns was worn smooth until they lost their accuracy, and our engines lost their power, but we had been fortunate so far in receiving replacements, cannibalised from spare tanks in India and flown in to us. There was no problem with the replacement of personnel. They were expendable and replaceable, and the training regiments ensured a steady flow of well-trained reinforcements who maintained our strength. Sometimes we had more officers than the official establishment. I was always amazed how fit Major Dorman was, despite the long hours he put in over and above those in action. He was often away at Brigade H.Q. for a conference and out in his jeep or on foot, making a recce with Lieutenant Ryman. I think that his secret was having an excellent batman who kept him in good condition.

Chapter 14

The Road to Mandalay

15th March 1945

Crossing the Irrawaddy was not very different from crossing the Chindwin. It was much wider and there were more hazards from shoals and islands, but we relaxed during a day of waiting for our turn for 'cruising down the river', when the words of the song could be heard above the noise of the power boats.

We drove off from near Myinmu, going west past Ywathetgyi until the river turned south to be joined by the Chindwin. Reports indicated little Jap activity on the other side and our crossing was tedious but uneventful. The rafts moved singly downstream in the current, and were driven to the other side by two DUKWs, one fixed on either side. We were all across and in a strong defensive box by the end of the day, ready to move towards the Ava Bridge and then to Mandalay.

Major Dorman came back from a Brigade conference absolutely livid. He called a parade of B Squadron and gave his sitrep, talking to us all as equals, quietly listing the various objectives that we had been given during the past few months, and which we had achieved.

"I have made myself very unpopular at Brigade. I can live with that. As you know, we had been told that our final objective was Mandalay and we had all been looking forward to that achievement. Now, I am told, C Squadron only will be involved in the attack on Mandalay. We will not be required. We have a new objective in the oil fields of Yenangyaung, 100 miles south of here. This will involve fighting our way through Myingyan, Pagan, another ancient capital of Burma full of pagodas, Mount Popa, an extinct volcano, Chauk, and so on.

I expressed my dissatisfaction with B Squadron being taken away from Mandalay, after leading the British 2nd Division all the way from India, and I demanded that a token force should be involved in that action. It was finally agreed that this could be done – by one tank! I will take my tank in the advance on Mandalay, representing you all, so that we can tell our children that B Squadron of the 3rd Carabiniers helped to recapture Mandalay from the Japanese. I'm sorry to disappoint you but it is the best that I could do."

There were a few weak cheers. Most of the men had had their fill of action anyway and a Jap is a Jap anywhere, whether he is in Mandalay or in any of these unpronounceable places yet to come. It was the same difference. Roll on the boat! Bet they tell us to go to Rangoon after we've cleared the oil fields!

20th March 1945

This was quite a day. We travelled nearly 50 miles on our tracks, together with lorried infantry, to the outskirts of Mandalay. One dark green battle-scarred [a] General Lee tank, with its seven man crew, was proudly showing the blue square sign on the turret to let everyone know that B Squadron was there.

On the way we saw the Ava Bridge from the east bank of the river, much closer this time. The Japs had fixed a wooden track across the broken gaps so that it could be used for men and mules to cross the river; but there was no passage for wheeled vehicles.

Mandalay itself looked at first sight like a large wholesome village but as we neared the centre, we saw more and more pagodas of all sizes and well-built, two-storeyed houses of brick and timber. The town was very spacious with many trees and open areas of grass. People were moving about on foot and some on bicycles. Roadside stalls were loaded with fruit and vegetables being offered for sale. We eventually came to the Palace and Fort Dufferin. The Fort covered a large square area, bordered by high thick, red brick walls and a moat. Each side was about a quarter of a mile long and had an entrance in the middle, with a road running over a short causeway

a Appendix A137

across the moat. On the western wall we could see a long scar in
the brickwork which had been caused by an R.A.F. mustang striking
it as it had crashed to the ground. The young pilot had survived and
lived on to become Air Vice-Marshal Sir Bernard Chacksfield, President of the Burma Star Association.

There was a broad sward of grass outside the moat, which helped
to create a peaceful and impressive sight. Inside the walls we could
see a wooded hill rising in the middle, with more pagodas and
buildings. Dotted along the inner walls there were a few ancient
cannon pointing outwards. We felt rather like tourists – until we
heard the machine guns firing inside the Fort.

The infantry went to ground and the Major took his chance. He
jumped down to speak with an officer and volunteered to help, so
we were soon able to fire a few rounds of 75 H.E. into suspected
bunkers. It was really a token shoot at a few Japs who were trying
to escape.

An hour later we moved out of the Fort area when we were asked
to help to release the inmates of an internment camp. We were to
be a show of strength to encourage the Jap prison officers to capitu-
late. The camp consisted of a few rows of huts with a perimeter of
a barbed wire fence.

As it turned out, our presence was not really necessary and the
gates opened soon after we arrived. The residents, who all appeared
to be female, came out slowly, carrying pathetic bundles of bedding.
Some were carrying babies who had been born in the camp. We
were told that they were mostly wives of suspect Burmese and that
they had been treated with surprising respect – because they were
married women. Unmarried women were another matter and were
often forced into service as comforts girls for the forces.

We had now done our bit in the relief of Mandalay and the Major
decided that we should return to our box, but not before we had bought
a few things to take back with us. He stopped the tank at a roadside
market and we all dismounted to have a look at the goods on offer.

We all felt the need for the delicious fruits and vegetables on
display and piled the tank with supplies. The strange thing was that

the high prices were marked in rupees but the locals would not accept the British Indian rupees in which we were paid. Instead they insisted that they wanted Japanese occupation rupees, which would not be the currency for much longer. As it happened, we had piles of Jap notes of all denominations, which the Japs printed in vast quantities on mobile presses. We had captured one of these presses a few weeks ago and had thought that the notes would have been useless except, perhaps, as souvenirs. Here was a chance to use some of it. I bought a box of matches for 100 Jap rupees and mangoes at 50 rupees each. The equivalent in Indian rupees would have been worth about £6 and £3, so we were delighted at being able to spend our captured notes. The remainder of the troop were similarly pleased with the fruit and vegetables on our return to camp.

———————————

I think we had known all along that we would look upon the recapture of Mandalay as our real objective, and there was a strong feeling of achievement in B Squadron. The next phase was something of an anti-climax.

The news from the European and Pacific theatres was mostly success and here, in Burma, the only real question was whether we could reach Rangoon before the expected monsoons made travelling almost impossible. The bad news of the V-bombs was censored and we learned of these new weapons only after we arrived back in the U.K. a year or more later.

There was no doubt that we would obliterate the remaining formations of the Japanese army in Burma. Many of them were already being crushed in and around Meiktila. Fair weather airstrips were being built in and near the area that could be described as 'the front', but most of them would become useless after the first week of heavy rain, due in April or May. The message came from the 14th Army H.Q. to press on to 'Rangoon or Bust'.

Our group were to push south more or less parallel with the east bank of the Irrawaddy, and once again the old procedures worked. I remember many days of driving, with the odd hour or so of shooting into bunches of retreating Japs. Pagan was unusual in the fact that the entire population had moved elsewhere. The town was simply covered with pagodas [a] of all sizes, some up to 30 feet high, and they were an impressive sight in the sunset. The sound of their tinkling bells in the breeze was soon drowned by the sporadic sniper and l.m.g.[b] fire directed at us. We spent two days removing the few Japs that we found.

Further south we came to Mount Popa. This was the only high feature in a flat plain and it appeared to be the hard core of a volcano, standing over 150 feet high with sheer sides. There were some suicidal Japs dug into the crevices and caves, and we required another two days of probing and shooting to eliminate them. And so we continued, with a mounting sense of urgency as the skies showed more clouds than we had seen for months. Kyaukpadaung and Chauk both needed attention from our tanks before they were clear of the enemy.

20th April 1945

It was at Kyaukpadaung that our M.O. 'Doc Griff' sought me out with a smile on his face. "Corporal Fenner, I haven't seen you for a few weeks. How is the sprue?"

"Much the same, thank you, sir. The trots average about six times a day, and I've learnt to live with it. I'm still hoping to go home on L.I.A.P."

"Well, I've got some good news for you," he said, opening his bag of tricks. "There have been some new drugs discovered recently that are very effective for problems like yours and I want you to try one of them." He produced a few yards of waxed paper strip containing a white tablet in each inch of the tape. He handed the lot to me. "Here you are. They are called Sulphaguanadine and you take fourteen now, followed by seven every four hours, until they are all gone.

It sounded very simple and Captain Griffiths was enthusiastic,

---

a Appendix A138
b Appendix A139

giving me a pat on the shoulder. "It's just what we have been waiting for. You'll soon be a different man." I was.

Instead of running to the latrines once an hour I stopped going at all. After one day, I told the lads I was cured. After the second day I knew that I was cured. On day three I began to wonder, because I remembered some of the tales told by the old soldiers of the dire consequences of not having a bowel action for more than twenty-four hours in the tropics. I had no success on day three and I had a restless night.

On day four I awoke, knowing that I would have to return to normal today. I had finished the tablets and I made my way to the latrine in our new box. To cut a long and painful story short, I was sitting and straining when I felt what I knew to be a bayonet rammed up my rear. I screamed and turned around with my tommy gun ready to fire. There was no Jap with a weapon behind me. There was nobody near at all but I was bleeding profusely and in great pain. I tidied myself and went to the M.O. truck, where luckily I saw Captain Griffiths. He was serious and diagnosed an anal fissure. "You should have told me that you were constipated and I could have helped you. You'll have to be evacuated now. Go and get your kit." It was as simple as that.

As I collected my small kit from the tank and handed in my tommy gun and ammo, the comments were all tinged with envy.

"Lucky bugger!"

"I knew he was trying to work his ticket, ever since Nunshigum!"

"He's split his ring!"

"No more guard duty now, Alan!"

It really hit me then. My immediate war was over for a few weeks. No doubt I would be back to rejoin them in time to pursue the Jap, all the way to Japan if necessary, but the whole Regiment would be pulled back to India during the monsoons, ready for our new tanks and to prepare for the invasion of Singapore. I intended to enjoy my spell in hospital. The Major saw me for a few minutes, when he thanked me for my help during the past three and a half months and wished me well. He agreed with my suggestion that Trooper Warrilow should take my place.

A 30 cwt. truck, ordered by the M.O., took me to the nearest airstrip, where I waited with more than a hundred other casualties for my turn to take a seat in one of the stream of Dakotas which landed and halted for a few minutes before taking off with a full load into the heavy clouds overhead. My Dakota had a Canadian crew and the wireless operator walked through to chat with his cargo. I was the only 'walking wounded' amongst the stretchers and, as soon as he knew that I was also a w/op, he invited me to go forward so that he could show me his set on the starboard side.

He showed me how he could wind the aerial out of its housing to become effective but he stopped me from doing so. "We don't wind it out in a monsoon cloud as it might attract lightning," he said to my horror.

"You mean – these clouds are dangerous?"

He nodded. "Yes, but don't tell the others. We don't want a panic. Look at those brown clouds – they are the real monsoon clouds and some of them are over 30,000 feet high and very boisterous. We lose the odd plane when its wings are torn off."

"You're pulling my leg," I said and went back to join the others for the remainder of the flight.

But he was not pulling my leg, as I found out after landing safely at Comilla, in Bengal. I learnt that five Dakotas had been lost during that day alone, all flying in the full knowledge of the risks. Apparently, these petrol-powered, twin-engined planes simply did not have the power to fly above the clouds and the pilots took their chances, trying to evade the darkest mass of storm. I take my hat off to those crews.

After a day in hospital at Comilla I was transferred to Dacca B.G.H. where I spent two weeks being tested and assessed. The worst part was the examination of my wound. A young doctor inserted an infernal device of levers and screws and cranked it open wider and wider until I again screamed in agony. This brought a group of medics, including his superior who spoke sharply to the junior, telling him to mop up the new arterial blood covering the bed. I refused any further inquisitional torture and it was mutually agreed that I needed rest and a good diet.

Two days later the specialist confirmed the treatment and said, "You are a Carabinier, aren't you? Your brigadier is in the officers' block and wants to see you. He was asking if any 254 Tank Brigade men were in and I've told him about you." I walked across to see him after tiffin.

Brigadier 'Culley' Scoones had commanded 254 Tank Brigade for more than a year, throughout the siege of Imphal and into Burma, where he had become a casualty only a week before I had. He was in bed, bored stiff with the restrictions, but he made me very welcome.

"Have a grape, Corporal," and he asked me about my problem. I told him the basic facts and he nodded sympathetically.

"I have a similar problem, only in my case I really did have a bayonet shoved up my backside."

Almost unbelieving, I said, "You mean the Japs got as close as that, sir?"

"No," he smiled, "they were at least ten yards away and I jumped into a ditch when they fired at me, but I rushed it and sat on my own bayonet!"

He was that sort of man – always wanting to be near the front and testing the action. I suppose that could be considered a fault in a brigadier, risking his own life, but the men admired him for it. His brother, who commanded 4 Corps at Imphal, was promoted much higher before retirement.

———

During my spell at Dacca, the patients were entertained by a party from E.N.S.A., who gave brief shows in the wards. Beryl Reed was my favourite, even though she raised a blush on my cheek by singing a love song to me only in a ward full of love-starved soldiers. She leant over me in the final verse and I could not escape; I didn't really try. A lovely lady.

My next move was a journey right across India, by hospital ship and train, to the 3 B.G.H., Poona. After a week of excellent food, including a pint of Export Guinness each day, I was discharged to the R.A.C. Depot, only three miles away. This was my old stamping ground of two years earlier.

I arrived at the gate to the Depot in my washed and well darned jungle green battledress, wearing an Australian-type bush hat issued from Dacca, only to be met by the R.S.M. He was a splendid specimen of W.O.1., in starched, almost white, khaki drill, with gleaming, polished badges. I expected trouble. He was standing in the entrance almost at attention and looking straight at me.

"Who are you, Corporal?"

"Corporal Fenner, B Squadron, 3rd Carabiniers, discharged from 3 B.G.H. and reporting for duty, sir." I stamped my feet and was covered in a cloud of dust.

"Is that how you were dressed when you went into hospital?" he asked.

"Yes sir, except for the hat. I was flown out from near Kyauk-padang, as a casualty."

He must have realised that that was in Burma and he relaxed, smiled and held out his hand to shake mine. "Welcome to Poona Depot, Corporal. We've been hearing about the 3rd Carbs in our news reports. Come with me."

We walked to the Depot Office, where he told a corporal clerk to look after me and to find me a bed and new kit from the Q.M. Stores. I was amazed at the warm welcome and enjoyed three days of relaxation before being sent to rejoin the Regiment, which had now arrived at Ahmednagar in the Deccan.

They had reached Rangoon at the end of April, as the heavy rains were making the roads extremely difficult. There had been a few actions after leaving the oil fields but I had not missed much. It was during that journey that the squadron had taken their first and only prisoner. One of our Indian sweepers,[a] who was travelling with

---

a Appendix A140

B Echelon, had gone outside the box, for reasons known only to himself, and had found a starving, sick Jap lying in the mud on the roadside. The sweeper had no weapon, only his brush, so he swept the pathetic Jap in front of him as he walked back into the box. "I had to keep the place tidy, sahib," was his excuse to the guard on duty.

The squadron had a wet and miserable last few days on the journey but they were very relieved when told to go straight to the dock area and leave their tanks there. The vehicles had been their homes and workshops for a long time but there was more excitement about going to India and leave. Some would be going back to Blighty on repatriation – anyway, they had survived a long and dangerous campaign. The holiday spirit lasted until after I rejoined them.

It was the end of May 1945 when I arrived at the Carabiniers lines at Ahmednagar and I was told to report to the Adjutant. This was an unusual order for an N.C.O. but I found him to be Captain Harry Blackburn, newly promoted. Another warm welcome from my old Signals Officer. "Come in, Alan. I have just the job for you – Intelligence Sergeant! How does that suit you?"

It was two shocks in one. Firstly, I had never been addressed by an officer by my Christian name and secondly the promotion was a very pleasant surprise.

"You will now be in H.Q. Squadron, but you will see your old friends in B Squadron often enough, that is, those who are still there. The Regiment is changing rapidly, preparing for the Shermans arriving soon, ready for the invasion of Malaya. I thought you had done enough at the sharp end, and we have plenty to do from the 'I' point of view."

As you know, the atom bomb was dropped soon after that and we were not required for any more action. The Regiment was sent north to Risalpur, in the North West Frontier area, near the Khyber Pass. We were there to strengthen the defences in case the Russians invaded India from Afghanistan and also to make a show of strength in that volatile area in order to dissuade the local tribesmen from creating any trouble. The rest is history.

Chapter 15

Back To Yorkshire 1982

16th April 1982

Chief Inspector Ackroyd called Inspector Bennet into his office.

"The Chief Superintendent wants our report this afternoon and we must be ready for him. What did you think of Alan Fenner's recital last night, Harry?"

"Very interesting. It's amazing what some of our Forces chaps had to put up with. He should write a book so that every one can see what war's really like. On that subject, I think the Chindits had the worst of the conditions and I'd like to read more about them.

"As far as it concerns our problem, I'd agree that someone like Alan Fenner could have gone round the bend and committed a murder once a year for thirty years, but, it'll be a big job to trace all the old Carabiniers who were at Imphal. It'll involve a lot of other Authorities throughout the country and possibly overseas. Some of them might have gone anywhere, South Africa, Australia, New Zealand, and then come back to the U.K. It would be a very big job. Tell me, sir, do you suspect Alan Fenner?"

The Chief Inspector looked at Harry. "Let me say that I have not removed his name from my list, but I don't have many names on it yet. Let's look at the other possibilities. Your jogger must be traced. We need more help from the public and I think you should prepare a statement for a press release. You've plenty of points that will arouse public interest when you ask for help to find a 30-year serial killer, aged about sixty, who jogs regularly and has an experience of jungle fighting. Someone must know of him and have seen him jogging in a blue or black outfit. Can you have that ready to show the Chief this afternoon?"

Harry nodded. "Anything more?"

"Just be completely up to date with any reports of sightings of our man or his car. I'll see you here at 2 o'clock, ready for the session."

2.30 p.m.

Chief Superintendent Strachan listened quietly to his two men, each giving his own review of the enquiry up to date. He read the proposed press release which was intended to encourage public interest and support in the search for the killer.

'Further to the reported murder of Mr Vince Hallet, President of the Colliery Workers Union, on 13th April 1982, information has now been received indicating that the man concerned in that attack may also have been involved in up to thirty other murders, dated on or near 13th April on each of the past 30 years.

The significance of this date is not yet clear but it could be connected with some trauma in the man's life, probably during the Second World War. It is believed that he spent some time in action, possibly in Burma or the Far East, and that, despite his age, he has kept fit with regular physical exercise, including jogging. He was last seen on 13th April this year, wearing a navy blue or black jogging outfit. He is intelligent and dangerous. Anyone knowing a person who fits this description should not approach him but should contact his local police station. The information will be welcomed and treated in confidence. It is vital that he is quickly traced and stopped.'

The Scot passed the paper back to Harry Bennet. "I like that, Harry. It creates interest and should produce some useful information. Get it out today, if possible. The idea of tracing every live war-time Carabinier rings no bells with me. It would not only be very expensive but it would be far too restrictive. In my view, it would exclude too many 'possibles', such as any other member of the 14th Army who was at Imphal at the time of Nunshigum and who could have picked 13th April because of the battle. Also, any person who had not even been there, but who had read some of the books written by those who were there and who had some bamboos growing nearby."

He smiled across the desk at his C.I. "That could be someone like you, James! No, it's an interesting theory, which could just prove to be correct, but I don't want you to pursue that angle, not just yet. Sheffield are still working on the red Cortina aspect, and your publicity approach is good. The point to remember is that we are investigating one murder here in Barnsley, not thirty. If the culprit is a serial killer, that will be a bonus when we find him, but we mustn't let it distract us from the job of resolving this one crime. How about contacting Crimestoppers? They are always helpful and often successful. Go to it."

On the way back to his office, Ackroyd said, "I've always said, 'three minds are better than two'. He's usually got something constructive to say. Let's press on, Harry."

17th April 1982

The local and national press made headlines of the murder. With little news coming from the Government recently, they had been delighted to splash the questions posed by Harry Bennet's press release.

'SOLO SERIAL KILLER'S 30 YEAR PROGRAMME.'
'ONE MAN JUDGE, JURY, EXECUTIONER.'
'NUTTER NEEDS NABBING.'
'D.I.Y. – THE ULTIMATE DETERRENT?'

These were only a few of the headlines which raised a surge of interest. Articles were printed that gave hints of connections with Nunshigum, Imphal and the 14th Army, posing questions such as: 'Is there a solitary, fit man in his 60's living near you? Does he disappear on 'business' at odd intervals? Are you living with or near a man like this? If so, tell your local police of the facts and let them eliminate a possible suspect from their enquiries.'

Harry Bennet began to wonder what he had started, especially when Yorkshire T.V. sent an interviewer and camera crew to his office. Was it a case of 'overkill'? Perhaps not; only time would tell how effective it would be.

19th April 1982

It was effective, but in a way that no one had forecast. During the previous night, the police facsimile machine had received the usual pile of messages from a variety of sources using the cheaper night rate, but one was included which was self-explanatory.

"To Inspector Harry Bennet, Barnsley Police.

From the Jogger.

You have succeeded in creating a lot of publicity for your case, but you are so wrong in your assumptions and you will not succeed in finding me.

No, I was not at Imphal or in Burma.

No, I was not in the 3rd Carabiniers.

Yes, I picked the date of the battle of Nunshigum, 13th April, 1944, for two reasons. Firstly, the 13th sounds unlucky and it was to prove so for the creatures I eliminated. Secondly, I was very impressed with the story of the battle, where, when all the officers were killed, the men carried on with the action to wipe out the invader. They succeeded and set an example to the rest of the 14th Army. Kohima was another example of a few determined, ordinary men refusing to accept defeat and clearing the land of evil.

Evil people are not all foreign invaders. There are too many of them in the British Isles and our government are not going to get rid of them, despite their election promises. They refuse to review capital punishment. They encourage the spread of cigarette smoking even when they know it kills thousands every year. They are far more interested in the welfare of the criminal than in helping the victims of crime. It is up to people like me to do all they can to make this country a better place.

If you check my list of successes, you will see that they are all child-abusers, rapists, black marketeers, crooks, trade union officials who try to destroy our way of life and who succeed only in destroying their market and the livelihood of their own members. They are all people who use their power for their own selfish ends, whether it is personal gain or extreme left or right wing politics. They do not deserve to live.

The press do nothing about it. In fact, at least one of the press barons needs to be studied and, if found guilty of such crimes, he will be punished. When that happens, think of me.

You refer to my hobby as a crime, when I am merely doing my bit towards punishing criminals. It has always been the right of any individual to protect himself, his family, and their way of life against any outside threat. We did that in Europe and the Far East in the Second World War and we have done it since in Korea and other places.

I shall continue as long as I have the health and strength to do so, but, as you are now aware of my existence, I will increase my output to more than one per year."

James Ackroyd read it through twice without comment and then burst out, "What a pompous ass! When did this arrive, Harry?"

"It's recorded as coming in at 2 o'clock this morning, sir. There is no indication of where it came from and the duty clerk merely found it in the machine, when he came back from the loo. This man seems to think he's smart, writing to us this way and eliminating any paper, prints and post marks."

"But, can't we get B.T. to trace a fax transmission to our number at about that time?"

"We can ask them but there must be a few hundred thousand accounts to check. There's no way of tracing the sender from our end and, knowing how bright our man is, I suspect that he would send it on someone else's machine and telephone line. He might even have used a portable fax and a public 'phone box. He wouldn't make a mistake like using his own number."

Ackroyd took a drink of coffee. "But he has made a mistake. And he'll make more. He's given us an insight into his mind, and our specialists can build up a profile of the man we're looking for. He may believe that he has the right to act as he does – how arrogant can he get? My first reaction to this message is that he thinks he is some sort of Robin Hood, looking after the welfare of the masses, and he wants to get more publicity for his so-called hobby. He will get plenty of that until we catch him.

"Let's keep up the pressure from the public with another press release, quoting from his fax, and it might just encourage him to write some more. We will get him sooner or later, because the general public always come up trumps in the end. They are not daft."

Appendices

Appendix A

1. P.T.I. Physical Training Instructor. Recognised by their red and black striped jerseys.

2. Chindits From the Burmese word 'Chinthi', the guardian of the temple. A member of the Long Range Penetration Group initiated by Orde Wingate, who led the first L.R.P.G. into Burma in 1942 and who was the first commander of the second, much larger, glider-borne expedition in 1944.

3. Punjis Made from split green bamboo, pointed and sharpened. Used by both sides in Burma for defence, especially when barbed wire was not available.

4. Paddy Paddy fields used for growing rice. Sometimes two crops a year were grown in Burma. They had no known Irish connection.

5. N.C.O. Non Commissioned Officer. Not to be saluted.
One Stripe – Lance Corporal. A temporary rank.
Two Stripes – Corporal.
Three Stripes – Lance Sergeant. A temporary rank.
Three Stripes – Sergeant.
Three Stripes and a crown – Staff Sergeant/Quarter master Sergeant.

6. Monsoons The winds which blow from the south of India, during May to July, bringing heavy rains. Often used to refer to these rains which could be two or three inches in the hour.

7. O.T.C. Officers Training Corps. A cadet force at some schools where the obtaining of a Certificate 'A' (Cert A) was helpful when applying for a commission in the infantry.

8. O.C.T.U. Officer Cadet Training Unit. Potential officers, already in the Army, were sent to O.C.T.U. for final appraisal and training prior to being granted a commission.

9. S.S.M. Squadron Sergeant Major. Warrant Officer Class II, (W.O.II). Warrant Officers were not usually loved by

their men and did not win friends easily. They sometimes won respect for their performance under fire but there were many songs sung which cast doubt on their parentage.

10. Lines — Cavalry-speak from the days when horses were tied to rope or chain 'lines'. Applied to the parking area for tanks or the living area for the troops.

11. A.F.V.s — Armoured Fighting Vehicles, tanks.

12. Picquet. — Guard.

13. 2359 hrs. — Midnight, using the 24 hour clock 1939/1945. Prior to that the twelve hour clock was used, together with ack emma or pip emma, a.m. or p.m. See Appendix E.

14. Basha — A bamboo hut or bungalow with a smooth earth floor. Usually well made and offering comfort and protection from the elements.

15. Muckers — Friends, mates.

16. Python — This was the code name for an official system of returning time-expired soldiers to Blighty (U.K.). All soldiers in India, peace-time regulars, war-time volunteers and conscripts, could expect to serve overseas for the duration of the war or until they had served 7 years abroad. (This period was later reduced to 6 years, then 5 years, and in 1945 to 4 years.) British Other Ranks, on Python leave in the U.K., were usually then posted to another unit stationed in Europe. This gave an advantage to old soldiers who were about to go into action in India or Burma. Some were sent home on Python leave only days or even hours before their colleagues drove off to attack a Japanese strongpoint. It was a disadvantage to the remainder of the tank crew, who found that they were depending upon an unknown new crew member. Such a newcomer learned very quickly how different an action was from his training experience in a base camp. Within 24 hours he would feel very experienced and be fully accepted by his new friends. He might even find that he was appointed the tank cook or barber if a more experienced holder of that position wished to delegate.

17. Trade Tested — A man who had passed a qualifying test in wireless, driving, etc. earned extra pay when he was mustered as a tradesman. One General asked a wireless operator trooper if he was mustered and was surprised to be told "I don't know if I'm as hot as all that, sir."

18. D.C.M.	Distinguished Conduct Medal, for Other Ranks.
19. Chaung	A deep ditch, in Burma, which may be natural or man-made, used for drainage. It was often dry, except during the monsoon period. Wet or dry, it was often a barrier for tanks. It was called a 'nullah' in India.
20. Officer	Personnel in the Army were divided into 'Officers' and 'Other Ranks' (B.O.R.s, British Other Ranks, I.O.R.s Indian Other Ranks). Officers held the King's Commission to wage war on his behalf. For this purpose they controlled the Other Ranks and promoted some of them up to N.C.O.s (See A5). During war-time it sometimes happened that successful N.C.O.'s were granted commissions – particularly quartermasters, who had learned how to organise supplies for their unit. See also A91 re V.C.O.s
21. Pahni	Water. Nimbu Pahni – drinking water. Pinky Pahni – water treated with Potassium Permanganate crystals, used for washing fruit and vegetables.
22. Q.M.S.	Quartermaster Sergeant. R.Q.M.S. – Regimental. S.Q.M.S. – Squadron.
23. Khud	Hill or mountain.
24. Gandhi Wallah	A follower of the Mahatma Gandhi, who preached non-cooperation with the British. He could be a member of the Congress Party, dedicated to encouraging the British to 'Quit India'. When they succeeded, after the end of the Second World War, internal strife cost over one million lives.
25. B Echelon	The support/supply half of each tank squadron, including clerks, cooks, medical staff, maintenance and storemen. These men had the basic training in the use of weapons so that they could defend themselves if attacked. They did this on numerous occasions.
26. Bully	Corned beef or mutton. Much enjoyed, either cold in slices, or hot, in stews.
27. 'Come and get it'	The clarion call of all army cooks – professional and amateur – to indicate that a meal has been prepared and is now ready for consumption. It implies that no complaint will be heard or considered.
28. Hiloes	Cavalry riding boots.
29. Batman	The personal servant of an officer. He was usually a trooper, trained in the use of all basic weapons, but whose main purpose in life was to keep his officer

looking smart and relieved of some of the normal chores of survival. He was invariably very protective of his officer against all higher and lower ranks.

30. Stuarts — A light American tank, often called a 'Honey', which carried a 37 mm gun in the turret, co-axially mounted with a Browning machine gun.

31. L.A.D. — Light Aid Detachment to give quick mechanical help. It was part of B Echelon in each tank (sabre) squadron.

32. Mods — Modifications, following afterthoughts. e.g. the Churchill tank had more than 1000 mods after being built and before being issued to the Army.

33. .300 — Browning ammunition was American, rimless and slightly smaller than the .303 British rounds. It was not interchangeable.

34. Net — A group of wireless sets operating on the same wavelength (frequency). See Appendix B.

35. Enfield — The Lee-Enfield rifle. The basic infantry weapon of the 1914/18 War. It used rimmed .303 ammunition and was very reliable for aimed, single shots.

36. P.1. — Qualification of a First Class Wireless Instructor in the UK. Similar to the Q.1. in India.

37. Tiffin — Lunch. The midday meal in India. Often consisted of a curry and fruit. On active service it was anything edible that was consumed during the middle of the day.

38. Tikh hai — O.K. Literally 'good is'.

39. Japani wallah hai — He is Japanese?

40. Charpoy — Bed. In India made from wood strung with jute cord and very attractive to bed bugs. In Manipur and Burma they were made entirely from bamboo and were much more wholesome.

41. Kukri — The Gurkha knife with a curved blade. Used as a weapon and as a tool. A man could remove the head from a bull, or an enemy, with one blow.

42. Ayo Gurkhali — The Gurkha battle-cry. The Gurkhas are coming.

43. Helio — Heliograph. A morse signal transmission system using the reflection of sunlight. Effective over many miles, especially in hot dry countries. Frequent adjustment was necessary because of the apparent movement of the sun.

44. R.H.Q. — Regimental Headquarters.

45. Sappers	Army engineers. R.E.s. Royal Engineers.
46. H.E.	High explosive. How Easy in the phonetic alphabet.
47. Co-ax.	Co-axially mounted machine gun. This referred to the Browning, fixed in the turret, mounted parallel with the 37 mm gun. This gave the turret gunner the choice of two weapons, using the same gunsight and trigger mechanisms.
48. Maidan	Pronounced 'my dan'. The open space in or near a town in India.
49. Shabash	Congratulations! A good show!
50. Bund	The packed earth barrier between paddy fields of different levels. Intended to maintain the correct levels of water in the wet season.
51. C.O.	The Commanding Officer of R.A.C. Regiments and Infantry Battalions. He held the rank of Lieutenant-Colonel.
52. Khaki Drill	The light cotton army uniform used in India and other hot stations. Known as K.D. it consisted of a bush shirt and belt, worn outside the trousers, and needed to be washed and starched each day.
53. L. of C.	Lines of Communication. Supply lines.
54. Lance-Corporal	Could be A.L.C., Acting Lance-Corporal, or P.U.L.C., Provisional Unpaid Lance-Corporal. The first step up the ladder. There is some doubt whether General Slim was ever a lance-corporal in the Army as it is recorded that he was commissioned directly from an O.T.C. (where he might have served as a Lance-Corporal).
55. R.S.M.	Regimental Sergeant Major. Warrant Officer Class One. W.O.I. Responsible for the disciplines carried out by his four W.O.II.s. R.S.M. Frank Wingrove was a gentleman and an immaculate W.O.I. I only knew him to be late for an appointment on one occasion, on Christmas Day, 1945, at Risalpur, when the camel race was delayed by one hour. The writer won that race, recalling that he was one of only a few who were able to make their mounts sit down, prior to climbing into the saddle, and capable of keeping on the racing camel and steering it, with a single rein, around a football pitch. We celebrated not only the end of the War, but also the two previous Christmases when we had been otherwise occupied.
56. Gungho	Over the top. Excessively over-optimistic.

57. According to plan	One of the expressions, used by Officers to give an air of confidence but which always created a sense of foreboding. 'It's all laid on' was another such expression, used to give the doubting Other Ranks an assurance that all arrangements had been completed and all precautions taken, to avoid any hiccup in the plan to achieve the objective. In practice, it was usually taken as a warning to expect a disaster that should not be blamed on the planners.
58. Pukkha Gen.	This was extremely accurate, prior information obtained directly from the Commanding Officer. In practice it was usually either a figment of the imagination or it had been passed on by a low caste camp follower.
59. Sitrep	Abbreviation for Situation Report.
60. S.E.A.C.	South East Asia Command, based in Ceylon. Also used as the name of the newspaper SEAC, edited by Frank Owen, printed in Calcutta and distributed by air to the 14th Army.
61. I.C.	Intercom. The internal communications system using the No. 19 wireless set in the tanks. See also Appendix B., No. 19 Set.
62. Mounted	Another reference to horses. It meant 'inside the tank' and ready to drive off.
63. Box	A defensive position, made by using whatever strengths were available – trees, buildings, chaungs, tanks etc. All weapons would be pointed outwards, slit trenches dug and reinforced, ready for an attack from any direction. Usually given a name, e.g. Oyster Box.
64. Victory Vs	A notorious brand of Indian cigarettes, sometimes issued to the troops, who cast doubts on the origin of the 'tobacco'.
65. Joe Nussey	Whilst 'J' was not his initial, he was always called 'Joe' after J. Stalin. They both had similar moustaches.
66. Humidity	One of the causes of 'prickly heat', a miserable irritation usually starting in the crutch and armpits before spreading over the body. The only relief was gained by cooling off in cold water or even standing outside in the rain.
67. Ventilator	When the 75 mm gun was fired, the recoil system ejected the used shell case into a container behind the gun. The burnt cordite fumes then escaped into the tank but they were soon expelled by the fan system

which air-cooled the seven-cylinder radial engine in the rear compartment.

68. F.O.O.

Forward Observation Officer. An artillery officer who tried to be near the point of impact of shells from his own guns, reporting adjustments necessary to hit the target. Considered a dangerous occupation.

69. Pugaree

The cloth bound round the head or head-dress in order to keep the head cool. e.g. the Sikh turban and Carabiniers' solar topee.

70. No. 9

The commander of a tank, troop, squadron or regiment. Not to be confused with Number nines – doctor's orders – a laxative.

71. Dannert

Coiled barbed wire which could be placed rapidly around a defensive position. If tin cans, containing pebbles were attached, they gave a warning sound when disturbed.

72. M.M.

Military Medal – for Other Ranks.

73. Nullah.

A 'chaung' in India. See A 19.

74. 17 Division

A famous Indian Infantry Division which already had more than two years' experience of fighting the Japanese in India and Burma. Their shoulder badges showed a black cat with an arched back.

75. Self-inflicted wound

This describes any deliberate damage inflicted on one's own body with the intention of becoming "unfit for duty". It rarely happened. Sunstroke was designated a self-inflicted wound as it was considered careless to expose the head to the sun (then known to be the cause of sunstroke). Walking in the sun without wearing a solar topee was a chargeable offence.

When it was later found that the likely cause of sunstroke was the lack of salt in the diet, all ranks were issued with salt tablets to be taken under orders each day, usually with the issued antimalarial tablets – mepacrine or pemaquin. These also had an unpleasant taste and were said to turn the skin yellow.

76. Kutchnai bibi, Kutchnai chute

No women, no crumpet.

77. Running hand

Plain English.
Cipher. Groups of five letters or figures – in code.

78. Valentine Scissors Bridger

One troop of Valentines was commanded by Captain Stanley Gibbons, who had transferred to the Royal Tank Regiment from the 26th Hussars when they were disbanded. His help was invaluable to the Carabiniers in achieving their objectives, especially during the monsoon rains. Lt Col. Younger was so impressed by this ex-cavalry officer that he insisted on his temporary appointment as a Troop Leader in the Carabiniers in action at a time of officer shortage.

79. Standing-to	Fully prepared for any defensive or offensive action.
80. High port	With the rifle and fixed bayonet held obliquely across the body, ready to shoot or stab.
81. 3rd/4th Bombay Grenadiers	Commanded throughout the Imphal and Burma campaigns by Lt. Col. R. A. Shebbeare, who insisted on the highest standards throughout his Battalion. His ancestors had commanded troops in India from the time of the Mutiny, one having been awarded the V.C. He was awarded the Ashoka Chakri Class III, the Indian equivalent of the M.C., for his bravery under fire when men, women and children on a train were being killed by over 2000 tribesmen at the time of the Partition.
82. Seven men	A full crew of the General Lee tank. Fourteen men in the same space would have been very uncomfortable, if not impossible. Fortunately, we never tried it.
83. Section	Of an infantry Company. Usually ten men.
84. Tumara officer kidder hai?	Where is your officer?
85. Nai malum, sahib	I don't know, sir.
86. Humara officer idher hai	My officer is here.
87. Lieutenant Cole	Soon after this action Lt. Cole returned to his original Troop in C Squadron. On 8th June he and three of his crew were killed by two direct hits from Japanese guns.
88. Pialla	Mug.
89. Garum char	Hot tea.
90. Stag	Guard duty.
91. V.C.O.s,	Viceroy Commissioned Officers. Indian and Gurkha officers in their own national regiments.
92. Chaguls	A cheap canvas bottle-shaped water container in which two pints of water could be kept cool by means of slow evaporation through the canvas. Dust tended to

collect in the neck and discolour the water when poured.

93. I.   Intelligence.

94. M.I. Room   Medical Inspection Room. An M.I. Parade, with the Other Ranks standing in line, was held regularly so that the M.O. could examine the men for any possible disease. Sometimes called the 'short arm parade'.

95. Sprue   Doc Griffiths told me that only three men in the Regiment were ill with tropical sprue, in which the lining of the stomach became ineffective, leading to starvation. The first two went into hospital and died, so he pressed me to stay with B Squadron for as long as possible.

96. B.G.H.   British General Hospital. No. 3 B.G.H. at Poona was one of only a few large, permanent hospitals in India and was staffed by Q.A.'s (Queen Alexandra's) military nursing staff. All nurses were commissioned and some of them applied strict military discipline to their patients.

97. 'You've had it' Means the exact opposite. You not only have not had it, you are extremely unlikely ever to have it. 'You're pushed' means the same as 'you've had it', also that you are late and will not be able to keep your appointment, arrive on time for the parade, etc. or achieve your ambition.

98. Padre   A minister or priest commissioned into the Army in order to take care of the spiritual needs of all ranks. Some of them carried side arms, for self defence, and most of them helped with the wounded and dying of all religions involved in the 14th Army.

99. Screaming shell A shell travelling at high speed made this noise as it passed overhead. If you heard it, it would not harm you.

100. M.C.   Military Cross. For officers only, for their individual bravery in action.

101. Q.   Quartermaster. See A 22.

102. Recce   Reconnaissance. A prerequisite for any successful action. If omitted, it was almost always regretted.

103. 82A Squad   A third member of 82A Squad, who was then in the Carabiniers, was Jack Clough from Bradford. He was Regimental Intelligence Corporal and his work involved the daunting task of frequently driving alone to the other scattered squadrons on a motor cycle or jeep. His knowledge of the Japanese language was of real

benefit to the Regiment, helping with the rapid translation of captured documents. After the war he joined the Territorial Army Military Intelligence and retired as a major.

104. Officers' Mess

The 'Holy Ground' used by officers for eating, drinking and any subsequent tom-foolery. It could be in buildings, tents or even in open ground when on active service. It was always tidy and never in a mess. Regimental cooks and barmen (all Other Ranks) were supported by local civilian bearers (waiters). Other Ranks were never admitted, unless as employees as above. When present, the Commanding Officer was God. No subaltern (junior officer) would speak, eat, drink or retire to his quarters without glancing towards the C.O. to check his possible reaction.

105. Tracers

A round used in medium guns and machine guns which glowed as it travelled towards the target. The gunner could follow the trajectory and see roughly where the projectile landed. In belted machine gun ammunition usually every fourth or fifth round was a tracer.

106. Samurai sword

The well-known curved sword used by some Japanese officers for ceremony and as a weapon. They were extremely well made and some of them have a very high value.

107. Napphi wallah

Barber. Usually an Indian but in action we had volunteers within the Squadron. Armed with scissors, comb and hand shears, they kept us reasonably tidy. Indian napphi wallahs used to finish the haircut with a neck massage and a sharp twist of the head in order to 'loosen' the top of the spine. Ouch!

108. Sword

See A 106. Not all Japanese officers were Samurai but they were mostly prepared to use their swords to behead prisoners or even reticent members of their own unit. The threat of this kept their infantry moving into the attack throughout the final stages of the fighting in Imphal and Burma. On one occasion a Jap officer climbed on to an A Squadron tank and killed the tank commander with his sword. He then climbed down into the turret and killed the 37 gunner before the loader shot him with six rounds from his Smith and Wesson pistol.

109. Bahout kharab Ooper jantha?

Very bad.
Can you get up there?

110. Kami kaze	Suicide attack. First heard of in the Pacific theatre where Japanese pilots deliberately crashed their planes into American ships in order to explode their bombs on a vital target.
111. Gauntlet	The men of B Echelon risked their lives many times bringing essential supplies to the tank crews.
112. Browned off or cheesed off	When spoken in a despondent tone this indicates that the speaker is gloomy, morose or 'fed-up'. e.g. a man can be 'fed-up' because he has not been fed for many hours, is extremely hungry, and he can see no prospect of any food.
113. Ista gan yam?	Are you going home?
114. Abbi bahout achcha hai	It's all right now.
115. Havildar	A sergeant in the Indian infantry.
116. Japani wallah etc.	The Japanese are evil, they gave me no food and their lovemaking is most unpleasant.
117. Kitna Japani ooder hai?	How many Japs are up there?
118. Idher aow	Come here.
119. I.O.	Intelligence Officer
120. Sergeants Mess	An area of Holy Ground, similar to the Officers' Mess, but, only to be used by Warrant Officers and Sergeants. Officers, on duty, have the right of entry but otherwise entry for Officers is 'not on' unless invited. On very rare occasions the Officers may be invited into the Sergeants' Mess for a drinks party. This might occur to celebrate something as important as the end of the 39/45 War. Members of the Sergeants' Mess would then have a moral duty to ensure that each officer is returned to his own bunk at the end of such an evening. Ties and belts would then be removed in order to allow the Officer to breathe and recover throughout the remainder of the night.
121. When we had horses	The cry of an old soldier in the cavalry. Now mechanised.
122. WASBI	Women's Auxiliary Services (Burma).
123.	Three Brigades of 2nd British Division. 9 Battalions.

4 Brigade,   Lancashire Fusiliers
                    Royal Scots
                    Norfolks
5 Brigade,   Worcesters

	Dorsets
	Cameronians
6 Brigade,	Durham Light Infantry
	Royal Welch Fusiliers
	Royal Berkshires

124. L.I.L.O.P. Leave in lieu of Python. See also A16. Similar to L.I.A.P. but was for at least 28 days leave in the U.K. for a soldier who was almost due to go on Python anyway. This helped to reduce the destabilisation of the unit caused by a drain of older, experienced officers and men. The return of these men, from L.I.L.O.P., maintained within the Regiment a nucleus of 'old hats' who could remember 'when we had horses' and 'before you joined'. It also reduced some of the need to give rapid promotion to men who were thinking 'roll on the boat'.

125. Field Rank Officers Majors and above. Those wearing red tabs on their collars were full Colonels, Brigadiers or Generals and were to be avoided at all costs by the Other Ranks.

126. Share I never heard of this happening. It would probably be considered 'a poor show'. This was the opposite of 'a good show'. Both these expressions, used by Officers only, mean what they say. e.g. 'A good show' would be used to congratulate men for (a) a smart turnout on parade, (b) a spotless barrack area, (c) a successful, or nearly successful, military action, particularly after suffering heavy casualties.

127. L.I.A.P. Leave in addition to Python. See also A 16. A soldier, due for Python leave in the next few years may be granted 14 days leave in the U.K. He would be flown there by the R.A.F. and expected back with the Regiment within three weeks. L.I.A.P. would not affect a man's entitlement to Python leave when it became due. L.I.A.P. was granted very rarely to a man of any rank who had fought well and hard over three or four months, in action on a daily or weekly basis. Such lucky men always returned to their unit on time. This was considered 'a good show'.

128. Interpreter Named Saw Perry Dwe, he was known as 'Perry' to all. He was a quiet, likeable young man in his early twenties who spoke perfect English, as well as Burmese and a few local dialects. Being a Karen, he originated in the south east of Burma, near the Siamese

(Thai) border, where his fellow Karens have resisted government rule ever since the communist military take-over in Burma. Currently, the Rangoon Government control, perhaps, only one fifth of the country, now called Myinmar. The remainder is in the hands of various tribal groups. North Eastern Burma forms part of the infamous poppy growing 'Triangle', with northern Thailand and Laos.

129. O.P.	Observation Point. See A 68.
130. Too late	It was not funny. We heard occasional reports of these men sometimes falling with the loads and being killed.
131. Only bridge	During periods of heavy rains and flooding over the centuries, the River Irrawaddy has changed its course many times in the area between Mandalay and Rangoon. Another expensive bridge, like that at Ava, could easily have been isolated and have become useless.
132. R.E.M.E.	Royal Electrical and Mechanical Engineers. The 'Experts'.
133. Ted Dyer	Known as 'Lobber' Dyer for his skills at serving food swiftly and fairly. This lean and fit man was loved by all his colleagues, many of them half his age.
134. Squadron Officers	It was traditional for Officers to serve their men with the Christmas Dinner each year.
135. Major Dorman	Whilst he gained the respect of all ranks for the efficient way in which he led B Squadron through Burma, he was never 'awarded' a nickname. Those who liked him called him 'the Major'. Those who did not referred to him as 'Dorman'. After the war he went to live in Australia.
136. Fishing rod aerial	Three metal sections, fitted into each other, enabled the rapid replacement of a damaged aerial – a frequent occurrence. They were obviously made by a fishing rod manufacturer and some of them were quietly modified by the crews, with welded loops, to convert them for this purpose. I never saw any fish caught with them and we all found that grenades were quicker and more effective when fish was needed for food.
137. Battle-scarred	This reminds the writer of a newspaper report about a retired general where he was described as 'the bottle-scarred old warrior'. This was hastily corrected, with an apology, the next day, saying "we should, of course, have referred to him as 'the battle-scared old warrior.'"
138. Pagodas	During a severe earthquake in the 1950 s, many of

these structures in Pagan were truncated, when the vibrations snapped off the top third. A large number of new pagodas have since been built there and have helped to regain the air of quiet peace which can still be found in Burma.

139. l.m.g.   Light machine gun.

140. Sweepers   The low caste Indians responsible for the cleanliness of the Regimental area. The 3rd Carabiniers carried a strength of fifty 'camp followers' with a 'Kotwol' in charge of them. He was a well-built Punjabi, speaking five or six languages and he maintained order by means of his assertive personality and the implied threat of his five-foot stick. These fifty men used 13 languages and dialects, creating problems of communication. The 'I' Sergeant sometimes used three interpreters at once on the pay parade, when they signed for their pittance with a thumb print on the payroll. During the twelve months of fighting we never saw any of them in B Squadron and carried out their chores ourselves.

Appendix B

Wireless Procedures

Over	I have switched to receive and await your reply.
Out	I have switched to receive and do not expect a reply.
Roger	Message received and understood.
Wilco	Message received and I will comply with the order.
All Stations	Addresses all main R.T. stations in the group. e.g. the Squadron Leader addressing all troop leaders: 'All Stations Able' is speaking to the four commanders of Troops 4, 5, 6 and 7, where the call sign for the day is 'Able'.
All Group Stations	Addresses every single station on the same wavelength. e.g. The Squadron Leader's operator to each station on the group: A1, A2, A3, A4, A4A, A4B, A5, A5A, A5B, etc. Used mostly for the checking of the accuracy of the wavelength setting and, occasionally for a vital alteration of orders.
Net	All the stations set on the same wavelength (frequency). This was done by the group leader's operator transmitting on a prearranged wavelength for a short period (known as a carrier wave) whilst all the other operators tuned in and locked their controls on that setting. With the No.19 set it was possible to lock on to two different wavelengths and change (flick) from one to the other when given a coded order from control. This was often used when interference from another group made communication difficult.
R.T.	Radio Telephony. The system of using the wireless for the rapid two-way communication in speech. In constant use between vehicles. Not at all secure, security could be improved by the use of code words.
W.T.	Wireless Telegraphy. The system of using morse signals to transmit messages. All operators were trained

to use this method but in the R.A.C. speeds of 15 words per minute were the best to be expected within the squadron. Lengthy regular training was required to achieve and maintain speeds of 30 w.p.m., which were expected when communicating back to Brigade H.Q. (Royal Signals operators).

No. 19 Set   A transmitter/receiver wireless set used widely in mobile warfare. It consisted of two sets. The 'A' set, with a range of perhaps 40/50 miles in the daytime, reduced to as little as 4/5 miles after dusk in the Burmese hills and jungle. W.T. was more effective than R.T. at night and was frequently used for reporting the results of a day's battle back to a rear H.Q. The variometer was used to 'tune' the aerial to give the strongest outgoing signal.

The 'B' set had a very short wavelength (V.H.F.) with settings numbered 1 to 10. It could be used for 'line of vision' communication only and frequently became useless in villages or amongst trees for that reason. It was sometimes useful where a number of troops were each wanting their own separate net, especially in open country. Inside the Lee tanks, the seven crew members each wore a plastic helmet incorporating a pair of earphones and microphone which had a 'pressel' switch. By picking up the microphone, each crew member could speak to all the others in the tank on I.C. (internal communication). By pressing the switch, everything he said was transmitted for all the others on the same net to hear. This would include every other tank crew member. This often happened in the excitement of battle, with various results – especially if the C.O. was on the same net. Within a squadron all voices were easily recognised and the inadvertent transmission of a young officer's conversation with his crew led to much 'ribbing' of all concerned when back in the box that night. If two 'A' sets were switched to 'send' at the same time this resulted in a loud howling noise (jamming) and little could be understood. The receiver was automatically switched off during a transmission.

Appendix C

Squadron Wireless Layout with the Call Sign 'Baker (B)'

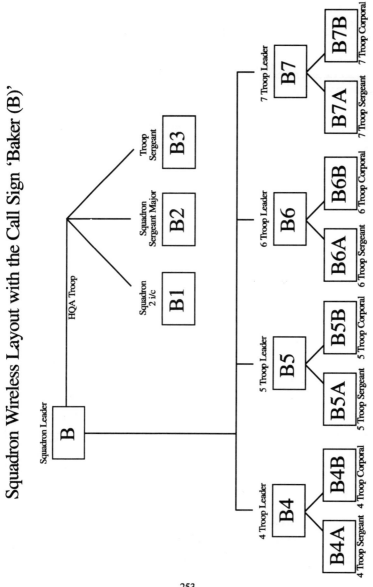

Appendix D

The Phonetic Alphabet

	1914/1918	1941/1945	1956
A	Ack	Able	Alfa
B	Beer	Baker	Bravo
C	Charlie	Charlie	Charlie
D	Don	Dog	Delta
E	Edward	Easy	Echo
F	Freddie	Fox	Foxtrot
G	George	George	Golf
H	Harry	How	Hotel
I	Ink	Item	India
J	Johnny	Jig	Juliett
K	King	King	Kilo
L	London	Love	Lima
M	Emma	Mike	Mike
N	Nuts	Nan	November
O	Orange	Oboe	Oscar
P	Pip	Peter	Papa
Q	Queen	Queen	Quebec
R	Robert	Roger	Romeo
S	Esses	Sugar	Sierra
T	Toc	Tare	Tango
U	Uncle	Uncle	Uniform
V	Vic	Victor	Victor
W	William	William	Whiskey
X	Xray	Xray	Xray
Y	Yorker	Yoke	Yankee
Z	Zebra	Zebra	Zulu

(Appendix D continued)

1. The author first learned the 1914/1918 version of the alphabet at school and recalls that in 1939 the British Anti-Aircraft guns were known to the entire population as 'the Ack-Ack'. There was a radio programme called 'Ack-Ack, Beer Beer' for the gunners and the Balloon Barrage defenders. They were never referred to as 'Able-Able' or 'Baker Baker'.

2. He learned the 1941/1945 version from Sergeant Chute (aptly pronounced 'shoot') of 82A Squad, 56th Training Regiment, R.A.C. Catterick. Sergeant Chute was a Londoner who pronounced the words: 'Ible, Biker, Charlie' etc. It was easy to realise that the first word was 'Able' but the author has always associated B for Baker with the vision of a man on a bicycle.

Appendix E

M3 General Lee Tanks

Specifications

Length	18.5 feet
Width	8.9 feet
Height	10.25 feet
Weight	30 tons
Armament	<u>One 75 mm gun</u> mounted in the sponson on the right of the driver. Traverse limited to 15° Fired H.E. (high explosive) and A.P. (armour piercing) shells. Projectile weight approx. 14lbs. <u>One 37 mm gun</u> mounted in the turret (360° traverse). Fired H.E., A.P. and canister (pellets). <u>Two Browning machine guns .300 ins.</u> Belt fed, (200 rounds per belt). <u>One mounted</u> co-axially with the 37 mm in the turret. <u>One mounted</u>, with elevation and depression only (no traverse), on the left of the driver. Controlled by the wireless operator. Mostly used dismounted for defence. <u>One smoke projector</u> mounted on the turret.
Engine	7-cylinder radial aero engine using high octane petrol.
Max. Speed	30 m.p.h.
Ammunition Stowage	Increased by modification to 120 rounds 75 mm and 170 rounds 37 mm Approximately 8000 rounds (40 belts) of .300 Browning ammunition were carried in the turret, mostly under the floor plates. Plus smoke canisters and Mills grenades.

The General Lee and General Grant tanks were designed and built in the U.S.A. in 1940/42. Over 6000 were produced in that very short period before being declared obsolete in April 1944. Superceded by the Sherman tank with the 75mm gun turret mounted.

The Fort Worth date stamp of 1922 must have been some sort of joke.

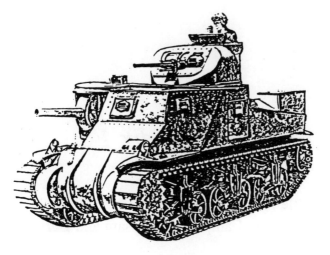

GENERAL LEE TANK CREW POSITIONS

PLAN

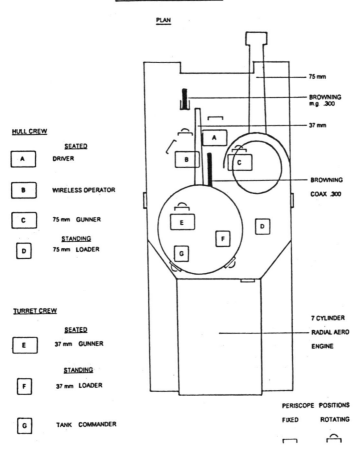

75 mm

BROWNING
m.g. .300

37 mm

HULL CREW

SEATED

A   DRIVER

B   WIRELESS OPERATOR

BROWNING

COAX .300

C   75 mm GUNNER

STANDING

D   75 mm LOADER

TURRET CREW

7 CYLINDER

RADIAL AERO

ENGINE

SEATED

E   37 mm GUNNER

STANDING

F   37 mm LOADER

G   TANK COMMANDER

PERISCOPE POSITIONS

FIXED   ROTATING

Appendix F

Battle Honours Awarded to the 3rd Carabiniers for the Campaign in Assam and Burma

3rd Carabiniers
Squadrons Involved

IMPHAL. 12th March–22nd June, 1944 — A.B.C.

TAMU ROAD. 12th March–14th April, 1944 — A.B.

NUNSHIGUM. 5th April–13th April, 1944 — B.

BISHENPUR. 14th April–22nd June, 1944 — A.B.

KANGLATONGBI. 21st April–22nd June, 1944 — C.

KENNEDY PEAK. 3rd October–7th November, 1944 — C.

SHWEBO. 6th January–9th January, 1945 — B.C.

SAGAING. 23rd January–12th February, 1945 — A.B.C.

MANDALAY. 12th February–21st March, 1945 — B.C.

AVA. 13th February–20th March, 1945 — A.C.

IRRAWADDY. 29th March–30th May, 1945 — A.B.C.

YENANYAUNG. 18th April–25th April, 1945 — B.C.

BURMA. 1944–1945 — A.B.C.

Appendix G

12 ARMY

14 ARMY

IV INDIAN CORPS

XV INDIAN CORPS

XXXIII INDIAN CORPS

2 BRITISH DIV.

"CHINDITS"

254 INDIAN TANK
BRIGADE

5 INDIAN DIV.

7 INDIAN DIV.

17 INDIAN DIV.

19 INDIAN DIV.

20 INDIAN DIV.

23 INDIAN DIV.

25 INDIAN DIV.

26 INDIAN DIV.

36 BRITISH DIV.

81 WEST AFRIC. DIV.

82 WEST AFRIC. DIV.

Badges of some of the formations with which the 3rd Carabiniers were associated during 1944/45

259

HYMERS
COLLEGE OTC
1936/38 and in the
L.D.V. & HOME
GUARD 1941

ROYAL
ARMOURED
CORPS, Catterick
1941/42

EAST RIDING
YEOMANRY 1942

47th ROYAL
TANK
REGIMENT,
Egypt and
R.A.C. DEPOT,
Poona 1943

26th HUSSARS
1943

3rd CARABINIERS
1943/46

ROYAL ARMY
ORDNANCE
CORPS for the 3
weeks 'secret'
train journey
1943

Cap badges worn by the author during his army service

THE ROYAL SCOTS DRAGOON GUARDS (CARABINIERS AND GREYS)

*This Regiment was formed on 2nd July, 1971 by the amalgamation of The
Royal Scots Greys (2nd Dragoons) and the 3rd Carabiniers (Prince of
Wales's Dragoon Guards)*

Author's Note

3rd Carabiniers (Prince of Wales's Dragoon Guards)

This is the story of a tank crew fighting in Assam and Burma towards the end of the Second World War, 1939/1945. It is an attempt to describe one of the secrets of how we beat a previously unstoppable enemy. The Japanese Army had a history of successes throughout the Far East and was spreading west through large parts of China, Siam, Burma and into India.

Led by General 'Uncle Bill' Slim, the 14th Army was based in and around Imphal, capital of Manipur State, in Assam, and in the Arakan to the south, waiting for the Japanese 15th Army to surround and attack them. British, Indian and Gurkha troops stood fast, supplied by air, throughout a siege lasting ten weeks. The desperate Japanese were fought to a standstill, followed by an ignominious retreat and, later, obliteration in Burma. Very few prisoners were taken by either side.

The majority of casualties were caused by a variety of tropical diseases, from which some of the survivors still suffer today. In this regiment of some 800 officers and men, there were more than 100% reported casualties, of whom 101 lost their lives. They received 95 Honours and Awards together with 13 Battle Honours. The effectiveness of this mechanised cavalry regiment, with a history of 300 years serving the Crown, was again proved many times whilst fighting through two monsoons and the dry months in between.

In 1971 the 3rd Carabiniers amalgamated with the Royal Scots Greys (Second Dragoons) at Holyrood Palace to become the Royal

Scots Dragoon Guards (Carabiniers and Greys). They are proud of the fact that Her Majesty Queen Elizabeth II is their Colonel-in-Chief. The strong family spirit continues with the new Regiment, who have already seen action in Iraq. Each year they celebrate two Battle Honours – Waterloo for the Greys and Nunshigum for the Carabiniers. On 13th April B Squadron of the Royal Scots Dragoon Guards parade without officers, as a reminder of that fateful date of 13th April 1944.

The introduction of a serial killer is fiction – a 'might-have-been'. The story of B Squadron, 3rd Carabiniers, is fact, based on war diaries for the dates and place names. The details come from a 50-year-old memory. There were many of us who believed that we were fighting to help to improve civilisation by eliminating aggression, greed and cruelty, but we soon realised that the job was not finished and that it is not likely to be completed.

Perhaps, on the 13th April each year, some of the jogger's potential targets will look over their shoulders and wonder!

A.F.F.